Enter the Dom

Enter the Dom

The No BS Book on Dominance

By Mario Tubone & Brandon the Dom

Table of Contents

Authors' Note

This book is intended for educational purposes only and is not a substitute for hands-on training, mentorship, or professional guidance in BDSM practices. The authors, Brandon and Mario, are experienced Dominants with extensive hours of practice in performing the actions and techniques discussed in this book. However, BDSM and other forms of sexual exploration carry inherent risks, and any attempt to replicate or engage in the activities described is done at the reader's own risk. Brandon and Mario assume no responsibility for any harm, injury, or consequences that may arise from such actions.

This book includes personal erotic stories based on our experiences. To protect the privacy of those involved, all names and identifying details have been altered. The individuals described in these stories were all consenting adults who participated of their own free will. If you choose to engage in similar activities, it is imperative that all parties involved are of legal age, fully informed, and consenting.

Readers should not attempt to recreate or perform the actions described in the erotic stories without first gaining a comprehensive understanding of the associated risks and learning proper techniques through reputable resources, experienced mentors, or hands-on training.

BDSM is built on principles of consent, negotiation, and safety. We strongly encourage you to educate yourself thoroughly, communicate openly with your partners, and prioritize physical and emotional well-being in all interactions. If you are new to BDSM, we urge you to seek out reputable sources, community education, and, when possible, experienced guidance before engaging in any high-risk activities.

By continuing to read this book, you acknowledge that you understand these disclaimers and accept full responsibility for your own choices and actions. Stay safe, stay informed, and always play consensually.

– Mario & Brandon

Dominance

What Exactly is Dominance?

CHAPTER ONE

The Essence of a Dominant Life

Why are you here?

Let's be honest—if you're reading this, it's because you know something is missing from your life.

Maybe it's a feeling. Maybe you've rationally concluded that you're not living in alignment with where you believe you're supposed to be. On the surface, your life might seem to be going well, but deep down, there's a hunch—a knot in your stomach—that tells you you're not experiencing your best sexual life.

Awareness is the first step in the adventurous journey this book will guide you through. It certainly was for Mario and Brandon when we embarked on our own paths—though separated by years and experiences, we both started from the same place.

What you're about to read is the book we wish we had when we began. Like you, we felt that same drive that led you here—not just to have more meaningful sex, but to get the most out of life.

Who This Book Is For

This book is primarily intended for men who share common struggles:

- The "nice guy" who feels chained to a societal role that doesn't fit.

- The confused (often young) man who doesn't fully understand relationship dynamics—especially intimate ones.
- The man whose sex life has become dull and unfulfilling.
- The man who is afraid to be his true self and is tired of staying silent about what he wants and needs.

I'm deliberately focusing on male/female dynamics and addressing you, the reader, as a **Dom**—short for Dominant in the Dominant/submissive power exchange of a relationship.

As you'll soon discover, **Doms are made, not born**. Every long journey begins with a single step. If you stay honest with yourself and put in the work, you'll see real transformation. Dominance isn't just about technical skills—it's a mindset that translates into action.

We fully acknowledge that Dominance isn't tied to gender, and plenty of Dominant women exist. However, Mario and Brandon are straight men, and we can only speak from our own experiences. We write from what we know and what we've observed through years in the BDSM world and self-development communities.

So, this book is for men looking to explore and develop their Dominance, maximize their potential, and experience a sex life beyond their imagination—with consenting, submissive women.

Of course, some principles we discuss may hold true universally, regardless of gender or sexual orientation. If you don't feel represented in these pages, don't take offense—this book simply may not be for you. And if you feel the need to send hate mail, direct it all to Brandon—he loves that.

How to Be a Dom That Women Will Submit To

There's an age-old debate in BDSM circles—one that's likely existed since the beginning of the culture—about whether Dominance is an inherent personality trait or something that can be learned.

Really? Another nature vs. nurture debate? We're so tired of these.

Here's the truth: **almost everything about being a Dom can be learned**—even the deeper aspects of inner Dominance that make a submissive woman truly *feel* your presence and believe you're a natural.

Except for one thing: **taking 100% responsibility for your life.**

If you're not willing to do that, we can't help you. No one can. As far as we can tell, that's the defining factor—it's in a man's nature, and some men will never take that step.

Now, here's the cold, hard truth:

- **Women will only submit to men they respect.**
- **Women will only respect you if you respect yourself.**
- **You can only respect yourself if you take full responsibility for your life.**

Being a Dom starts *long* before the bedroom. It starts before you learn any technical skills, before you approach a submissive woman, and before you even consider a power exchange dynamic. You have to **master yourself** before you can be a master of another person.

Luckily for you, that's exactly what this book is going to teach you.

Two Doms Walk Into a Bar...

At this point, you might be wondering: **Who the hell are these random guys from the internet telling me what to do and what to believe?** Why should you listen to us?

That's a fair question. Being skeptical is actually a good thing, especially when it comes to advice from the internet.

Remember when we said, **"Doms are made, not born"**? Neither Mario nor Brandon started out as the Dominants we are today. In fact, we were far from it.

Just like you, we had to learn how to unlock that part of ourselves and express it fully.

So, let us share a few parts of our stories. Maybe you'll see a bit of yourself in them.

Mario's Story

I come from a classic lower middle-class family with two children. We still had a nice house and food on the table every day; however, I distinctly remember asking my mom, "Why are we so poor?"

In reality, we weren't doing that badly. We had a comfortable apartment in a nice area, food, clothing, and my sister and I even attended a private school managed by nuns! I simply had an inferiority complex, being the poorest kid in a class of children from wealthier families.

My mother always wanted the best for us, and so did my father. As an aspiring entrepreneur building his business, he wanted to excel no matter what. They both worked long and hard to provide for my sister and me, leaving us to be cared for by our conservative, southern Italian grandmother.

With absent parents, I spent most of my childhood days in religious school, school practices, and when I reached the right age, my parents signed me up for the Christian boy scouts.

Growing up, I felt ashamed that I was attracted to symbols that directly contrasted with my religious teachings. While on one hand I was listening to the parables, I was also drawn to MTV and the rock stars who were all about "sex, drugs, and rock and roll." My coping mechanism was to push these feelings down and repress them while simultaneously dreaming of being one of those guys with long hair and painted nails.

Then puberty hit, and suddenly I started to see my female schoolmates as interesting instead of as annoying girls dressed in pink school aprons. When nudity appeared on television, I felt so embarrassed in front of my parents because nudity and sex were sinful, and I didn't want to show how much interest and arousal I was getting from those images.

Thanks to the boy scouts, we merged with a mixed group of boys and girls in the same 13 to 17 age group, and I started hanging out with guys and girls who seemed to know much more about these matters than I did.

My equally horny friends and I started getting our little hands on tapes and magazines (hello 90s!), and I was shocked the first time we saw porn. Some of my friends still believed having sex meant holding hands, looking into each other's eyes, and saying "I love you." Meanwhile, some of the best extreme porn actors Italy has ever produced made quite an impression on me. While some of my friends were shocked by the performance, I was thrilled. It was like a volcanic eruption, bringing all the repressed horniness and feelings toward women up like a giant wave.

My next encounters with girls only increased my arousal more and more, as I started to engage in the great teenage pastime "spin the bottle," having random makeout sessions or seeing two girls kissing each other—instantly giving me a boner. After another platonic kiss by a girl I thought was attractive, I knew I had to lose my virginity ASAP! And destiny wanted it to happen quite soon...

Finally Burning My Virginity Membership Card

There was a girl in the Scouts with me who started being direct in her interest. As you can imagine, with me being completely incompetent, this frustrated her quite a bit as she had to take the lead on making things happen: the texting, the phone calls (you know, back in the day people used to call each other), the "let's hang a little bit Saturday" invitations. Then one sunny afternoon, she texted me "I'm home alone," to which I replied, not understanding what that meant, "OK, do you plan to do something fun?" She had to explain to the naive me, "Yes, if you come here."

I showed up at her place, parked my scooter, and she greeted me half-naked at the door, pumping my hormones to a level never experienced before. I sat down on her bed while she danced to the music cranking out of a relatively new CD player sound system, adjusting myself on the bouncing mattress covered in a sheet with a big cat on it.

Suddenly, the heat started being too much for me to handle as I felt sweat streaming down my forehead, my arms deprived of all strength, legs shaking. I was uttering single-word answers to her questions as she drew closer and closer until her head was on my chest. As she looked up at me, the effort to maintain eye contact felt like lifting hundreds of timber logs. She'd push upward to kiss me only to immediately jerk back and start laughing while I was stuck in my head trying to process everything. I couldn't even comprehend where I was at that moment, meanwhile having a full-blown erection that was almost painful.

I leapt forward like a spring, reaching her still-grinning and giggling face, and planted my lips firmly against her teeth. That fraction of a second felt like an eternity, where the universe froze, before she reacted to my risqué move by closing her lips and kissing me back. We started making out as passionately as two horny teenagers can and undressed each other with a primal hunger for each other's body.

The first real woman I ever saw naked was my mother after going into our family bathroom without knocking, feeling extremely ashamed of myself. So after wrestling with this girl's bra like it was some sort of bear trap, revealing a generous, soft, and white breast, I had feelings of shame, embarrassment, and guilt shake and stir with the excitement of finally having sex.

She instructed me through foreplay, almost as an experienced mistress would. As she stood up she started jerking me furiously as if we were survivors on a desert island stroking wood twigs to light a fire.

I swear there must be some sort of male orgasm detector in a woman's head because as I started to fall into the pre-orgasm trance, she whispered if I had a condom, dragging me back to reality like a bungee rope snaps back when it reaches the end of the line.

"WHAT?!" I boomed.

The terror in my eyes must have caught her by surprise as she immediately became defensive, apologizing, "I'm afraid of getting pregnant so young," while looking down. "But I have one if it's OK," she continued. I said, "Of course." I would have done anything to score, especially when so close to burning, once and for all, my virginity membership club card. She stood up and retrieved from a small wallet hidden in the desk drawer across the room a bright orange square that felt like a summer gadget from promotional events at the beach.

I had absolutely no clue what to do once she deposited the tropical tea bag-shaped latex rubber protector in my hands. Seeing my curiosity, she inquisitively asked if I knew how to use it, to which the proudest and clueless version of me answered with a "of course" so fake a polygraph would have sparked with laughter.

After figuring out which side was correct to unroll along my penis, I was finally ready. I was about to go all in and finally emulate my favorite adult movie star, only to then struggle to enter her young and nervous body. By the sheer power of being a super horny teenager, I finally managed to push inside. At that moment, I knew I would be hooked for life to this feeling.

Now it was time to perform like Rocco, but I was keeping my eyes closed and doing the equivalent of a plank at the gym with small, short, fast thrusts that still embarrass me to this day. But the oddity wasn't done, as I felt a massive tingling feeling in my balls, like I needed to go to the bathroom, while feeling good at the same time, making me want to chase that warm and addicting sensation.

So I kept thrusting with my hips like I had to hammer a nail with my penis, taking aim before every single thrust in the same robotic way a machine seals bottles of soda before they're ready for the store, sweating so much that I would make Finnish sauna-enthusiasts envious, squeezing my eyelids closed almost making my eyeballs hurt until I reached the magic moment I'd only seen in the dusty VHS cassettes.

I was having an orgasm!

I buried my head deep inside the pillow next to hers, completely forgetting there was another person there with me, as my penis transformed into a bilge pump that with every squeeze sent shock waves through my body, making me unable to realize what was happening around me. My only thought was to not let any sounds escape my mouth, like a muzzled dog seeing a cat through a door window. That was it—I officially burned my virginity card.

As my entire body collapsed over hers, making her join my sweat fest, I was enjoying the rush of hormones coursing through my body, resembling a caterpillar about to transform into a butterfly with all the shaking and trembling. As I opened my eyes, I saw her big eyes staring directly into mine, catapulting me into the "after sex" world with the same intensity a space rocket defies gravity.

I had no idea what to do or say—after all, this wasn't documented in the "educational" material I was trying to emulate—so with the most candid voice my throat could produce, I asked, "Did you like this?" I would have never thought the next sentence would change my life...

"Mmm...yeah..."

Mmm yeah?! The tonality sounded more like a no or an "I'll think about it..." I was lying on my back, covered in sweat from head to toe with an equally drenched woman next to me, and my head wondered if I was any good at this, if I was a "natural" talent. Would I make my unknown mentor proud or revolt in disgust? Would I get compliments from all the girls who would queue at my door for the ultimate experience of joy?

A few years later, being a goal-oriented person, I realized how that one experience had massively influenced what my sexual goals would soon become: **to mesmerize every woman I would have a sexual encounter with.**

Of course, a teenager is justified in having such goals because what do they know? The idea of becoming "the best version" is simply flawed because there is no "best" version, as it would imply that there is a worst version of yourself that could potentially exist too.

You will see that the goal should have been to be "competent." What is competency, you might ask? Competency is a combination of skills, knowledge, and abilities that enable someone to perform a task or job effectively.

Of course, as a teenager, you would think that great sex is the combination of physical fitness and hammering a woman long and hard with your dick. Which, of course, is wrong because it leaves out the real big elephant in the room: **the mind**. What we should be striving for is the ultimate achievement as a Dom: fuck her mind as well as her body.

Entering the Secret World of BDSM

Fast forward a decade after giving up my virgin card, I was doing pretty well in terms of relationships with the opposite sex. I was having plenty of sexual encounters, working as a club promoter in the summer, giving me access to a lot of girls on holiday who, as the song goes, "just wanna have fun."

One night while in the club I was promoting and flirting with all the girls that passed by, I was having a conversation with a colleague about kinks and other sex techniques (squirting was the big thing back then, and I was trying to grab every resource I could find on the internet, in the process collecting viruses as trophies). He suggested we should go to the local swinger club. I was immediately curious. He had been practicing swinging with his girlfriend, and I felt the intrigue rising.

Upon arriving at the swingers club, I noticed the place looked somewhat bizarre—a giant beautiful villa that was probably built by local nobility. Little did they know what their manor would transform into a few centuries later. The inside was a mix of your local shitty disco with an average sound system and lights that favored darkness and shadows at the sides. There was a buffet of three-day-old-looking food served in disposable white plastic dishes sitting alone in a corner overlooking the internal courtyard, lit by elegant lamps that must have been copied from the most elegant streets of Paris. The upper floor, where the "fun" was happening, had plenty of small rooms with just a curtain made of red lace to provide privacy for their occupants. There was also a little cubic-shaped room with a chair in the middle surrounded by wooden walls filed with holes in them (little did I know back then the purpose of it) closing the small maze of the second floor.

Having fun with my friend and his girlfriend sitting at the side of the DJ booth overlooking the small dance floor, I spotted a girl who really caught my attention. She was almost as tall as me, with a slim athletic toned body with visible tattoos, dark hair with dark eyes that complemented her tanned skin that was exposed by revealing black latex clothing.

As the cocky, fueled-up-by-testosterone Casanova I thought I was, I went straight in approaching her, spitting my best game. She asked me if I smoked, and we proceeded to introduce each other while lighting up a Camel Blue.

"Cami," she firmly said while extending her tattooed hand in front of my chest.

"So what do you do here?" I asked.

"I'm doing a squirt show." She must have known I was a complete novice there because my puzzled face prompted her to explain further. "You see the cage over there? I will be inside in a short moment, and I will squirt a lot. Come and have a look."

I replied, "I know how to make women squirt, but I have never seen a squirt show."

"Here is your chance," she giggled.

As we finished the cigarette, she excused herself as she had to get ready to go inside the cage diametrically opposed to the DJ booth in an equally elevated position, so all the guests could have a perfect view of whatever would happen inside. She stepped into the cage with another older woman dressed in red lingerie holding a giant pink dildo in her right hand, while the DJ was pumping up the audience by yelling loudly in the microphone that the best duo in town was about to raise the temperature of the room.

As the older woman was behind Cami, they both started swinging their hips to the music, the older woman holding her waist with one hand and caressing Cami's face with the tip of the dildo, slowly moving it downwards the erogenous zones of her

11

fit body. A few minutes of this erotic foreplaying led to Cami dropping her pants and throwing them with the heel of her long stilettos in the face of a guest that was straight in the line of fire, making him go wild like an ape inside a cage when food is taunted in front of it.

The music slowed down and a more sensual acoustic guitar started to accompany the scene.

Both women sat down, with Cami spreading her legs revealing her vagina to the line of men surrounding the cage. The older women played with the massive dildo around Cami's vagina and with a steady hand started to rub the shaft portion of the dildo over her clitoris, making both women moan at the same time like wild coyotes on a full moon.

The momentum kept growing as the music started to grow louder and louder, until the older woman slowly started to push the beer bottle sized dildo inside of Cami's vagina, making her head tilting backwards swiftly exploding in a loud moan. Without hesitation, the older woman started moving the pink dildo back and forth, with a steady motion like a piston in a cylinder, with every push making Cami shout short-wailing noises growing louder and longer as the speed of the penetration increased.

I was looking from the other side of the room with curiosity, not to the spectacle itself, but to the atmosphere. Clearly this was an adult only thing, but it wasn't only men interested in this contrary to my beliefs, there was also two women in their 50's that were stroking each other's genitalia on a couch not too far from where I was observing, as well as other females in the small crowd that assembled around the fake gold painted cage from which Cami was brutally penetrated. A thought started to form in my head that perhaps women were also interested in erotic and porn imagery and it wasn't just a Men's club. Porn didn't have gender barriers and it was made for everyone that had an interest in it.

Cami started yelling as if she was about to give birth, only to push the giant dildo out of herself and start squirting so hard that I immediately thought "it's a fountain!" splashing the face of the few front rowers that were hugging the cage barrels.

I knew what was happening, but I had no idea how it was happening, like an astrologist seeing how a star is formed for the first time after reading the process in the scientific papers. I knew I was hooked. In my quest to become much better at sex, if I could give women experiences like this one, I would be, hands down, the best one in the world. The thought was soon replaced because getting sprayed by human fluids wasn't the only kind of degeneracy that this place offered.

"Did you see me?" Cami asked me after she changed into a black leather bikini, surprising me while drinking a very watery gin and tonic.

"I did, it was funny" was the most nonchalant, pretending to not be an excited answer.

We continued the conversation about how she performs it, how she prepared for it, if she enjoyed performing, until she confessed to me "well I would like to perform something with you..." I was taken back - I knew we could have sex but I wasn't expecting it to happen that fast.

Trying to sound as much as Casanova as possible, I did my best seductive tone saying, "What do you have in mind, girl?"

"Let's go to the dungeon!" she happily declared while taking my hands and leading the way.

We crossed the dance floor that was now filled with couples of all ages and a bunch of single guys in their mid 20's that annoyingly tried to dance in front of the women, showcasing their bad dance moves. We entered a massive wooden door painted in jet black that was conveniently camouflaged by the darkness of the room and the wall painted in a lighter shade of black.

As soon as Cami turned the door knob and we stepped in, I had a deer in the headlights moment to process what I was looking at. The room was painted with a bright red and every other detail in black. A collection of wooden and metal furniture and medieval torture machines was filling the crammed room. There was a man with a latex mask tied to a black cross that resembled the shape of an X, while next to him stood a woman dressed as a police officer, if police officers wore all black leather and tiny skirts with huge heels, who whipped him violently in the back with a horse whip. The woman smiled and opened her arms in a dramatic way making it clear it was an invitation towards Cami as she hugged back.

"She is Clio, the Domme of this place," Cami said, introducing me.

I robotically held my hand out in front of me while Domme clawed her forearm behind my neck, pulling me down to kiss me on the cheeks. She must have detected my embarrassment and feeling of awkwardness because smilingly with bright white teeth chiseled in bright red lips said, "we are less formal here and way more fun."

"It's your first time here?" she questioned me.

"Yes, I never seen a place like this, aside from the museum of torture," I half jokingly smiled.

Knowing she was dealing with a novice, she smiled caringly like you would do with a child when they ask why the sky is blue. "Very similar tools for a very different purpose" she winked at me and immediately went back to whipping the back of the man tied to the cross that exploded in a whine of pain while she yelled at him "shut up filthy pig!"

Cami must have seen I was still absorbing everything and she asked me if I wanted to tie her to a nearby wooden column with straps chained to the sides to just "play a little bit." She leaned with her chest into the pole almost like she wanted to hug the wooden phallic-like pillar. I struggled with the straps, having no idea how they worked and using them for the first time. The only knowledge I had about restricting movement was to pin the wrists of my partners over their head while having sex in missionary. So this was a new concept and game to me. Carefully closing the velcro of the straps with the same accuracy a climber checks the knots of his ropes before attempting a rappel descend, I looked at how I had this beautiful girl tied as she was pushing her glutes out towards me, letting her arms fall down only to be suspended by the straps that forced the chains to go in full traction.

"Spank me" she seductively said while looking at me by turning her head in my direction.

Now I had seen a few hardcore scenes, so I understood the concept of spanking, and had thrown a few timid slaps here and there in my previous sexual intercourses. What I was lacking was the know how, the warming up, how pain and pleasure work in tandem, everything that makes impact play more fun and safe for both of us. I just simply thought you approach the whole situation like a baseball player approaches the batting cage, just swing as hard as you can and send the ball in the parking lot. I loaded my body weight on my back foot while raising my flattened hand ready to high five with maximum force on her right gluteus maximus. I was ready to make her feel the pain. If that's what she wanted, she will get it.

Springing fast, my hand descended upon her like thunder hits the ground, fast and deafening. The skin of my hand slammed hard into her skin that was all tensed up by the leg stretch and the anticipation of the hit. It felt like hitting the border of a hand drum, hard in some area and squishier towards the center. Cami exploded in a loud wail filled with pain while immediately squatting to the ground hugging the pole surrounding it entirely with her inner elbows, hurling something at me that I didn't process because I didn't expect this reaction. I mean after all she asked me to do this. In retrospect, there was a lesson to be learned there, which is to not assume how any activity is supposed to be done just because you think it's how it is supposed to be.

I wasn't the only one that felt something was wrong, as Clio stepped next to me looking straight into my eyes with bossy body language pushing her face towards mine.

"WHAT. ARE. YOU. DOING???!"

"She asked me to be slapped!" I defended myself in front of the BDSM judge.

"But don't you see you almost injured her? Do you know what you are doing?!"

Now, usually in this situation, another Dom/Domme doesn't interfere with the play of another Dom simply because there is no knowledge of the scene and the agreements that the parties involved have. Even dungeon monitors usually refrain from interrupting while keeping an observing eye making sure that everyone is safe. However, Clio was the monitor and friends with Cami, having seen her playing and having played with her before, she knew what she was used to and had to intervene.

Without knowing it, she changed my life forever.

Then she went back to the tied up masked man at the cross. Feeling ashamed of my action, I joined Cami's still squatting body as I stuttered a lousy apology while reaching for the strap to release her. She drove her right hand immediately on her glutes starting to vigorously caress the area affected by my negligent hit.

"Why did you hit me so hard so soon?" she protested.

"I thought that's what you wanted," I excused myself while not maintaining eye contact.

I must have really messed up since she didn't offer any further comment while I was removing the straps, as the sensual and hedonistic vibe was immediately killed by the glacial air perceived in the room. Clio leaned in with Cami, making sure she was good, checking how she was feeling, and sending a couple of air jabs my way, half-jokingly saying that she'll whip me if I attempt again to do such a thing without proper care.

The three of us stood in a small circle where Clio schooled me on the principles of spanking, how play should be negotiated beforehand, how to get real time feedback from the submissive, and that the main job of the Dom is to deliver not only what the Sub is asking, but delivering it correctly (which is harder than it sounds).

From that night on, I was hooked by the feelings and the dynamics, but I also realized how incompetent I was in this sphere, and how it made me question my manhood: Was I the incredible sex machine that I thought I was? Was I capable of delivering the pleasure that I was so sure I was giving to women by trying to "drill" their uteruses with my penis?

As the place started closing, I praised Clio for her knowledge and exchanged contact details with Cami, just to never write to her out of the embarrassment of my poor performance. The ride back home with my friend and his girlfriend was a mix of debriefing and reflection time. As I told the story I experienced, detail by detail, both started to chime in with feedback pointing out what I did wrong, what I should have done, and some internet resources that I should look at if I intended to go deeper into the rabbit hole.

Not only was I completely ready to deep dive into this, I was unwillingly preparing to embark on a journey that would take me around the world, meeting fantastic new people, and bringing my more "vanilla" friends to sex-positive events, shibari nights, and tutoring them in their first steps into this brand new world.

I started to look for every bit of knowledge possible, reading every website that wouldn't low-key give my computer a virus, shady blogs from anonymous self-affirmed Doms and experts, looking at all possible porn (even though I realized it was a bad idea because, most of the time, porn is not a correct reflection of reality and how things should be done)—anything below mastery wasn't going to be accepted. It was during that time that I took a new job that included traveling abroad for business meetings, bringing me to the kinky capitals of Europe: Berlin, London, and Amsterdam. That's where, by attending sex-positive parties, mysterious meetups in formal clothing in bars and cafes, and conventions, I started to learn more and more from others' experiences and stories, absorbing them like a sponge, every particular detail about what was so fascinating about this world.

I hope my words will help you get inspiration to deeply explore a world that is trying its hardest to present itself in the best light to mainstream culture. As you will see, this journey will force you to self-reflect and gain a better understanding of yourself, uncovering feelings and beliefs that you had confined in the back of your mind and never manifested into your everyday reality, just as it did for me.

Brandon's Story

While I have some personality traits that could lean me towards being Dominant, I'm also a product of my environment, just like everyone else. I had a lot to learn, and frankly, more that I had to unlearn, in order to become the Dom I am today.

I grew up in a broken home, a poor kid from the trailer park, raised by a single mother. My father was an "every once in a while" dad, with some years in my childhood him being very heavy into drug use. My mother was a strong, caring woman who played both the masculine and feminine role in the household very well, although she often leaned more masculine. She had to. She was raising a boy all on her own, one with a strong, independent mind, so she had to keep me disciplined. However, she also had her own shortcomings with mental health issues, depression, and epilepsy, on top of working 40-50 hours a week. I had to learn to grow up and become "the man of the house" very quickly.

In addition to being strict about my studies, so I would excel and one day get out of the trailer park, she also conditioned me to treat a woman as a lady with respect, compassion and care and to find a woman who would equally support me. My mother taught me about working hard, honor, trust, respect, and kindness for others. These are all wonderful for treating women as equals, yet when it came to seduction and sexual dynamics between men and women, I was so utterly underprepared.

As far as I can remember, I've always been interested in the opposite sex, even before puberty. I had my first girlfriend in the 3rd grade after I gave her a ring during recess. I've always been a lover boy and romantic.

When I finally did hit puberty, oh my god. The sexual drive was debilitating. By that time school was so easy for me that my mind was often free to be preoccupied with girls and sex. I grew up during the age of the internet, but the only computer we had was in the dining room that my mother and I shared. So sometimes when she'd go off to bed after working all day, I'd get on the computer and google image search for boobs or lesbians making out so I didn't get a virus on the computer from going to a porn site. Of course, I did accidentally do that from time to time too.

Then I spent one summer with my father working construction and actually got paid for the work. The first thing I did when I got home was buy an iPod touch so I could surf the internet in the privacy of my room.

The world of porn was unlocked for me.

Despite what the media will have you believe, I never kept looking for more and more extreme stuff. I usually stuck to my favorites, which most of the time was POV porn. But damn, I must have spent hours jacking off back then and several times a day. So many hormones pulsing through my blood, it seemed to never go down.

I had many different girls I was interested in throughout middle and high school, but one girl imprinted my mind harder than any other. She was a blonde dancer and fire spinner who then went on to become a cheerleader. I was **infatuated** with this girl. We became friends and shared the same friends group throughout middle and high school. I really wanted to date this girl, so I ran the script that I was taught, be a nice guy, care for her, treat her "right", even spending money on her, but never blatantly making my interest known or being direct about my intentions.

What I received in return was being strung along, maybe she likes me, but we're more like brother and sister, but also being super affectionate towards me at times, and then seeing her repeatedly get into relationships with abusive boyfriends, with one actually physically hurting her.

I didn't understand at all and I spent many years in what felt like the worst agony of my life. The girl had burned a hole in my psyche and it took a long time for it to heal. From that point on, I knew whatever I was doing was not working, but I had no idea what to do...

An Experience Like No Other

I left high school still a virgin and went off to college. Because I had no idea what I was doing, and really knew that, I wasn't even attempting to attract girls. I just focused on my studies. That didn't get rid of my annoyingly high sex drive though. During the summer break between freshman and sophomore year, I had somehow found my way to Craigslist casual encounters.

You know, the online dating and hookups side of craigslist before dating apps existed. Despite some of the ads being really shady, some were pretty genuine. I can't recall if it was my ad or having replied to hers, but I ended up chatting with a girl who was a couple years older than me and by happenstance lived a block away from me, in the neighborhood that my childhood best friends and I used to hang out. I told her I was a virgin and had no experience. She was the sweetest girl and said she would teach me. Then she surprised me and told me she was a cam girl on Chaturbate and that I should watch her that night and then come over the following night. So me and my trusty iPod spent the whole night together as I watched this curvy redhead fuck herself with a dildo. I repeatedly kept edging myself as I watched, but didn't want to cum. I wanted to save it for her.

The following night I snuck out the back door of my childhood home to walk up the street to this beauty's apartment. I nervously knocked on the door and was greeted by what felt like an angel to me at the time. She was sweet but surprisingly a bit timid and seemed as nervous as I did. We went to the living room, she poured me a drink, and turned on a movie. I never had done this before, so I just nervously sat there wondering how I was going to kiss this girl let alone get her clothes off.

Luckily, she turned to me and said, "you don't actually want to watch this movie, do you? Come here and kiss me." THANK YOU! To this day, I love kissing, and to my surprise, I was actually pretty decent at it without having any experience. Both of us leaned in, cheeks flush, and what felt like electricity pulsing through me. I started fondling her as she reached over to my pants and started rubbing the very obvious erection I had.

Quickly we started peeling clothes off, at least till we had to pause so she could help me get her bra off because I was struggling harder than someone trying to get into Fort Knox. Then, with me standing up and an erection that could cut diamonds, this adorable girl dropped to her knees and consumed my cock with her wet, warm mouth.

I had watched this a thousand times in porn, but to finally feel it was unbelievable. It was better than I could have ever imagined.

I was so excited that I put my hand on the back of her head and started thrusting my cock as quickly as I could into her face. She let me fuck her face for several thrusts before she gagged and tapped me. As I pulled my cock out of her slobbery mouth, she said "don't forget to let me breathe, sweety." Ohhh, right, I guess this might make it hard to do that...

Again, I had no idea what I was doing, so I didn't know how to lead this to anything else, so kept letting her suck me off until she asked if we should move this to the bedroom. She stood up and we stumbled our way down the hallway, running into walls because our faces were locked into each other the entire time. When we finally got to the bed, I was so eager to try the next thing: eating a girl out. I'd love to remember how I actually did, because I've learned much better techniques since then, but all I do remember was how much it turned me on hearing her scream and moan as she orgasmed with me between her legs.

Then it was time, I was finally going to do what every horny teenage boy thinks about for 365 days in the year. I was finally going to get to fuck a girl. I came prepared with the condoms from the box that my mom had bought me years earlier telling me to "wrap it or slap it". I'd even practiced a few times before, so I didn't look like an idiot when I'd finally get to use one. So I slipped on this rubber, positioned myself between her legs, and slid into what felt like heaven. Now you'd think that because I had been edging myself the night before, that I was ready to explode, but instead I was so hyper focused with 100% awareness of the sensations that were happening to me and how she was reacting, that I just kept fucking without stopping. It felt like forever. We just kept switching positions in every configuration I could think off and fucking like two wild animals. You'd think I could remember how I finally came, but truth be told, I don't. All I remember is how amazing it felt to be inside of her and hearing her moan over and over and over again.

Afterwards we cuddled, and she said there was no way I was a virgin and asked me if that was some scheme to have sex with girls. I laughed and I told her no, that I legitimately was a virgin. She was shocked and told me I was really, *really* good at everything. At the moment, my little hormone-drowned teenage brain lit up like fireworks and the only thing that crossed my mind was **"I want to be a sex god!"**

Awakening the Dominant Inside

We'll fast forward the story some, but in college I wound up getting a cute, spitfire redheaded girlfriend (something about these redheads...) after learning the power of pre-selection and the halo effect of being seen with attractive girls, even if those girls were just being friendly at the time.

This girl and I were in the same program together and also had physics together, which meant we needed to do a lot of homework together. After learning she was into me during a college party, I went to her apartment for physics homework. I was studious, so we *actually* did our homework, and then proceeded to watch the entire Batman series because I was too afraid to actually make a move. But before I left, I finally gained the courage to do what felt like the scariest thing of my life, I kissed her, and when I left, I was shaking like an earthquake had hit me. A week later, I took her virginity, and we started a marathon of fucking like jack rabbits, multiple times a day, several times a week.

I credit this period to the seedlings of awakening my kinky tendencies, because we couldn't keep our hands off each other (or more like my dick out of her) and played many times in various ways in public. I have fond, fond memories in the movie theater, at the park, in the back of our friend's car, the back of a charter bus, in the alleyways of Chicago, and more. This also when I started becoming a sex nerd, learning and studying new sex techniques so I could fulfill that fantasy of being a sex god. I remember purchasing some course on how to eat a girl out from some PUA that I can't even recall his name, but it's the same technique I often use today and it's always gotten me stellar reviews.

Eventually we both graduated and moved back to my hometown. We still had sex quite often, but of course, the realities of the real world started to creep in and we did not have the time freedom we had as college students. Some of my favorite memories were when we'd order pizza for a cheat meal on the weekend and just have all day long sex sessions. Of course, my curiosity kept wanting to push the bounds of what we did sexually, but I didn't really know what there was, more than oral and intercourse. I actually found my way to Tantra before I did kink, but that's a story for another book.

I'd been dating this girl for four years, and we shared a lot of love and genuine friendship with each other. So I decided to propose. We got married, bought a house, and started living the life I'd been told was the goal. My first introduction to any kind of inclination of Dominant desires came when we were in our bedroom one day. I was tickling her and play wrestling with her, something that we had engaged in many times before, and sometimes it led to sex, but I never really thought anything of it.

What was different this time was I had grabbed her wrists and was using a lot more force, because she was resisting a lot. I ended up pinning her hands to the bed next to her head, with my body on top of hers and in between her legs. She kept squirming and resisting, and saying "noooooo. Stooooop it. noooo." trying to get her hands up. She alternated between laughing and seeming to like it, but then sounding genuine in her no, but then still looking like she enjoyed it. What frightened me was that... *I was enjoying it*.

Immediately a tsunami of shame came over me. I quickly let her go, got off her, and sat there, disgusted with myself. All I could think about was, "**what kind fucking monster am I?**" It was like my mind was clashing up against a football league of linebackers carrying every single lesson that I had learned about how you're supposed to treat a woman and *that* was not it. I did not tell my wife what was wrong, because I was terrible at expressing emotions or needs back then. Instead I shoved that deep down and told myself I would never do it again.

But of course, you can never truly repress your sexuality. It always finds a way back out. Later in the marriage I would learn of my wife's love of smut novels and taking a liking to 50 Shades of Grey, especially when the movies came out.

With time I did a lot of self work in a weekly men's group I started 6 years ago and still lead to this day. My wife and I were able to explore a little bit of kink, but we never fully stepped into D/s, even though I think she would have really enjoyed it. Looking back at the relationship now, there were also small things we'd done outside of the bedroom that are classic D/s dynamics, like her having a goal to be fit, so she gave me control to make her meal plans and workout routines.

In the meantime, our sex lives had started dwindling, and I take responsibility for that because I was largely repressing mine, even though I was longing for what we once had. To be honest, I just wasn't man enough to be a Dom yet. I also had a strong desire to have multiple partners. We had one discussion about opening the marriage, but she was a strongly monogamous woman, so I dropped the pursuit. This in combination with diverging values and life paths led to a divorce, but not the end of our friendship. We both strongly respect, care for, and wish the best of each other and check in on each other quite often.

With the divorce though, I was now free to explore what I was too ashamed to share with my ex-wife, and also learn to start unraveling all the nice guy tendencies, deconstructing the Madonna/whore complex, and actually step into my natural leadership capabilities that allowed me to be the Dom I am today.

I spent hours reading books and blogs, learning from dozens of courses, talking with mentors far more experienced than I, posting on forums, and diving head first into the local community in Texas. My first play party was one of the largest in the area which can get 700-900 people in a single night. I've volunteered with them for a few years now, taking their training including those to be a dungeon monitor. I also started leading a munch (just a kinky meetup where people network and talk about sex rather than business). I have thrown a few play parties myself too. I've also shared my bed with many wonderful, submissive women and done things far more intense than simply pinning a woman down during missionary. That thought makes me chuckle at my naive, past self a little.

I'm incredibly grateful to the many mentors I learned from during this journey, with a huge amount of appreciation for Mario. He saw something in me that I couldn't see in myself when I started and graciously gave his guidance to a fledgling Dom so I could become the powerful individual I am today.

My additions to this book are those lessons I learned. I hope they help you step into your power, too.

What Is Dominance, Really?

This book isn't just about becoming a better Dom in the bedroom (though don't worry, we'll help with that too). What we've come to understand, through time and self-reflection, is that our journeys to becoming highly Dominant were, in fact, compensations for what we truly wanted: **control over our lives**.

When we realized that we had to take charge of our decisions and face the consequences of our actions, we understood that the only way to feel truly aligned was to be dominant *both in and out* of the bedroom.

Being Dominant isn't just about exercising control over someone else; it's first and foremost about exercising control over **yourself**.

One of Mario's favorite Latin phrases is:

"Potentia supra ipso, Potentia supra Aliis"

which roughly translates to, **"Power over self is power over others."** There's no truer form of Dominance than the Dominance we exercise over ourselves.

This book is far from the "tough-navy-seal-run-marathons-while-shitting-yourself" type of approach, or a bullet-point list of to-dos like "make your bed and fight lobsters." No, this is our personal journey—how we improved from a place of insecurity and hope to one of confidence and fulfillment.

While the original structure of this book was outlined by Mario in 2022 on a remote beach in Mexico, the subsequent reviews include Brandon's excellent additions, plus the work in structuring the book and simplifying concepts that require more explanation than a live demonstration. And, of course, we've included more experiences we both gathered along the way.

For the remainder of Section 1, you'll get a concise definition of what Dominance is.

Section 2 will guide you in developing your **Inner Dominance**, detailing the specific traits and mental beliefs you need to master within yourself in order to have women wanting to submit to you.

Section 3 will then focus on your **Outer Dominance**, including techniques and hands-on skills to demonstrate your Dominance in the real world and build relationships with submissive women.

We wrote this book with a few key elements throughout:

- **Principles:** the mindsets and behaviors that underlie Dominance, because if you don't understand the why, you'll just be a robotic Dom.
- **Practices:** the juicy stuff where you learn how to do the actions of a Dom, after you first understood where they come from.
- **Stories:** where you can see how we think, act and behave. You'll see disclaimers at the beginning of every story since names and locations were edited for privacy reasons and conversations were edited to fit the flow of the book.

Honestly, we could have written this book without many of the traits and skills we're about to teach you and just shown you the process to roleplay as a Dom. That's what most BDSM education does. However, every woman who submits to you in the future would feel that something was off. It just wouldn't *feel* right to her—that you were a fake Dom. She'd never be able to fully surrender or be in complete submission. The relationships would be short-lived, and you'd be ghosted.

The traits you'll learn in Section 2 and the skills in Section 3 are the prerequisites to actually **be** a Dom, not just roleplay one. You'll build a strong, masculine, inner frame where Dominance truly comes from—one that allows you to make her feel everything she wants to feel in full submission to you.

CHAPTER TWO

Dominance & Submission

What is Dominance & Submission?

Dominance and submission—also referred to as D/s and Dom/sub—is a relationship dynamic in which the Dominant exercises control, and the submissive willingly surrenders control, all within mutually agreed-upon boundaries and guidelines.

Dominance and submission is one of the foundational dynamics of BDSM, which also includes bondage and discipline, dominance and submission, and sadism and masochism. As you'll learn later in this book, being a Dom does not necessarily mean you must be a sadist. In fact, you can be a Dom without ever engaging in any of the other BDSM practices. It's also important to note that there is a vast world of kinks and fetishes that you could explore without ever taking on the role of a Dom—and many people do.

What is a Dom?

A Dom (or Dominant) is the person who assumes the role of authority, control, and power over the submissive. In our experience, being a Dom is about leadership, which requires understanding the goals and desires of each person and creating a clear vision for how to achieve those goals. A Dom is in service to the dynamic— the mutual vision for the relationship. These goals could range from something as simple as both partners reaching the heights of ecstasy, to something as complex as guiding both of your lives. In pursuit of that, the Dom is responsible for creating structure, providing safety, building trust, allowing for play and pleasure, and caring for the submissive.

Dominant vs. Domineering

Being Dominant means you exercise control, influence, or authority over others **in service of both partners.**

Being domineering means asserting your will over others in an overbearing or authoritarian manner, **solely to serve your own needs**. Being Dominant is *not* about aggression, manipulation, or abuse.

Fake Doms

One of the biggest concerns of submissives is submitting to the right Dom and avoiding falling prey to a "Fake Dom."

Typically, Doms who are labeled as Fake Doms fall into one of two categories:

1. They are inexperienced.
2. They are manipulative.

The first category isn't necessarily "fake." They simply need to level up in their role as a Dom. No big deal—that's why you're reading this book, and kudos to you for doing so.

The second category is far more insidious because these individuals seek to use a submissive's desire to submit to fulfill their own needs, with no regard for the submissive's needs or whether consent has been given. In this case, they are not truly acting as a Dom.

It's not uncommon for us to hear from women who've had bad experiences with Fake Doms—individuals who, in one way or another, were solely focused on fulfilling their own pleasure, entirely neglecting the submissive partner, who should be their responsibility.

What is a Sub?

Generally, a submissive is a person who willingly consents to relinquish control, authority, and decision-making to their Dominant partner. Submissives take on the role of being obedient, compliant, and responsive to the wishes and desires of their Dominant, within the agreed-upon boundaries of the relationship.

Submissive vs. People-Pleasing (or Being a Doormat)

Being submissive means *consciously choosing* to give over control, influence, or authority to another person because they have the sub's best interests at heart— and because the sub *wants* to serve them.

People-pleasing, or being a doormat, means serving others while disregarding your own needs, often due to unconscious choice, insecurity, or even a desire to please— sometimes even when you don't want to serve them.

The major difference is that being submissive means your needs are actively considered and addressed (whether they are met or not is up for negotiation between the Dom and sub). The submissive consciously chooses to be subservient to the Dom, rather than letting others take control of their life without their consent.

Being submissive is also not a passive role. Subs don't simply let things happen to them. Receiving is a skillful act. Both sides of the slash must contribute and actively participate to create a mutually beneficial and enjoyable experience.

Who Actually Has the Power and Control in the Dynamic?

At first glance, and to anyone unfamiliar with BDSM dynamics, it might seem that the Dominant has all the power and control. The Dominant is the one deciding what the submissive does, when it's done, how it's done, and for whose pleasure.

However, what you might not see is that the submissive has *voluntarily* given up control and retains the power to end the interaction at any moment by using a safeword or revoking consent. The entire power granted to the Dom can be removed at any time. It's this choice that differentiates a healthy BDSM relationship from an abusive or manipulative one.

So, does that mean the submissive holds all the power and control, since they can essentially "turn it off" at any moment? While this is the common view in the BDSM community, we believe it undermines the importance of the Dominant's role in the dynamic. The Dominant takes on the responsibility for both people in the relationship, and if the Dom decides that the relationship is no longer worth pursuing, he too has the right to revoke his consent and withdraw the leadership he provides.

This point is crucial because some Doms may undervalue their own Dominance and the kinds of experiences they can create because of their leadership—experiences that many women deeply crave.

Since the relationship is built on mutual consent, and neither side is obligated to continue, we believe the power is equally held—though this may seem counterintuitive given the nature of the relationship.

Why Be a Dom?

The obvious reason you might think being a Dom would be great is because you get to have full control over another person to satisfy your every whim and desire, right?

To some extent, that's true—but not in the way you might imagine. In reality, being the Dom often means *more* work, not less. You're now responsible for two people. As much as she is there to serve and attend to your needs, you must also attend to hers, without taking advantage of her eagerness to please. It's a balance—you can't give nothing in return.

So then, what is the benefit?

Brandon's Perspective

For me, witnessing her sink into her sweet feminine energy and release all of her inhibitions is a beautiful thing. And frankly, seeing her go from composed, proper "good girl" to a feral, sex-driven nympho is incredibly hot, too.

But more than that, when she looks at me with those doe eyes—completely surrendered, fixated on me—I am her entire world in that moment. I find women to be one of the greatest creations of beauty, and for that brief moment, I get to own that beauty completely. It feels as though I'm God, because, in that world, I am. I'm the Alpha and the Omega of *her world*. The trust, devotion, and confidence she places in me to lead her, and her desire to serve me out of appreciation, is a true power trip. I get to feel her admiration, respect, and ultimately her love. That feeling makes me feel invincible—like I could slay dragons. It fuels my soul, so that the next day I can continue working hard to make us both better people.

Dominance feels authentic to me. I have a saying: how you see me show up in the scene is how you'll see me show up in all aspects of life. I'm not stepping into a role; I'm being more of who I am. It's simply part of my personality to want my own way, to lead from the front, to retain control, and to do things on my terms. It feels incredibly validating to have a woman who loves to serve and please a man like that.

But the least obvious reason is that the work required to be a Dom makes me a better version of myself. Seeing her kneel before me is just icing on the cake.

Mario's Perspective

Aside from the thrill of controlling (within the limits of negotiated boundaries) one, two, or more human beings, Dominance naturally resonates with me because I'm a natural leader in life. In modern-day life, it's not like I'm always forced to lead or take responsibility, so when it comes to my sexuality, I run toward the opposite. I feel at ease when occupying the "boss" chair—it's where I belong.

Dominance also forces you to have a deeper conversation with yourself, since the stakes are higher. Now, not only do you have to take care of yourself, but also of others. What will you do? How will you react? What if... ? These questions make exploring the deeper parts of your mind easier, especially when you're in an aroused state.

Obviously, I'd be lying if I didn't mention, at least for me, how much I enjoy "unleashing the monster" inside and letting it roar in a safe, controlled environment.

Why Would a Woman Want to Be Submissive?

The surface answer might be that they find it hot. The idea of raw masculine energy wanting to rip her clothes off, claim her, own her body so he can have her anytime he wants, because she turns him on **all the time**.

But it's much deeper than that.

Why on earth would a woman want to willingly give control of herself over to a Dom? For some, going as far as becoming a slave to them?

The answer is simple: The Dom *cares*.

Let's take a step back. Think back to when you were a child. Unless you had a completely traumatic childhood, most of the time, you were willing to let your parents have a say over your life because you trusted they had your best interests at heart. You trusted they cared about you.

Submission is about trust. Submissives look for someone who will have their best interests at heart—someone who will care for them when they are at their most vulnerable, with complete surrender of control. It's the feeling of being so loved and desired that someone is willing to care for them and keep them safe, no matter what.

To some degree, all of us hand over control of our lives to all sorts of people every day. We make that exchange because we believe the other party—whether an employer, a corporation, or a government—will benefit us in some way. The most prominent benefit is that we don't have to worry about the logistical challenges of getting our basic needs met.

So, is it really so far-fetched that she would willingly give over control in order to have her mental, physical, and emotional needs met too—especially if she knows that person cares about her?

She gets to feel:

- **Free**: She doesn't have to worry. She doesn't have to be on alert. She can relax and let you take care of everything. All she has to do is have fun, enjoy herself, and do as she's told. No stress about planning, being prepared, or worrying about what comes next. She's free from the hassles of everyday life. You will take care of it.

- **Safe**: She wants to know you have the capacity to be dangerous, to be a threat, but can control it and deliberately exude that power without causing her harm. She wants to know you will take care of her and keep her safe.

- **Desired**: Being ravished by you makes her feel wanted. To be "owned" means someone values you, someone likes having you around.

- **Important**: She feels satisfaction in pleasing you, accomplishing her tasks correctly, and earning praise.

- **Appreciated**: In a world where people are quick to criticize and judge, it's deeply satisfying to hear someone truly mean it when they say, "You're a good girl."

- **Accepted**: When she sees you pursue your desires unabashedly, she can release and pursue hers without judgment. She wants to be the sex-crazed nympho for you and not be shamed for doing so.

- **Loved**: Someone has taken the time to learn about her—her desires, her boundaries, what brings her pleasure. And in doing so, they've hit all the other emotions above. All of these things make her feel cared for and, ultimately, loved.

The dream for a sub is that as long as they do what the Dom says, everything will be great. They won't have to make any decisions, accept responsibility for what happens, or worry about anything—period. It's liberation and freedom from worry, anxiety, uncertainty, and the stressful realities of life. Yet, they'll still be cared for and taken care of.

Submission allows the sub to enter a state of tranquility, fully sinking into the pleasure of the fantasy realm—a special bubble without stress or pressure. It recharges her mental, emotional, and spiritual batteries so she can battle through another week of life.

She only has one responsibility: pleasing her Dom. The Dom will take care of the rest.

It's as close to a utopia, heaven on earth, or **pure bliss** as she'll ever get.

The Latvian Brat Who Met Her Torturer

A real story of Mario's. To protect the privacy of those involved, all names and identifying details have been altered. The individuals described in these stories were all consenting adults who participated of their own free will. If you choose to engage in similar activities, it is imperative that all parties involved are of legal age, fully informed, and consenting.

The Baltic countries offer more than what tourist guides present: crazy must-see locations, questionable food selections, and a very good range of craft beers, plus a *surprisingly* kinky community.

I was visiting some friends for a national celebration, where the locals enjoy a whole night of partying like there's no tomorrow, fueled by alcohol, songs, and debauchery. As tradition has it, this celebration was a pagan ritual to celebrate the hard summer work of harvesting the fields at a big banquet where then, with the favors of the fertility gods, humans would reproduce and make new offspring that will repeat the same process again and again. That hay ain't gonna make itself, son.

Fast forward a hundred years, the local fertility gods' favors and decisions on who does what to whom have been replaced by the algorithm of a dating app. Such algorithms decided to put me and Ieva on the same path, at least the type of path that lasts for a full night of lust.

Enter the Dom

We exchanged a few messages about both being disappointed since our respective celebrations were rather dull and uneventful and that we needed some adrenaline to make up for it. That adrenaline is exactly what I got once I texted Leva's phone number, with her replying to my initial text with a few nudes and a not-so-shy "hi stranger."

Looking at the hot Slavic features of her face, complemented by shoulder-length ashy blonde hair on a tall, slender, toned body with tattoos visible on her legs and upper chest, I made the decision that I wasn't just going to have an orgasm tonight, but I was going to get much more fun in the process.

"Hello you," I texted back. "Seems like the perfect body that can withstand some pain," I doubled down.

"Oh yes but only for the strong ones," she enthusiastically replied. Ah, gotta love that attitude. We were on the right road for some good fun together.

A few texts later, we set up a date at the bar at the corner of my place to check each other out and proceed straight back. While getting a glass of wine and sitting comfortably on my couch, Leva was wearing a skimpy, silky black summer dress with black boots laced up to her ankles and absolutely no underwear, something she proudly said as soon as she sat on the couch. I was hovering over her providing wine and water and trying to be a good host while not being distracted by this *important* piece of information.

"So what do you like in the bedroom?" I opened while I lounged next to her on the couch offering a toast.

"I don't know... I guess a bit of everything," she offered with a hint of disinterest at my question.

"Really? So let's say that you would meet a strong man and he would pull your hair, whisper naughty things in your ears, and tie you to a bed, how would that make you feel?"

"I don't know... I need to see if he is strong first," she said with a cheeky tone, giving me the look that only bratty girls can give you.

She didn't know yet, but that sentence was all I needed to search in my arsenal of "how to punish a brat" for a proper brat tamer tool.

"Oh of course, let's pretend you are going to meet such a man one day, would you give him control over you and let him play with you?"

"That sounds hot!"

Say no more, girl. I know what I'm going to give you.

My eyes turned darker and my smile descended into a smirk as I started to look at Leva like a wolf looks at a lamb. She broke eye contact first, looking down at her wine with a smile then taking a big gulp from the chalice, as I slowly moved my body closer and closer to her.

I placed my right hand over her shoulder with a gentle but firm top-bottom placement that would allow an easy "you stay down here" push down while my right thumb was creating small circles under her collarbone right where the skin and the silk of the dress met.

My left hand started stroking her right leg, crossing all the way, making us closer and closer, cupping the knee in my hand and stroking all the way up to her hip slowly with all the calm in the world, making her body squirm and slowly tremble.

"Look at me," I ordered in a neutral yet authoritarian tone.

She blushed and turned her head the other way around, emitting in a shy and playful tone, "No..."

I grabbed her left cheek with my full hand and pressed my left thumb on her chin and turned her directly towards me. "Look... at... me."

With our faces inches away from each other, she kept her eyes closed and repeated a more firm yet still playful "No."

Making sure I never broke contact with her skin, I slowly moved my left hand from her cheek down on her throat, not applying too much pressure but still making sure she would feel my hand on the sides of her neck as I rose above her and grabbed a chunk of her blonde thick hair and jerk her head up, making her gasp with her mouth and eyes wide.

"Good, you are listening now," I said while keeping eye contact.

I slowly pressed my lips against hers, which she abandoned by fiercely pressing her tongue against mine in an intense and passionate kiss that felt like it lasted forever. Once I broke from her lips, while still holding her in my hands, she gave me a voracious look like someone who had tasted just a small sip of water while stranded in the desert.

"Kiss me but harder this time," I demanded while pulling her head closer to me. She obliged, throwing herself at me and grabbing my face with both hands.

"Keep your hands on your chest." I erupted with a stern tone of voice, breaking immediate physical contact.

"You will touch me when I say so." to which she immediately complied.

"Very good," before I offered a full passionate and deep kiss.

We kept kissing with my hands moving her head up or to the side depending on where I positioned myself. I then noticed her hands rubbing her generous breasts. This was the signal I needed before I decided to stand up while holding her hair still and pulling her up towards me.

"Undress," I ordered.

"What if I don't want to?" she objected.

"Then we will do things my way," I shot back without hesitation or a hint of doubt, while grabbing her shoulders with both hands and rotating her together with me before sending her over the bed.

She exploded in a small excited scream of pleasure and a smile, looking to see what I would do next to her in such a defenseless position.

I undid my black leather belt, placed my knees on the bed, and slowly made my way to her chest, making her tremble in anticipation of what would happen next. I grabbed her wrists and wrapped them together with the belt at one of the corners of the bed.

I dismounted from the top position with my right knee placing it right next to her right hip, looking with mischief straight into her eyes before announcing the destination of my hands.

"I hope your cunt is not wet... It would be a shame what follows if it is..." I sweetly threatened her.

I placed both my hands flat on her belly and then slowly drove them apart, my left hand towards her neck, while my right went towards her pussy. I made sure that I would advance so slowly even a snail could keep up with me. I spread my arms to their respective destinations, anchoring my left hand gently at her throat and my right hand finally reaching her slit. By placing my right and middle finger on top of both lips, I could feel a spasm already.

"Now I will see if you are a good one or..." I declared before pushing the first phalanx of my right finger straight in her, appreciating with a smile how wet she was but without showing her.

"Or definitely not... I will show you what is my way now. I will start to rub your clit and count from 10 to 1. For every number I say, I will get faster and faster. When I arrive at 1 and I order you to cum, you will cum, but only then, OK? No lies, do you understand me?"

"YES PLEASE! TOUCH ME!" she begged back with the anxiety of one who desires nothing more than being played with.

"Very well," as I gently and softly whispered "TEN" with my hand following in sync with the lustful hip movement of Leva.

Enter the Dom

"Nine," long pause looking firmly in her eyes.

"Eight," still holding eye contact.

"Seven," noticeable speed increase in my fingers.

"Six," Leva tried to close her eyes to not show how much she was enjoying this, but her facial expression and breathing were betraying her.

"Five," now my hands were moving as fast as you would do when trying to dry a passport photo from the photo booth.

"Four," more intensity.

"Three," Leva moaned subtly with squeamish pleasure and when she least expected it, I removed my hand.

Her eyes beamed at me like a lighthouse would blind you in the middle of the night, confused, unsure what to say, her right brain fighting tooth and nail with the left one. That's when I knew I had her right where I wanted her.

"It seems you enjoyed it too much," I grimaced.

"WHY DID YOU STOP? I WAS CUMMING!"

"That's exactly why." I grabbed her throat and looked dangerously in her eyes. "You will cum when I decide it."

She looked back at me with a mix of fear and excitement. "DO YOU UNDERSTAND?" I growled in a low and dark tone.

"Yes, yes, I understand," she offered back in an excusatory voice. "Let's start again."

I repeated this cycle about four times, every time interrupting one number below the previous one, grabbing her, pushing my hand in her mouth, telling her to taste how much she wanted to cum.

Until the fifth time... I could feel her body being traversed by shockwaves that culminated in a body-shaking orgasm and a loud "Waaaghhhh" from her voice. She

41

was squeezing her eyes so much that I could notice a tear forming from the moisture of clenching the eyelids so hard. Her hips and boots bounced up and down a few times while her legs shook as if trying to warm up after being exposed to the cold.

I immediately undid the belt and placed my back against the bedpost, holding Leva in my arms, with her hands now folded over her belly with mine on top of hers, gently caressing her and whispering in her right ear, "You have been so good," and other gentle phrases in a sweet, calming, and with a hint of *self-pride* tone of voice.

She asked me if I enjoyed playing with her to which I replied "Delightful," and continued the aftercare and cuddles that ended up with her hands searching for my cock, and pulling it out of my trousers.

She remarked, "Now let me please you like I should do."

We had sex very shortly after and had most of it in doggy style, which ended up with me ordering her to get on her knees with her mouth under my crotch and cover her sweaty body with my sperm.

We cleaned each other up, exchanged more hugs and kisses and words of gratitude from both sides. I walked her to the door so she could catch her bus home, the last image of her walking down the hallway swaying her hips left to right in that black silky dress.

SECTION TWO

Inner Dominance

Become the Man She'll Submit To

CHAPTER THREE

Dominance As a Mental Set of Beliefs

When most people think of dominance, they typically associate it with physical traits, such as being tall or muscular, or personality characteristics, like being sanguine and driven. These, of course, are simplifications and generalizations.

There is no single trait, like a bullet point on a list, that will make you be perceived as dominant. For example, while being taller than the average person can help with the perception of dominance, not every tall person is actually dominant. The same applies to the personality trait of decisiveness—though many decisive individuals may seem dominant, not every decisive person exhibits true dominance.

Dominance is a product of beliefs, behaviors, physical traits, and actions that influence how the universe and the people around us perceive us.

Let's consider a quick example: Two men walk into a bar within a short time of each other.

The first man is 6′4″, walks with his back straight, is dressed in an elegant all-black suit and tie, and wears a confident smirk as he heads toward the bar without hesitation.

Shortly after, a 5′11″ man enters. He pauses at the entrance to survey the room, walks hesitantly through the crowd, and sits on a stool at the end of the bar, next to the wall.

Who is more dominant? The answer: We cannot possibly know.

If you say the first man, you've been fooled by his appearance and behavior into assuming he is dominant, but we can't be 100% sure. While how others perceive you can help—especially when signaling dominance—it doesn't necessarily make you dominant.

To be truly dominant, we must start with the most challenging aspect of this journey: changing your mindset. Specifically, we need to change how you think about yourself, the world we live in, the people around you, and what is possible.

The Hardest Case of All: Nice Guys

In Mario's years of traveling around the world, he's had the great fortune of meeting a wide variety of interesting people from all walks of life, from millionaire tech entrepreneurs to sales bros on company trips, to antiquity market hunters.

The fascinating part of these encounters was gaining different perspectives on the world and learning the peculiarities of how business is conducted in various fields. What stood out most was when conversations turned to sex and behavior in the bedroom. It was rare for Mario to meet someone who shared his views and ideas (sometimes he even received confused or shocked looks when expressing his preferences, with new acquaintances asking, "What do you mean by spitting in your girl's mouth while pulling her hair and slapping her in the face right after?").

It was always a variation of the same "mind virus" we've seen time and time again: the "Nice Guy" mentality.

Now, generally speaking, being nice is a good thing in society. Being kind and generous are valuable traits when interacting with others. However, the harsh reality is that when it comes to getting what you want and navigating intersexual dynamics, nice guys tend to finish last, as the saying goes. It's true that men who show more disagreeable traits often experience more success in various fields. Yet, many guys continue to believe that bending over backwards and placing others on a pedestal above them is what it means to be "nice."

Anyone want to guess why?

Let us explain:

- You have been programmed by society to follow a set of beliefs that don't align with reality.
- You seek validation from others and ignore your own opinion.
- You've conditioned yourself to act meek when you should have been doing the opposite.
- You've been weak all your life.
- You never stopped to ask the critical question: "What do I truly want?" and "If I'm not getting what I want, but someone else is, what am I doing differently than them?"
- You lack masculine role models.

Well, that's it. I guess the book could end here—the solution is right above, and we could all high-five each other, right? Not so fast.

If you truly want to overcome this, it's time to show you what's been behind the curtain all this time, and for you to start asking some important questions. Are you ready?

Deprogramming Yourself

Society, media, religion, and local culture have done an outstanding job of instilling beliefs in our minds about how the world works and how we should live.

Think for a moment about Mario's ancestors in ancient Italy. They truly believed the Earth was flat and that at the edge of it was a black hole that would suck you into the deepest ring of hell. Today you might laugh at this, but imagine how fiercely someone would have defended this belief. At the same time, people were burned at the stake for their beliefs because they went against what was preached and (wrongly) accepted as truth back in the day. If that doesn't make you appreciate modern life, we don't know what will.

Beliefs are the real reason we act the way we do, and they dictate the direction of our thinking. They become part of our identity, and after being brainwashed all your life, it's incredibly difficult to change them... but not impossible.

As an exercise, complete the following sentences:

- "Every time I talk to an attractive woman, I ..."
- "When I express what I want, I feel like ..."
- "I want to do (insert sexual act) because ..."
- "When I push for what I want, I get ..."
- "When others force me to do something I don't like, I ..."

There are many beliefs holding you back right now. It would be impossible to uncover all of them in a book, but we encourage you to sit down with pen and paper and start thinking about your life, your sexual life, and how you and others interact with each other.

The second step in changing your beliefs is to question them:

- Where do these beliefs come from?
- Do I believe this because I have hard proof or tangible evidence (e.g., touching a hot stove will burn me, and I will feel pain)?
- Did I learn this belief from a specific moment in my life, perhaps when I was a child?
- Did someone tell me to believe this? My parents? Culture? Society?

To become the Dominant man you want to be, you need to identify if your weaknesses stem from the beliefs, religion, culture, lifestyle, and habits that have been programmed into you and executed throughout your life.

When Mario decided to work on himself, he wrote down all the patterns, thoughts, and behaviors that kept recurring, then identified the underlying beliefs that caused him to think, project, and act in a certain way. He would continually ask "Why?"— at least five times.

As you will see, when you start looking under the hood, there are plenty of components working either for or against you, and you might not even be aware of them. You must work on your beliefs before anything else because they will change how you think and act.

The Nice Guy Cures

Approve of Yourself

Your entire life, you've been seeking others' approval and validation for your actions—or worse, for your very existence. You shy away from confidently being who you are because you're afraid of going against the grain of what others think and tell you you *should* be.

Yet, why is it that the very guys *who do* go against the grain, break the rules, and have a "I do whatever the f*ck I want" attitude seems to be more attractive? It's not because they live irresponsibly. In fact, it would probably be better if they got their act together. It's because they approve of themselves, irrespective of others' approval. They believe they have value and worth and live their life in accordance with their own values.

Society (or any group of people, from your family to your culture) has sets of rules. These rules define what that group deems appropriate for reaching their goal or what they define as success. For example, a Catholic family might say no sex before marriage because it's a sin (rule), and if you sin, you don't get into heaven (goal).

Here's the kicker: You get to decide what your goals are and the most effective way to reach them. You don't need anyone's approval to have a goal or to pursue it. More importantly, you're just as worthy as anyone else to be pursuing those goals.

Now, you may need to follow the rules occasionally to function and cooperate with others in that group of people. Laws typically exist for good reasons, and we don't advocate breaking them.

However, Mario and Brandon like to think of themselves as pirates, where the rules of society are more like guidelines than anything else. Hell, Brandon went from working behind a desk, being married, and owning a two-story home to becoming a digital nomad, being non-monogamous, dating multiple women, and traveling the U.S. in a van. The world bends to your will more than you know.

Put Yourself First

An absolute plague in the male universe is the virus of people-pleasing and putting everyone else's desires and pleasures ahead of your own. This stems from an insecurity that you are unworthy of receiving love or having your needs met.

People-pleasers do a disservice to themselves, thinking that by putting someone else before them, they will get reciprocity and get what they secretly want. This is known as a covert contract: "I do X for you, and you will do Y for me, but I'm not going to tell you what Y is or that I need Y..."

Not only is this a road to dissatisfaction, but in our experience, it's the surest way to create a bunch of misogynists who hate women in online forums. They've bent over backward trying to please women, completely disregarding their own needs. When women don't reciprocate, they become bitter, resentful, and hurtful towards women.

Get this clear in your head: no one owes you anything. Even if you satisfy their needs, they are under no obligation to give you anything back.

People-pleasers often fall into one of two traps:

1. They don't make what they want and need known (to protect themselves from being hurt by that person saying no).
2. They don't have anything of real value to offer the other person (so they just hope the other person will be nice to them).

Dominants get what they want because they:

- Have the confidence to ask for what they want and take responsibility for getting those needs fulfilled.
- Are aware of who they are, what value they have, and how to exchange that for what they want.

Yes, you read that right—we said "exchange," because everything is based on an exchange between parties, and you've been offering free samples this entire time.

Putting yourself first doesn't mean you need to step over others or tear them down, but it does mean you need to treat yourself with respect and go to bat for yourself as much as you do for other people.

Act with Courage

Most people are simply cowards. That's it. We said it. We create nightmare scenarios in our heads about the future that will never happen, keeping us from taking action.

There was one time when Mario was sitting in a café in Budapest. He saw a cute girl reading a book and decided to get her number. Right after that, two guys approached him and bombarded him with questions: How did he pull it off? What did he say to her? What would he have done if she rejected him? What if she called the police? It was as if these guys had just seen a Martian land from a spaceship!

Let's get something clear: There's danger, and then there's fear. Danger is a potential situation that could cause damage and inflict real pain, with a variable probability that it will happen. Fear is a response to that danger. How you decide to respond to fear makes all the difference.

When you're "afraid" of getting rejected by a woman at a bar, asking for a promotion at work, or negotiating a larger discount, you're imagining an invisible threat or irrationally blowing the odds of it happening out of proportion. You spend too much time thinking about past experiences, or make the same mistake thinking about "what ifs" in the future—and rarely do either come to pass. There is only the here and now, and it requires you to be fully present to push yourself toward what you really want. When you feel the sting of fear kicking in, it's time to embrace it, take a deep breath, and do exactly what you are afraid of.

Mario will always remember when he used to be afraid of asking for sexual acts from his partners. His mind would race: "What if they think I'm a deviant? What if they change their opinion about me? Can I stomach their reaction and potential disgust?"

There was one time it took him a while to find the courage to ask an ex-girlfriend, after a night out with friends, for a blowjob in the alley behind the club. He was so deep inside his head trying to figure out how to ask that all the noises around him sounded muffled, the lights were blurry, and he couldn't understand a single word his ex-girlfriend was saying. He had to snap out of his mental prison and ask her straight to her face, with a seriousness and tone more like asking for a kidney donation than a sexual favor. Obviously, she was taken aback by the body language and randomness of the ask, but she showed a great deal of eagerness to do it for him. While he enjoyed the lovely gesture from his ex-partner, leaning against a wall in a dark alley at 4:30 a.m., all he could do was question how many things he had been missing out on because he was too afraid to ask.

Be brave and ask for what you want with courage.

Set Boundaries

When you don't value yourself, you fear speaking up for what you want and need. You don't want to rock the boat too much with other people, *especially women*. You quickly neglect setting boundaries, allowing people to cross them, especially in romantic or sexual contexts.

Boundaries are the hard lines you don't want people crossing. They protect your time, energy, and resources from being drained beyond the point of suffering. They keep others from imposing their will on your life and forcing you to live outside your values. Boundaries are normal and healthy.

How often have you done things you're not proud of to impress a pretty girl? How many times have you let her run amok in your life, doing as she pleases, even if you didn't want her to?

You do this because you're afraid that if you set a boundary or tell her "no," she'll leave. Guess what: if she's going to be running all over your boundaries, do you really want her in your life anyway?

The first time Brandon vividly remembers setting a boundary with a woman was in high school. He had been giving this cute Latina from his sex-ed class (oh, the irony!) rides everywhere because he thought being a nice guy was the surefire way to get her to like him. One day, when he was walking to his buddy's house, she called asking if she could borrow a couple hundred dollars to pay for something. Being a poor teen living in a trailer park, that was a lot! Standing on the sidewalk, something broke in his head, and his "spidey senses" kicked in. He asked himself, "Why on earth would I give you money for no reason? Who does this girl think she is?" So, for the first time, he told her no. They hung out a couple of times after that, but he stopped giving her rides and dropped the rose-colored glasses he'd been wearing before.

Boundaries aren't just for you—they're for other people, too. They tell others how you want to be treated. Most healthy people enjoy hearing what your boundaries are because then they don't have to guess. Not knowing your boundaries is uncomfortable for women because:

1. They don't know how you'll react if one is crossed.
2. If you don't respect your own boundaries, there's a good chance you won't respect hers.

Who Do You Admire as a Man?

If you are anything like Mario or Brandon, growing up as a young male wasn't easy. Mario is pretty sure that most of his manhood insecurities stemmed from the '80s macho era, where Stallone and Arnold were the two main stars, followed by Bruce

Willis. No, don't scream "toxic masculinity" just yet. Men throughout history have always been strong and competent. However, instead of having a supportive and positive male figure in his life, Mario found himself searching for a role model everywhere else, and trying to emulate those he admired only left him feeling uncomfortable and disillusioned. (To this day, he still hasn't achieved the muscle mass of Arnold... who would have thought that as a teen, right?)

Without a father figure around most of the time, Brandon pieced his masculine identity together from the video games he played. He wanted to be as courageous as Master Chief, as much of a lady's man as Ezio Auditore da Firenze, and as jacked as the testosterone-fueled guys from Gears of War (let's face it, no one can achieve that level of muscle mass without steroids...). The problem was, these are not even real people. How could he ever aspire to be something like that?

Take a look around you. Do you have positive, strong, dominant male figures you can look up to in your everyday life? Do you have a role model who embodies true Dominance? Does this person radiate a strong but warm energy that inspires you to take action? If so, you are experiencing what true Dominance looks like: a commanding yet nurturing presence that naturally draws you in. Observe everything—the way they move, how they speak, what they do, and most importantly, how they think.

Once we understood that our role models were merely sources of disappointment and frustration, we sought out more relatable and useful figures to surround ourselves with. We wanted to understand what we were doing wrong versus what they were doing right.

Now, this might be difficult because maybe you don't have many friends, or the friends you do have aren't exactly what you're looking for. But don't despair. This is a sign that you need to make changes in your life to become the person you aspire to be.

Brandon took action by starting a men's group that met once a week. It began with just him and one other guy he met at the airport on his way to a business conference. The next member was someone he'd taken an online course with. With each new man, he had to gather the courage to ask if they would be interested in joining. Slowly but surely, he added more powerful, respected men into his life—men who took responsibility for themselves, their families, and their communities. He's now been running the group for over five years, and during that time, more than a dozen strong, influential men have come and gone.

He also had the benefit of connecting with Mario in the depths of online forums. At that time, Brandon was a young, naive, budding Dom who could use a little tough love when it came to understanding intersexual dynamics. (Mario is probably as close as you'll get to a real-life Ezio Auditore da Firenze, if Ezio were a kinky, degenerate character).

Our advice for finding a mentor who's walked the path before you:

1. **Show initiative and start working on improving yourself**, even if you're not entirely sure how. Let your effort and progress speak for themselves.
2. When they notice (and they will), and offer a little guidance, **listen to them**. At least try to put into practice what they suggest.
3. **Show respect**, but don't belittle yourself.
4. **Give gratitude** and credit them when it's due.

Start looking elsewhere, broaden your horizons, and push yourself out of your comfort zone. We know it's tough at first, especially when you can't quite picture what you're looking for, but there's so much more out there than you realize.

CHAPTER FOUR

Leadership

If we had to distill Dominance into a single essential trait, it would be leadership. Submissive women expect you to lead every aspect of the interaction—from seduction to lifelong partnership. The Dom must lead the dynamic, lead the submissive, and, most importantly, lead themselves. Of course, the traits discussed in the following chapters will also help you become a more effective leader.

Leading Yourself

Before we dive into the deeper, internal aspects of leadership, let's start with something more tangible. In the world of startups and business, leadership can be broken down into three fundamental functions:

1. **Setting a vision for the team:** A vision is a collective story of a better future—one compelling enough to inspire the team to put in long, grueling hours to make it a reality. It provides both meaning and direction.
2. **Building the team:** Lofty visions require talented people to bring them to life. A leader must identify and evaluate who will best serve the vision, then delegate tasks based on each person's skills.
3. **Acquiring resources for the team:** This often includes capital, land, software, or any other assets necessary to build and sustain what has been envisioned.

Leading yourself follows the same principles. To build a successful life, you must:

- **Set a vision for your life:** If you don't know where you want to go, how will you ever get there? How will you recognize the right people to have in your life? How will you know what resources you need?
- **Build a support network:** No one—truly no one—succeeds alone. Even the so-called "self-made man" has received help from hundreds, if not thousands, of people along the way. The more intentional you are about curating your network—from intimate relationships to colleagues, friends, and business partners—the more likely you are to achieve your vision.
- **Acquire resources for success:** Money is just one resource. Time, knowledge, and skills are equally valuable. Fortunately for you, reading this book will save you years of trial and error while equipping you with new knowledge and skills to put into practice.

As you implement these principles in your own life, your capacity for leadership will expand. You'll naturally begin leading others—a skill that will be crucial in any kind of relationship, but especially in a Dominant/submissive dynamic.

To put it bluntly: If you get your shit together, others will want your leadership in getting theirs together, too.

But it all starts with you.

Take 100% Responsibility for Your Life

If you can't take responsibility for your own life, how can you possibly take responsibility for someone submitting to you? How can you lead another person if you can't lead yourself?

Taking full responsibility means that—regardless of circumstances—you actively identify and address your shortcomings, move your life forward, and solve the problems that arise. **No matter the circumstances.**

You cannot be a victim. Victimhood means powerlessness and a lack of control—two things that are completely incompatible with being a Dominant.

Look, we get it. Everyone is dealt a shitty hand in life. Some people have it harder than others. Some systems are built to put you at a disadvantage. Life is unfair and unpredictable. Sometimes, terrible, ungodly things happen to good people.

So what are you going to do about it?

You can either let your circumstances control you, or you can overcome them. Your road to becoming the person you want to be may be longer and more arduous than someone else's. It doesn't matter. You still have to walk it.

When you do, you'll start to realize something: Either you directly contributed to your problems, or you were complicit in creating the conditions you claim you don't want. Either way, it comes back to you.

This is critical to understand because you won't play the blame game when you're in a relationship. If something doesn't go the way you wanted, you'll have the humility to examine how **you** contributed to the situation. Then, you can work on yourself—because you can't change other people. The only person you can change is you.

One of the essential responsibilities of a Dominant is to create order and structure for their submissive. If your own life is chaotic, you won't have the capacity to bring order to someone else's. You'll be a hypocrite, and your submissive will see right through you. So take control. Identify what's wrong in your life, and start putting it in order.

Grab a journal and assess where you stand. You can use whatever categories make sense for you, but consider the following:

- Health
- Wealth
- Career
- Relationships with family
- Relationships with friends
- Relationship with yourself
- Romantic relationships

- Sex life
- Creative outlets or hobbies
- Learning and development
- Spirituality
- Community contribution

For each category, ask yourself two critical questions:

1. What does this area of my life look like, objectively?
2. How did I help create the conditions I'm in?

As you go through this exercise, do your best to remain neutral. Don't label anything as "good" or "bad." Don't praise yourself, and don't criticize yourself. The goal isn't to beat yourself up. The goal is to take full responsibility for where you are—because once you do, **you gain the power to change it.**

Set a Vision for Your Life

Leaders create visions for the future. That vision *attracts* followers—people who share the same goals but lack the ability to reach them on their own. If you want a woman to follow and submit to you, your vision must be **clear and compelling** enough to *attract* her.

But you can't figure out where you want to go if you don't first understand where you are now—which is why you started by taking full responsibility for your life. This means taking a cold, hard look at your reality. No self-pity. No wishing things were different. This is where you are.

But it doesn't have to be where you stay.

It's time to create a vision for your life.

This doesn't need to be complicated. In fact, the more you overcomplicate it, the worse it will be.

So ask yourself: **What do I truly want in every area of my life?**

Simple to ask. Hard to answer.

Why? Because:

- You've been oblivious to who you really are.
- You've been doing what others expect of you.
- You've been afraid to admit what you want because the gap between where you are and where you want to be seems insurmountable.
- You've been avoiding the responsibility of doing the work.

There's that word again—**responsibility.** Taking responsibility for your life means taking responsibility for what you want and doing the necessary work to make it happen.

This is crucial in a Dominant/submissive relationship. When you and your submissive define what your dynamic will look like, she needs to know that you're a man who can make it a reality. If you don't have a clear vision, you'll be pulled in every direction by others—including your submissive—and eventually, you'll become angry, bitter, resentful, and weak.

That is not the foundation of a strong relationship.

So, get your journal back out. (Trust us, it's going to become your best friend.)

Using the same categories from earlier, write down a vision for what you want your life to look and feel like in each area.

Ask yourself:

1. What do I truly want, irrespective of what others expect of me?
2. If I were living a life I was proud of, what would it look like?

Write freely. Don't censor yourself. If you can't be honest with yourself about what you want, you'll never be able to express it to others, gain the support you need, or see your dreams come true.

Define Your Values

So, you've taken responsibility for your life. You have a vision. Now, how will you get there?

There are countless ways to achieve a goal. For example, acquiring money can be done through:

- Employment
- Entrepreneurship
- Investing
- Stealing
- Extortion
- Selling kidneys on the black market...

Some of those options probably resonated with you more than others. That resonance is a hint at your values. Values determine which strategies you're willing to use to achieve your vision. Your actions are always downstream of your values.

If you don't know your values, you'll unconsciously choose strategies that conflict with them—creating internal turmoil and problems down the road.

Taking responsibility for your life means taking responsibility for how you achieve what you want.

Shall I tell you to get your journal, again? Because I will... Get out your journal. You're going to define the values by which you want to live.

To define your values:

1. Use a website like personalvalu.es or any other online resource to brainstorm values that are important to you.
2. Narrow your list down to fewer than ten—ideally five to seven.
3. Rank them from most important to least important. This will help you make decisions when values come into conflict.

4. Clearly define each value in your own words. Write down what it looks like in action.

Let your list sit for a few days, then revisit it. Do these values still ring true? Adjust if necessary.

Take Action in Alignment with Your Values

Once you know your vision and values, you have to take actions that are congruent with what you say you want and what you value.

Put simply:

- Do what you want to do
- Don't do what you don't want to do

This doesn't mean being lazy and completely hedonistic because you don't want to do the work necessary to bring what you *actually* want to reality.

It means that when someone, society, or life circumstances tries to make you take an action that is out of alignment with your values or takes you farther away from your vision, you don't buckle and give in, but instead find another action that is in alignment with your values.

For example, life has tasked you with the necessity of making an income. You chose to be employed because that's the strategy everyone chooses and is easiest, right? Yet you value freedom or autonomy. So you feel your soul decaying every day you drive to work rather than doing the hard work necessary to be an entrepreneur.

This applies directly to being a Dom. Your values shape:

- Who you choose as your submissive
- How you treat her
- How you lead her

A man who knows who he is—and where he will not bend—exudes true Dominance. This kind of solidity gives a submissive woman the safety and confidence to follow your lead.

Of course, taking action requires a plan.

So let's build one.

For each area of life you define a vision for, outline a *very rough plan* to achieve it.

We say rough because:

- You've never been there before, so you can't be certain of the path.
- As you progress, you inevitably discover that some of the things you said you wanted, you don't actually want.
- Life is unpredictable. Adaptation is necessary.

It can be helpful to take your large vision and break it down into smaller milestones that can serve as mini goals on the path towards your vision.

For example, maybe you have a vision to be a best selling author in something you're an expert in. Working backwards, you can break that into milestones: Large post publishing marketing campaigns to gain sales, publishing the book, editing the final draft, writing the rough draft, coming up with the topic for the book. Each of these could be broken down further such as writing one chapter at a time for the rough draft.

Leading Submissive Women

Section 3 of this book will equip you with a range of skills to effectively lead a submissive woman. What's important to understand now is the mindset: you will always be the one in the driver's seat—setting the direction and moving the relationship forward.

This means having a clear vision of where you want to go and then providing her with clear direction while offering ample opportunities for her to buy into the next steps. Let's illustrate this with examples from opposite ends of the relationship escalator: a first date versus marriage.

Example: First Date

To even get a first date, you had to take the initiative—whether by approaching her in person, messaging her on social media, or reaching out on a dating app. Yes, some women might approach you or slide into your DMs first, but this is rare, especially for an attractive, submissive woman. It's your responsibility to initiate the conversation.

From that first interaction, it's also your responsibility to move the conversation toward setting up the date. You must demonstrate that you're not a creep, that you're someone she would enjoy spending time with, and then take the lead in getting her number. Once you do, it's on you to decide when and where to meet— ideally within 10 minutes of your place, should things go well and you both want to continue the evening there.

When you're on the date, it's up to you to ensure it flows smoothly and progresses in the direction you desire. You'll pick a seating arrangement that fosters intimacy—next to each other rather than across—so you can lower your voice when discussing more personal topics (especially when transitioning to discussions about sex) and create opportunities for physical touch. You'll guide the conversation from small talk to deeper subjects to sexual topics. You'll invite her presence with moments of silence and eye contact. You'll initiate light physical contact—touching her hand, hair, arms, or thighs. You'll openly communicate about relationship expectations, whether you have other partners, and what she can expect from you in the bedroom. Finally, you'll be the one to extend an invitation—whether that's back to your place or for a second date, depending on the vibe.

Every step of this process requires your leadership. You are responsible for how the date unfolds. You might argue that this isn't fair, that effort should be equal, and yet you'll find yourself frustrated when she doesn't take the initiative.

Here's the reality: Most people—including you—think that "things just happen." They don't. Someone has to take the initiative to set a series of events in motion. Think about your friend group—there's always that one guy who organizes get-togethers, makes plans, and ensures things happen. In a relationship, it's just the two of you. Either you take the lead, or she does.

And let's be honest—you're seeking a *submissive* woman, someone who wants to *follow* your lead. Sure, she could approach you first, make the plans, direct the conversation, and invite you back to her place—but in that case, who's really the Dom?

How you start a relationship—even in the very first interactions—sets the precedent for the entire dynamic. Whether consciously or not, she is evaluating your ability to lead. She's asking herself:

- Will this man be able to guide me in the relationship?
- Will he be able to lead in the bedroom?
- Can I trust his direction?

Life isn't fair, bud. You can fight that fact, or you can take responsibility and make things happen.

Example: Marriage

Well, that escalated quickly...

Let's start by acknowledging that reaching the point of marriage required you to take the lead. You were the one who had to get down on one knee and pop the question. In a D/s relationship, this leadership extends beyond the proposal—you are the one who establishes the structure of the dynamic, setting expectations and agreements, including a contract (which we will discuss in Section 3).

In marriage, as a Dom, you take on the role of CEO of your household. The business analogy we used earlier becomes even more relevant. You are responsible for setting the vision, making decisions, supporting your submissive, assigning duties, and securing resources. Your leadership is the foundation upon which the relationship thrives.

To illustrate this, Brandon will share a story from his past marriage.

Brandon the Married Dom

My ex-wife and I were not in a formal D/s dynamic. At the time, I barely even knew what Dominance was, aside from the distorted depictions in *Fifty Shades of Grey*. That said, certain aspects of my personality naturally compelled me to step up and take responsibility for leading our marriage. Of course, I owe a great deal of that growth to my ex-wife, for which I will always be grateful.

I once told Mario that women are like mirrors for all your bullshit. You experience this in a cold approach or on a date, where you get instant feedback about how you're presenting yourself to the world. Women sense insecurities and bring them to the surface. In those situations, you at least have the option to retreat, regain your composure, and try again with a more polished version of yourself.

But in a long-term relationship—especially when you live together—it's like having that mirror held up *all the time*. There's no retreat. You are constantly confronted with your shortcomings. In my experience, a good woman will not only reveal those shortcomings but also support you through them (though not fix them for you). A bad one will only point them out, and a worse one will belittle you for them. My ex-wife was a good woman and a great mirror. She undoubtedly helped create the space for my Dominance to develop in those early stages.

During our marriage, I took the lead in managing our finances, planning our meals and workouts, and establishing structure through weekly relationship check-ins—dedicated time where we'd go somewhere for a couple of hours to discuss the state of our relationship. I also made larger decisions about where we lived, buying our home, acquiring rental tenants, and navigating career transitions.

One example of this leadership came during the 2020 COVID-19 lockdowns. While most people were hunkering down, waiting for life to resume, I was preparing to move us across the country in pursuit of better opportunities. At the time, I had a vision for a startup and wanted to create a more exciting life for us as a couple. I had initially hoped to use a PhD program as an incubator for my idea, but after receiving rejection letters, I shifted my strategy. I researched cities with growing startup scenes, compiled a whiteboard of potential locations, and listed the values my ex-wife and I prioritized. Together, we narrowed it down to a few choices, ultimately deciding on Austin.

I reached out to a friend, a real estate agent looking to invest, and arranged to sell our house to him—netting us over $100K in profit.

Then, just an hour into our move, as we crossed the first mountain pass, our car's engine blew a cylinder. It was completely shot. Instead of panicking, I focused on solving the problem. I arranged for a tow truck, called our friend—who had family in the town where we got stranded—and secured a place for us to stay for a couple of days. After a few hours of weighing our options, I came up with a plan: we rented a large U-Haul, transferred all of our belongings from our trailer into it, and rented a separate trailer to tow our dead car behind the U-Haul. Throughout the ordeal, my wife was anxious but reassured by the fact that I was handling the situation calmly. A week later, we finally arrived in Austin.

You might read that and think it wasn't a big deal. But put yourself in that situation: you've just sold your home to move to a city you've never been to, for opportunities that may or may not pan out. You have no family or friends there. All of your belongings are packed behind you, and then—out of nowhere—your car becomes completely unusable. How well would you lead in that moment? Hell, how well did you lead *any* part of your life during the pandemic? Most people didn't do too hot.

If you're going to step into Dominance, you have to lead all the way through— even to the very end. After several months in Austin, I initiated a divorce because I believed we would both be happier and more fulfilled apart. This wasn't a one-sided decision. After many relationship check-ins, it became clear that we had grown in different directions. I could see how unhappy she was, and I knew my own feelings as well. So, during what would be our last relationship check-in walk, I told her I believed we should get a divorce. She agreed without argument, and we both cried for a long time.

Later that week, we had our final dinner date together. In the months that followed, I made sure the transition was as smooth as possible. Because of that, I was able to walk away with not only a clean break but also an enduring friendship with my ex-wife. To this day, I can text, call, or even visit her during my travels.

From beginning to end, you are the one who must lead.

STORY TIME

The Polish Girl Who Couldn't Stop

A real story of Mario's. To protect the privacy of those involved, all names and identifying details have been altered. The individuals described in these stories were all consenting adults who participated of their own free will. If you choose to engage in similar activities, it is imperative that all parties involved are of legal age, fully informed, and consenting.

Poland to me is an interesting country. A traditional, hardworking, conservative nation in contrast with a hedonistic, rebellious, and kinky side.

Anytime I'm in the country and the topic of sex comes up, I'm met with a hurl of defensiveness and stereotypes, to which my closing statement is just to observe the amount of sex shops spread around the country. If it was so holy, there wouldn't be such businesses around—and that's before I learned about the amazing parcel system operating in Poland.

Well, where were we? Ah, Poland, specifically the city of Poznań—an amazing little jewel in the west that definitely warrants a weekend visit.

The center is an amazing example of architecture (well, at least to me; I'll leave Brandon to make the aesthetic remarks) and well-thought-out spaces where one can socialize, simply go shopping, or just sit down in a hip café and enjoy a well-made roasted blend.

Enter the Dom

And that's exactly where I met Julka.

Julka appeared in front of me waiting for her coffee after she had already tapped her bank card in the terminal to pay. Immediately, scanning her body frame hidden under a baggy puffer black jacket but paired with very tight black yoga pants, I could tell her body was very fit which was very attractive to me. Later I discovered it was shaped by hours of bartending and kickboxing lessons, and the dirty blond hair sitting on her chest already proposed strange ideas to me.

Her blue eyes made quick contact with mine while she turned around, and in the fraction of a millisecond, I swore to myself I saw a smile forming on her lips. I had to talk to her.

"Excuse me, I know this is quite direct, but I thought you were super cute, and I thought perhaps we could both enjoy a coffee and meet a stranger at the same time."

She smiled with all her face shining and offered a pleased "Sure, why not" back to me.

We introduced each other and spent the next half hour talking about her life and a bit of mine while traveling in her country. I made a few teases about being a Negroni fan (which I am) and thought maybe I could pass by and see if she was capable of handling my tastes; of course, the innuendos were pretty obvious.

We hugged outside the coffee shop and went in different directions.

That night I sat at the stool straight in front of her and pretty much didn't pay attention to her, with the exception of inquiring about her body and arms filled with tattoos, creating a very interesting contrast: face of an angel, body of a devil. Especially since she had massive boobs that were begging to jump out of her bra, or at least that's what I felt.

Instead, I spent most of the time interacting with the DJ girl seated on my right, who reminded me why I would never date DJs, and another patron on my left who argued that the best city in the world was Kiev because it was safe, cheap, and filled with beautiful women. I guess he must have developed a certain sadness right now.

The evening was going smoothly until Julka told me she was on a smoke break and to meet her outside, where she would take a smoke break hidden in the gateway to an inner yard belonging to a residential complex. Once I got close to her, she simply locked her wrists behind my neck and offered me a "You are so damn sexy when you talk," and then our tongues twisted with each other until she had to go back to her workplace.

I had previously informed her that I couldn't stay up all night waiting for her shift to end because in the morning I had a train to Berlin to catch. On her second break, 90 minutes later, I invited her to join me when she had her day off, since I would be in town for a while.

The plan was simple, I told her: "Sex, more sex, even more sex, some steaks and naps, and more sex." Little did we know when she agreed to drive the distance separating the two cities that we would end up in a spiral of hardcore BDSM for a whole day and night.

We kept sexting and sending nudes and videos of each other for the next five days until, around lunchtime, she parked her car with Polish plates in the underground parking near the building where I was renting an Airbnb in Charlottenburg.

During the sexting conversations, a few very spicy details came out about her sex life and the things she liked the most. Now, I don't want to give the story away now, but let's say that when a play partner sends you a text with an alphabetical order of the things she would like to do, you know you will have your hands busy and you will have to bring your A game.

The apartment was set for a sex marathon. I had good food and training the days prior, went to sleep early—naaah, are you kidding me? In Berlin? I met with an ex-Tinder date of mine who performed on sex cam websites, and we ended up blind drunk and having sex a few times. *Talk about bringing your A game...*

Enter the Dom

Anyway, I set up my apartment with all the tools of the trade. I knew that Julka was an "ass play" girl, meaning she loved anything revolving around anal sex.

She confided in me that she had taken the biggest cock of her life deep inside without using any lube, and after meeting a few more girls like that, I think it's just a talent.

I welcomed Julka straight into my apartment and immediately went for a kiss, which she complied with, but I could feel some resistance from her side.

I invited her to sit on the couch and make herself feel at home.

"Do you want to take a shower after the long car trip?" I offered. "I promise I won't sneak in," I winked—little did I know about her shower plans when she jumped right in while carrying her backpack into the bathroom.

After what had been more like 30 minutes, she elegantly came out of the door with a red body fishnet and red collants, complimenting her gorgeous shape and contrasting with her angelic face. Now, obviously it doesn't take 30 minutes to shower and put on a fishnet... I didn't know then, but the girl with the ass always ready had indeed prepared her ass with some in-depth cleaning—talk about being courteous to guests.

We immediately started to jump on each other like we hadn't had sex for years and had to catch up where we left off.

I grabbed her neck with my left hand while ordering her to suck my right thumb as she was grinding her panties over my cock, still prisoners of my trousers.

The foreplay moved to my spanking her on the bed with her ankles tied together with a bandana I carried with me all the time. They say it's a clothing item out of fashion, but if people could be a little bit more creative... (funny, Brandon also carries a bandana in his leather jacket.)

I kept alternating some good spanking with making her squirt, which I could get feedback from through her loud moans, ignoring the fountain she was making on the floor straight from the edge of the bed.

I placed her head, manipulating it by holding a good chunk of her hair, on the edge of the bed, right where her bum was getting punished prior, and after ordering her to keep her mouth wide open and tongue out, I proceeded to fuck her throat until I got pleased with the hardness of my erection.

I placed her in doggy, the position she revealed to me she loved the most, and started ramming her as hard as I could while holding her head back with my left hand tightly anchored to her hair, while with my right hand I performed one of my favorite metal songs' drum solos. Isn't it all art anyway?

After a while, I slowed down to catch my breath. Julka must have interpreted this as a signal for a change, as she turned her head toward me and said, "Don't you want to fuck my ass?" How could you resist such a *delightful* request?

I rolled up a condom and started pressing my tip around her butthole or feigning penetration just to tease. What happened next literally shocked me in a positive way.

She squeezed her tight hole as much as possible and, when releasing, it swallowed my whole cock's head entirely. Now, I've done plenty of anal sex in my life, but it was always accompanied by a lot of patience, reassuring, and family-size lube bottles. This was literally the first time witnessing such a miracle.

Trusting that the hardest part of the job was done in such a smooth manner, I proceeded to hammer her ass hard for what she was calling during the process "such a good rough fuck," to which I replied with some degrading slurs and encouraging positive words. We must have kept going and going on, with some breaks in between to towel-dry my body from sweat and get a blowjob while playing with a magic wand on her pussy.

All of a sudden, I noticed the street lights were on, a stark contrast from the bright daylight creeping in from the windows when we started playing. I asked myself if perhaps I had depleted my balls too much prior to this meeting, since it seemed to me I couldn't reach an orgasm, which I was very much craving. I wanted to allow myself to catch a break with some aftercare—my hips were hurting, and my back and glutes were on fire. I cannot recall even the heaviest one-rep max squat I've done in my life leaving me this way. I knew I couldn't cum in those conditions, and the awareness of my physical status started to affect my cock as well. I had to come up with a plan B before losing my erection entirely and, with it, my honor.

I pulled out and grabbed the dildo from the bag positioned on the chair next to the bed (I wonder if most people see the same cuck-meaning of furniture placed in such a place) and, after wrapping another condom on it from a 30-pack, I started hammering it as deep as possible. I forgot the dimension of it when I bought it, but I know for a fact it was bigger than a half-liter water bottle by comparison. Pressing it all deep inside and pulling it almost out with the maximum amount of speed I could generate, while pressing the wand on her clit, Julka told me she would cum again, so I endured the physical punishment of pleasing her until she did, her making another puddle at the end of the bed.

I took the opportunity to step back, towel-dry, and bring us two water bottles I had bought at the store, offering one tenderly to her.

"Damn, I'm so horny," she started after a big gulp from the bottle.

My heart sank. While getting the bottles, I realized that it was almost past dinnertime when we started playing. This was basically a *marathon*. I was feeling like once I crossed the finish line completely drained, one of the officials would approach me and inform me I had just finished a lap.

"Well, it's going to be a long night," I offered with a very fake sense of confidence and sexual prowess. In reality, I was hoping she would ask to stop for food or to cuddle and talk, but none of that happened. Instead, she took another big sip from the bottle and said, "Yes, I want your cock all night." My soul left my trembling and hydration-depleted body right there.

I accept challenges when faced with them, but the idea of being sleep-deprived again from another night of sex sent a small shiver down my spine. After all, I didn't have to do anything I didn't want to do, but my pride was on the line, and I needed to get some time to think myself out of this situation.

"Yes, but I promised steaks also, so get dressed and let's get some food to prepare for part two." I knew the hour spent at dinner and getting food in me would help me recover. Plus, I thought if I could get some electrolytes and magnesium from the conveniently located downstairs drugstore, I could give my body a chance for a bit more of a fight.

We spent dinner talking about the sex we had and how much she enjoyed it. She confirmed to me her opinion was that I could fuck well, but she didn't expect me to be this good, and she was on a personal mission to finish me off, while lightly kicking my feet under the table.

I realized that if I would play this game, I would be knocked off shortly. I was frustrated at myself for not being able to cum and have a plausible explanation to ask for some sleep, especially given the fact that I had spoken highly of myself as a sex machine and felt I had to deliver a crazy performance. There was absolutely no way I could keep up with this pace.

Thankfully, being in the Dominant position means you have ways and means to control the situation. I formulated a plan that would make me waste as little energy as possible. I came up with a series of challenges, commands, and actions to be performed by her while I would comfortably watch from the cuck chair next to the bed and just use my voice.

I started by telling her we wouldn't leave the restaurant until she got her pussy wet, to which she said, "But I am already!" *Dang, bad move, Mr.*

"Good, go to the toilet, touch yourself, and make a video out of it that I want to watch when you are back." She laughed at my request, to which I replied, "The more you laugh, the more I will punish you by not giving you what you came for."

Swiftly, she stood up and left for the ladies' room.

Five minutes of sweet rest for me. Then she came back to the table and showed me a quick preview of the video, saying it was very hot and now she was wetter and ready for more.

Enter the Dom

Once we walked back into the apartment, I told her to strip and seduce me as if she was a stripper in a club. I was getting horny again, but my hips were more locked and tight than a high-security museum.

"Go on the bed facing me and touch yourself, first slowly, and then as hard as you can," I ordered.

She played with her clit long enough to have another orgasm, which I let her enjoy for a bit before I practiced my squirting routine on her. I felt I was running out of ideas, and I said to myself, *I've been good enough; she can write a bad review tomorrow if she didn't enjoy it.*

I tied the bandana like a gag to her mouth and played with her nipples, twisting, pulling, and biting them, which made her moan more and more.

I pretended to choke her with one hand while slapping her boobs with the other, and I could finally feel some energy resurging in me.

"Fuck your ass with the dildo while you suck me," I commanded while pulling down the bandana, now soaking wet with her saliva, from her mouth.

My wimpy cock got another round of erection after she vacuum-sealed her lips at the base of it and moved her tongue back and forth, never breaking contact.

I ordered her to wank me, and for some magical reason, I felt I could be close to an orgasm. I took back control of my cock and jerked as hard as possible to relieve myself of some sperm, which landed straight on her chest.

I collapsed next to her in bed and was panting hard while she went to the toilet to commence the cleanup operations.

She took a long shower, which must have lasted long enough for me to completely fall asleep. The only thing I can remember is that I was so tired even my eyes would hurt.

I woke up with Julka wrapped around me and the morning sun creeping in. I gently left the hold of her hands to go to the toilet and grabbed my phone along the way.

It was already 10 a.m., and Julka had to make the trip back to be ready for work at 3 p.m. This could mean making a quickie by waking her up now, or waiting to finish my morning routine and do something for half an hour before inviting her to breakfast.

I consider myself quite a permanently horny guy, but that morning was a reminder that nothing is permanent.

Being the sweet host, I prepared a coffee for her and jumped in bed, tactfully waking her up. We spent a few minutes cuddling and exchanging pleasantries. Once she placed her back against the bed wall and drank her coffee, she made a comment on how I fell asleep so soundly that she didn't want to wake me up but felt tempted to suck me to keep me awake. I thanked my lucky stars she had mercy on me after the all-day and evening sex encounter.

I informed her about the time and how she should get ready so we could get some breakfast together, to which she protested that she wanted to have sex.

"You will have to wait until next time I'm in town, which will be very soon," I apologetically replied.

More protesting but a sense of acceptance from her side made her step out of the bed and collect her things. We made it to the breakfast place and got some German-Turkish mix special breakfast with a lot of caffeine on the side.

After that, we kissed goodbye at the entrance of the parking lot. I saw her driving off on the road, for the last time in my life, since after this event, our communication became sporadic until it stopped entirely.

Never make a promise you cannot fulfill.

CHAPTER FIVE

Power

Power—the ultimate aphrodisiac, the driving force behind every struggle, every ambition, every game we play. It has always been about power, and it always will be.

But what exactly is power?

At its core, power is the ability to act freely—when you want, how you want—without external forces dictating your choices. It's the capacity to take a vision in your mind and turn it into reality without restriction or interference.

Consider your job. If your manager walks in at 4 p.m. on a Friday with a stack of documents and asks you to complete them, who holds the power in that scenario?

Now imagine you're the CEO's son, and you don't really want to work at the company anymore. You casually reply, "Thanks, but I have other commitments and can't do this right now." Who holds the power then?

Power is the weight we place on one side or the other of a leverage point. We use it as leverage to get what we want—or what we think we want. Understanding power is fundamental to all relationships, including the one you have with yourself.

But why is power so *damn* attractive?

The simple answer: Power grants control over an abundance of whatever currency holds value in a given social context. It might be manpower and social status (politics), money, or other resources that shape a particular society.

Our monkey brains, wired for survival, have evolved from a state of scarcity. We instinctively seek security, and abundance provides the illusion of comfort and safety. This drives us to accumulate resources—and to depend on those who have them.

As human societies developed, the world became a marketplace of exchanged resources. We trade what we have for what we crave. If you're cold and hungry in a cave, constantly hunting for your next meal, you're willing to bargain—even to the point of relinquishing power over yourself to someone with greater resources.

Beyond evolutionary psychology, power has long carried a halo effect, embodying the characteristics of kings and rulers. You either submit to their will or face the consequences—often a direct threat to survival.

At certain points in history, not only were you expected to obey those in power, but you also had to think and believe as they dictated—or suffer severe punishment. It's no mystery how we arrived at this moment, where power remains the most potent and desirable quality. It rules over everything.

Power Today

Power is fluid, ever-changing, taking whatever form best suits the moment. As of this writing (2022–2024), power has evolved yet again, shaped by societal shifts and advancing technology.

The legacy of kings and rulers still lingers in our collective memory, but today, power operates on different levels.

Consider social media influencers. A YouTuber with millions of subscribers or an Instagram personality with a massive following—surely, they must hold power, right? (Aside from those who buy fake followers or rely on provocative photos.)

Technology and attention have reshaped how we *perceive* power. But real power can only be measured when it's tested.

Does an influencer truly have power? That becomes clear when they attempt to leverage their audience—whether by launching a business, starting a movement, or mobilizing people to take action. Many times, what looks like power turns out to be a house of cards.

In today's world, wielding power effectively requires two key elements:

1. **Real Power** – The ability to acquire and control resources that can be exchanged or used to shape reality.
2. **Perceived Power** – The way you present yourself to the world. Perception shapes how people respond to you before they even meet you.

As Denzel Washington's character famously said in *Training Day*, "It's not about what you know; it's about what you can prove."

In the attention economy, if you have real power but remain invisible, you'll be overlooked. If you have only perceived power with nothing to back it up, you'll eventually be exposed as a fraud.

What Lies at the Heart of Power

What do you think lies at the heart of power? For most people, the first thing that comes to mind is control, right? After all, we've just explained that the person who holds power controls the resources—and that's what makes it so attractive.

But control only comes once power has been attained. How did they *get* that power? And why do people continue to willingly *give* that person power?

Look, just because you have power and people perceive you as powerful doesn't mean they'll remain under your spell forever. Sure, if you're a king or an S&P 500 CEO, even if someone beneath you thinks you're a total tool, they'll still have to comply with your dramatic tantrums. That's one of the perks of power. But why rely solely on a seat and a symbol? After all, even kings were overthrown when they failed to serve their people properly.

People generally yield power to you in exchange for what they need and want. Think about this for a moment: To some degree, all of us hand over control of our lives to all sorts of people every day. We make this exchange because we believe the other party—whether it's an employer, a corporation, or a government—will benefit us in some way. The most prominent benefit is that we don't have to worry about the logistical challenges of meeting our basic needs. Hell, people will accept tyranny if it provides safety and food on the table.

What lies at the heart of power is not control, but **responsibility**.

If you take responsibility for providing people with what they want and need, they will hand over their resources—and sometimes even some level of control. These exchanges occur because you have more power (remember: the ability to do or say something) than the other person and can make things happen. This means those who yield power must be able to understand, read, and feel what others want and deliver it in exchange for control.

The greatest skill for gaining more power in your life isn't about gaining physical strength or amassing an army of supporters (though it doesn't hurt). It's the ability to understand what people in front of you secretly crave and take responsibility for delivering it. There are many tools, both online and offline, that can help you develop this soft skill. If you're serious about power, make it a goal to work on these.

Power in a D/s Relationship

Now that you understand how power works on a broader level, how does this concept apply to power exchange relationships?

It's simple: Submissives will yield their power to you if they feel you have the strength and responsibility to ensure their safety and well-being as the Dominant.

Power in a D/s relationship is exchanged based on the idea that all parties get what they want. If, as the Dominant, you're able to identify what your submissive truly desires—and you promise to deliver—you will gain their submission in exchange for everything that dynamic entails. You might be starting to see that this relationship resembles a contractual agreement, and you're right. Later in Section 3, we'll discuss contracts, which are a cornerstone of serious D/s relationships. For now, you can imagine that even the most casual of relationships still operate under an unwritten contract of exchanged wants and needs.

This trade is continuously updated by both parties' decisions and actions, whether it's for short-term sexual play or a long-term romantic relationship, until one or both parties decide to break the agreement or no longer wish to continue the exchange after the play is over. The invisible contract is always in flux, and the Dominant remains in charge only because the submissive agrees to it every time. If you forget to uphold your end of the contract by failing to live up to your promise of responsibility, the submissive will revoke power and kick your ass to the curb.

How to Become More Powerful

Take Responsibility for What You Want in Life

To become more powerful, you need to understand the ramifications and consequences of your actions and words—and learn to live with them if they align with what you want.

In Mario's previous job, he wanted to take a trip to Southeast Asia with his friends for a couple of months. This would require asking his boss for permission to work remotely (before remote work became the norm). He tentatively presented the idea, only to be rejected immediately. He sat in his office chair, feeling sorry for himself, and thought that no job in life was worth missing the memories he could be making with his friends while still young. (Some of those memories still comfort him many years later.) At that moment, he realized he was ready to face the consequences of his actions, whatever they might be. Even though he was scared of being "officially" fired for the first time in his life, and potentially facing difficulty finding a similar job that he liked, he knew what he wanted more and what had greater value for him. He prepared his pitch properly, confronted his boss with newfound confidence, and handled every objection his boss raised. The result? A week later, he was on a plane to Thailand to make memories that would last a lifetime while keeping his job.

Face What You Are Afraid Of and Slay It

You need to find what scares you and deliberately face it.

Are you afraid of rejection? Being canceled? Going broke? What thought in your mind censors the original message your gut wanted to send?

Fear is an honest indicator that something is taking power away from you and using it against you.

Mario was once afraid of being rejected or negatively labeled because of a particular sexual kink. The idea of asking for what pleased him terrified him to the point that he had to suppress his desires, pushing them to the back of his mind. He spent so much time engaging in internal dialogues while he was supposed to be enjoying himself. He kept asking himself, "How bad am I for wanting such a thing?"

What you'll learn when you allow yourself to accept what you want and start asking for it directly is this: people will either accept it or not, but how they react to what you want is their problem, not yours.

Live with Integrity

You say you're taking responsibility for your life. You say these are the things you want. You say this is who you are and fully live and feel that to your core...

Is that true?

Every time a woman "tests" you, she is actually asking this question. She's conducting an integrity check. Because if she cannot trust you, she will never feel safe and will never submit to you. It's not that she's trying to actively distrust you or be your adversary—it's that she's putting herself in an incredibly vulnerable position by trusting you, and she needs reassurance that the person you say you are—the Dominant leader—is actually true. Otherwise, at best, she'll feel led nowhere, and at worst, she'll be led into pain.

Your job is to live with integrity.

Integrity is pretty simple:

- Only speak the truth
- Do what you say
- Say what you mean
- Be who you say you are

Only Speak the Truth

For anyone to believe what you say, your words and actions need to be grounded in reality. The more aligned you are with reality, the more true your words and actions will be.

Part of seeing reality was done in Chapter 3 when you took 100% responsibility for your life. In order to take responsibility, you have to be brutally honest about where you are right now. It's okay if you have a lot of improvement to do, but you have to be honest with her about that. It's her decision if she wants to be part of that or not.

Also, when you set a vision for yourself and state your values, you can't lie about what you truly want or value. If you do, you won't be in alignment with the reality of your personality or your true nature.

Do What You Say

Your word is the most important tool you have in your relationships with others. If you say you're going to do something—big or small—and you *actually* follow through, others will give you more support in the future. They'll see that you're a man who can turn potential futures into reality. They will relinquish power to you.

If you say you're going to do something and then fail to deliver, either through lying or negligence, people won't align with you. You'll be all talk, no action. They won't trust a word you say, and they'll never give you power over them.

Which man do you think a woman would trust with the responsibility of her submission?

There's more to this, though.

Doing what you say requires that you follow through—even when it's hard. Especially when it's hard. This means you assert yourself in the face of obstacles, whether they're people or circumstances, in order to bring your vision to life.

As you take action in the world, you must do so in a way that's in accordance with your values. Otherwise, you'll be out of integrity, and your vision may come to life at any cost—including the cost of her. When you're acting within your values, you're predictable, and she can assess whether you're the type of man she'd want to submit to and follow. When you're not acting within your values, you're unpredictable, which causes anxiety, and she can't trust or feel safe with you.

Say What You Mean

You can't lie about your intentions, emotional experiences, or expectations because that will only cause grief for both of you. You won't get what you want because you didn't speak up, and she'll feel betrayed because you weren't honest.

You also can't edit your speech to please others or fit their values, because often you don't share their values. Editing yourself may directly contradict your values. If you don't have the courage to say exactly what you mean in terms of your vision and values, she can never effectively follow you. She'll never trust that you'll take her where she wants to go.

Be Who You Say You Are

Being yourself means you don't change your vision, values, self, or emotional experiences to better fit your circumstances. Doing so would mean following the whims of life and everyone else. That would be relinquishing your power to others. Instead, you change your circumstances to better fit you. That's leading.

This applies to women, too. You don't change who you are to win her approval. You find the woman who needs your approval to fit into your life because, in the end, you're the one leading it, right?

Seek More Responsibility

If you truly want to amass power in your life, you need to start viewing every moment as an opportunity to assume responsibility. Every day, you're given chances to step up and lead where others might rather abdicate responsibility. Let's look at some simple examples.

Back when Brandon was still married, he owned a house on a corner lot with a large bay window that had a direct view of the intersection of the roads he lived on. He would eat his breakfast there every morning with his wife. One day, he noticed someone leaving a piece of furniture on the corner opposite his. In the days that followed, he saw more garbage and furniture being left behind until there was a sizable pile. None of that junk was his, nor was it technically his problem to deal with, but he decided he was tired of seeing it every morning. So, he rented a truck, loaded up the junk, and took it to the dump. Interestingly enough, when he was loading the stuff, one of the neighbors came to help him and thanked him. Was any of this his responsibility? No. But do you think the next time he needed something from a neighbor, they would be more willing to help? Absolutely. That's power.

Let's extend this mentality. When Brandon got into the BDSM scene in Austin, he noticed many people mentioning that they wished there were more munches in the southern part of the city. He also noticed that events specifically for the younger kinky demographic were limited. As he listened to people's concerns about what they didn't like about other munches, he decided to start a new munch called *Young and Kinky* in South Austin to better serve that community. Again, was this his responsibility? No. In fact, he was fairly new to the scene in that city. Nobody would expect a newcomer to take on the responsibility of making the community stronger. But he did it anyway.

This same mentality is what drives successful businessmen, politicians, and community powerhouses. In the context of D/s relationships, the more you're able to say, "I'm going to take responsibility for you and our dynamic," the more power a submissive woman will want to relinquish to you. In BDSM, there is a dynamic known as Total Power Exchange, where the submissive gives 100% of her power to her Dom (often called her Master). That means he has 100% control over her. But do you know what else it means? He also has 100% responsibility for her in every area of her life.

So, if you want to become powerful, start by taking responsibility for yourself, then seek responsibility for others.

CHAPTER SIX

Strength

Strength—both physical and mental—is a force that transcends its immediate, tangible effects. Consider gravity: an invisible force, yet one that governs everything on Earth, from how we walk to how the oceans move.

Strength operates similarly in human interactions. It may not always be overtly visible, but its presence is felt, and its absence is starkly noticeable. Whether it's the confidence of a solid handshake or the calm decisiveness of a person under pressure, strength—real, palpable strength—is magnetic. It shapes how others perceive you, how they respond to you, and even how they treat you.

Invisible forces like strength govern much of our lives and the lives of those around us. It is the foundation of reliability, trust, and leadership. But for strength to be complete, it must manifest both physically and mentally—one reinforcing the other in a powerful feedback loop that makes a person unshakable.

During Mario's gym days, he was fortunate to meet many different types of athletes. The most intriguing were the bodybuilders—mountains of muscle—who, despite their imposing physiques, struggled to hold eye contact because of extreme shyness.

The Halo Effect of Physical Strength

As mentioned earlier, there's a reason we expect someone as physically imposing as "Mr. Muscle" to behave differently. When we see a person with such an impressive physique, we naturally assume they won't be so shy and timid that they cannot hold eye contact with other less muscular beings.

Physical strength is more than just the ability to lift heavy objects or excel in athletic pursuits—it contributes to the **halo effect**, a psychological phenomenon where one positive attribute (such as looking strong) leads people to assume other positive qualities. When you appear strong, people instinctively perceive you as capable, disciplined, and resilient, even if they've never seen those qualities in action.

Why? Because physical strength symbolizes effort. It represents someone who has committed time and energy to shaping their body, someone who has the discipline to maintain a demanding regimen. This visible proof of strength creates an unspoken message: *I am someone who can overcome challenges.*

In moments of crisis or high-stakes situations, people naturally gravitate toward those who appear strong because strength suggests safety and capability. It communicates, *I can carry the weight—literally and figuratively.* Simply by looking strong, you project an aura of competence that earns respect and opens doors without a word being spoken.

We've discussed before how people are willing to trade almost anything for comfort and security. Becoming the strong, illuminated leader places you in an elite and highly sought-after circle.

But physical strength is more than just a social advantage—it is a reflection of how you see yourself. Training your body to be strong isn't merely about aesthetics; it is about cultivating a mindset.

If you are willing to endure the sacrifices, the pain, and the costs—if you adopt a *whatever it takes to get it done* mentality—you demonstrate a far more profound type of strength to the world.

Mental Strength Assumes Physical Strength

There is a profound link between mental and physical strength. To achieve physical strength, you must first develop mental strength. The discipline to wake up early, hit the gym after a long day, and push through fatigue when your body tells you to quit—all of this is a mental game. Physical strength is merely the visible manifestation of countless acts of mental resilience. You don't need to go full *David Goggins mode*, but it's easy to see why figures like him command attention.

The benefit of developing mental strength is that it transfers to every other area of life. The discipline required to get into the gym every day is the same discipline needed to succeed in dating, business, or any other meaningful pursuit.

In fact, how do you think Mario and Brandon got this book done? Writing is no easy task. We had to show up day after day, putting words on paper despite creative blocks, imposter syndrome, and even the temptations of our own lifestyles.

Mental strength is about endurance, adaptability, and remaining calm under pressure. Just as a strong body can withstand a physical test, a strong mind can weather emotional and psychological challenges. A mentally strong person doesn't crumble in the face of adversity—they adjust, adapt, and push forward, no matter what.

You are the captain of the ship in stormy weather, not one of the rowers below deck.

Strength Over Yourself Equals Strength Over Others

True power begins with mastery over yourself. The ability to control your impulses, emotions, cravings, and actions is the cornerstone of both mental and physical strength. This self-mastery creates a ripple effect, influencing how others perceive and interact with you.

Imagine two men in a high-pressure situation. One is visibly frazzled—his voice shakes, his movements are erratic. The other remains calm, his demeanor steady, his voice controlled. Which one would you trust to handle the situation?

Mario was once terrified of flying, convinced that every bit of turbulence signaled impending disaster. That changed when a close friend—an airline pilot with 20 years of experience—offered him a simple piece of advice: "Take a good look at the flight attendants, if they aren't shaken, it means it's all good. "

Strength over yourself is what enables you to be the calm one in the storm. It keeps you from reacting impulsively or being swayed by fear or anger. It allows you to make decisions from a place of clarity and confidence, not chaos. When others see that you are in control of yourself, they naturally look to you for guidance and support.

Brandon became acutely aware of this aura of strength during an event he was helping to set up. As he stood calmly next to one of the event leaders—who was visibly stressed over scheduling and logistics—she turned to him and said, "Please don't move from standing next to me. Your energy and calmness feel really good to me right now. " In that moment, he became her rock in an ocean of chaos.

The ability to remain composed under pressure, to think clearly when others are panicking, and to act decisively when others are frozen—these are all signs of strength. They demonstrate reliability and the capacity to bear responsibility. In a world where many struggle to manage their own lives, this level of self-possession makes you stand out.

OK, I get it, but what the heck does all of this have to do with becoming more Dominant and more important, in a sexual environment?

Good question. If you're asking that, you're already thinking about how your mindset shapes your reality. (Awareness)

Beyond the benefits of how others perceive and react to you, strengthening yourself mentally and physically directly enhances the quality of your life— **including your sex life**.

Being stronger—both in mind and body—translates to better sexual relationships. Not only will your body be more physically attuned to whatever experiences you choose to explore, but your partner(s) will feel safer with you. And when a woman feels safe, she allows herself to surrender more fully to the experience.

Think about it from this perspective: a woman who does not feel safe will have a difficult time experiencing pleasure. Her ability to enjoy any interaction with you—from giving you her number to walking into your apartment—is predicated on her sense of security.

Sure, she might like knowing you could physically protect her from a potential threat on the street, but what matters even more is *mental* safety. She needs to trust that she doesn't have to keep her guard up around you—that you won't fly off the handle if she says something you don't like, that you won't judge her, and, most importantly, that if she says *no* to your advances, you won't become aggressive.

When a woman feels safe, her nervous system shifts out of *fight, flight, freeze, or fawn* mode and into *rest and relaxation*—which, by the way, increases blood flow to all of her erogenous zones (*wink wink*). You'll know she feels safe with you when you see her body physically relax—like she's just taken a deep breath and exhaled with an *"ahhhh"* of relief, as if she's at the spa.

Back in the day, before Instagram and high-resolution smartphone cameras, even within the shibari and rope bondage community, there was extensive vetting before engaging with a new play partner. In Mario's experience, finding respected teachers or trustworthy partners required effort.

Sure, you could ask clever questions, observe how someone negotiated boundaries, or even check with others they had played with. But ultimately, a significant part of trust came down to *gut feeling*. And that principle still holds true today.

Want your woman to be more submissive?

Want your submissive to be more into you?

Want more people to instinctively trust and respect you?

Simple. **Become stronger.**

Physical and Mental Strength in Practice

Developing strength is not a passive process. *"One does not simply become stronger"* should be a meme. Strength requires deliberate effort, consistency, and a willingness to embrace discomfort—*a lot* of it.

Building Physical Strength

Pick a program and stick to it: Building strength isn't about occasional bursts of effort—it's about showing up day after day. Whatever your thing is, lifting weights, practicing martial arts, select something that makes you sweat and stick to it. Consistency is key.

Push Your Limits: Growth happens at the edge of your comfort zone. When you push your body to do more than it thinks it can, you train it to adapt and grow stronger.

Rest and Recovery: Something that took us a while to understand: strength isn't built in the gym; it's built during recovery. Proper sleep, nutrition, and self-care are just as important as your workouts.

Cultivating Mental Strength

Embrace Discomfort: Mental toughness is forged in moments of challenge. Seek out situations that test your limits and push through the discomfort. A recurring theme in our stories is that Mario and Brandon repeatedly put themselves in uncomfortable situations—sometimes deliberately, sometimes recklessly—but growth never happens without discomfort. *Sorry, champ—there are no shortcuts.*

Practice Discipline: The ability to delay gratification and stay committed to your goals even when motivation fades is the foundation of mental strength. Ever wonder why a six-pack is considered sexy in today's society? In a world of hyper-engineered, addictive food, *discipline* is rare. Start small, and progressively push

yourself   further.
When Mario quit smoking, he didn't go cold turkey (in hindsight, that probably would have been the best approach—but hey, lesson learned). Instead, he pushed his first cigarette back by 30 minutes each day until he was down to only smoking after lunch. Small, incremental discipline led to a major change.

Reflect and Learn: Take time to evaluate your actions and decisions. *What worked? What didn't?* Every experience—good or bad—is a chance to learn.

Go deep in your analysis: *Why did I react that way? Where did I learn that behavior?* Coach yourself. Keep your focus on the immediate next step instead of the overwhelming big picture. Don't think, *"Oh boy, I have to lift this heavy thing 10 more times."* Instead, focus on *"I'm going to lift this now."* Then repeat.

How Meditation and Mindfulness Made Us Stronger

One of the stereotypes Mario unfortunately embodied as a southern Italian was having a temper—erupting like a volcano. Some might see it as a "personality" quirk or a folkloric trait of his country, but the reality is that it was simply learned poor behavior. And poor behavior leads to more problems than it solves.

Sudden bursts of rage in key situations do far more damage than just making you look like a jerk. Instead of inspiring trust in his partners, Mario often scared them. Standing before them was a muscular 6'2" man with eyes filled with rage. He couldn't blame them one bit for feeling unsafe around him.

Through mindfulness training and meditation, he learned to harness that energy—to control it and use it constructively. Even in the heat of the moment, he practiced staying calm and present, learning to "slide" through the emotion, observing it instead of letting it take over. As an added benefit, he trained himself to stay in the present rather than being pulled into the past or future. Needless to say, it made a world of difference in his relationships.

Brandon began meditating shortly after graduating from college, right before he married his then-girlfriend. At the time, he struggled with anxiety and noticed he wasn't fully present with her—even when sitting right next to her, supposedly spending quality time together.

So, he committed to just 10 minutes a day. (Remember: consistency and discipline.) He did that every day for years. The only time he skipped was for an early morning flight—and even then, he'd try to meditate on the plane. Today, he practices for 24 minutes in the morning and another 24 in the afternoon.

Within the first couple of years, he noticed significant changes. He was more present with his wife, less emotionally reactive, and able to stay calm under stress. His thinking became clearer. He started truly listening—not just hearing the words, but understanding the emotions behind them. (A critical skill if you ever plan on getting married!)

A few years later, he noticed something else: people around him seemed more at ease. They displayed fewer nervous tics when speaking to him. He could focus his attention entirely on whoever was talking, making them feel truly seen, heard, and understood—a rarity in today's world.

When he got divorced and re-entered the dating market, he was met with an unexpected realization. Time after time, women told him they had never felt so safe, comfortable, and vulnerable with a man—especially on a first date. He frequently heard things like:

- *"I've never come for a man like that the first time we had sex."*
- *"You're incredibly easy to talk to about anything."*

During interactions, his mind was almost entirely silent—fully present with her, free from intrusive thoughts, worries, or distractions.

A quiet, focused mind—one not preoccupied with its own anxieties—becomes a source of strength for others. It creates a space where a woman can fully express herself, letting go of the burdens that plague her mind, too.

May the Force Be With You

Strength, in all its forms, isn't just about power.

It's about being a force that shapes the world around you. It's about having the discipline to master yourself, the courage to face challenges head-on, and the resilience to keep going when others would quit. Strength allows you to bear the weight of responsibility without being crushed by it. It enables you to lead—not through force, but through example. To be **Dominant, not domineering**.

When you cultivate both physical and mental strength, you become more than just a strong individual. You become a reliable presence in the lives of others—a source of confidence and stability.

You don't just react to the forces of life.

You *become* the force to be reckoned with.

CHAPTER SEVEN

Awareness

No, we're not about to get all new-agey on you. However, we invite you to set aside any preconceived notions about what you think awareness means before dismissing this chapter. Truth be told, awareness is a trait that will set you far above many other Doms, simply because few take the time to cultivate it.

Awareness, in simple terms, is the ability to observe, without judgment, what is happening inside you and around you.

Why does this matter for being a Dom?

Let me illustrate with a simple example: A submissive agrees to impact play in order to please the Dom but doesn't want to say "yellow" or "red" when things become too intense because they want to be a "good submissive." When the Dom swats the sub and their body flinches, that's a clear signal that the Dom should check in to see if the impact play is becoming too much. The sub is verbally saying yes, but their body may be saying no. If the Dom continues without checking in, the sub may regret the interaction later.

Without awareness of the situation, the Dom is unlikely to pick up on these subtle cues that something isn't right. Awareness means the Dom is present in the moment, not lost in their own head. They are attuned to what's happening in both their body and the sub's. With this awareness, they can sense when a sub is truly enjoying themselves and lean into that, or when the sub may be nervous or in their own head. In such cases, the Dom can invite them to reconnect with their sensations and breath.

In this example, the Dom had to be aware of:

- **Their internal state**—assessing the intentions and energy behind each blow (such as whether they are hitting out of fun or out of anger), and not beating themselves up if the sub doesn't respond as expected.
- **The amount of force** being used, so they can calibrate accordingly.
- **The sub's internal state**—for if the impact play has been going on for an extended period, she may be in the altered state known as subspace, which makes it harder for her to gauge her own pain tolerance.
- **The sub's body language**, particularly if she is flinching or tensing too much, too often.
- **The environment and surroundings**—because it may not be the impact itself but the temperature of the room, the unease of people watching her, or a dozen other variables life presents in any given moment.

As you can see, that's a lot to hold in your mind at once. But have you ever felt "in the zone" when doing something? You know, when you're intensely focused not just on one thing, but on everything around you, too? That is awareness.

However, if you're caught up in your own head—worrying about how you'll perform as a Dom, getting lost in your emotions, or simply ignoring the present moment—you'll miss all the signals happening in real time.

Now that you understand why awareness is important, let's discuss how you can cultivate it.

Cultivating Awareness In Yourself

I'm not talking about being self-aware in the sense of examining your belief structures or stories about yourself—that will be discussed in the next chapter on confidence. Instead, I'm referring to being aware of your internal state, mainly your thoughts, emotions, and body. All of these will affect your interactions. The more aware you are of them, the more you can influence them toward your desired outcome.

Thoughts

We're starting with thoughts because they are likely what you identify with most. You have a thought in your head, and you seemingly believe that thought is true—it's who you are, and you are the one saying it.

However, we have hundreds of thoughts each day, some of which contradict each other, some that are irrelevant, some positive, some negative, some useful, and others not. The more you observe your thoughts with objectivity—not putting a ton of emotional energy behind them and not tying them to your identity—the more you'll notice that many of your thoughts stem from preconditioning and programming you've learned from other people (parents, family, friends, media, society, etc.). Your thoughts are no more a representation of you than a slogan on a billboard in the middle of Wyoming.

The problem is that you become so enamored with your thoughts that you grasp onto them as if they are gold. This prevents you from experiencing reality, where the true information about what's happening resides. As a result, you misunderstand people, misconstrue situations, misinterpret others' emotions, speech, and body language, and ultimately cause yourself a lot of misery because the world doesn't match what you *think it should be* in your head. The world doesn't exist in your head. *She doesn't exist in your head.*

If you want to show up as a powerful person, not just a powerful Dom, you'll need to get out of your head. You need to stop clinging to every single thought that crosses your monkey mind, learning to discern which are useful for the moment and which are just noise.

A Few Activities That Will Help:

- **Meditation:** teaches you to focus on the present moment and not grasp onto thoughts.

98

- **Journaling:** by writing your thoughts on paper, you can view them more objectively, separating them from the rest of your mind and the emotions you attach to them.
- **Talk Therapy:** by expressing your thoughts to another person, you can borrow their discernment in order to observe them objectively.

Many people have tried meditating and feel that they are failing because they can't quiet their thoughts.

The goal of meditation is not to quiet the mind (though, eventually, that may happen to some degree), but rather to help you see that your thoughts are irrelevant to everything else happening in your awareness—that they do not need to be clung to.

In fact, if you have a very active mind full of thoughts, consider yourself lucky because you get more practice and repetitions in learning to notice a thought and just let it pass!

Simple Breath-Focused Meditation:

- You can do this anywhere and in any position, but if you make this a daily practice, choose a spot where you can sit with your feet flat on the floor or with your legs crossed.
- Next, briefly bring to mind why you're doing this practice. Why do you want to cultivate awareness in yourself? Then notice that desire, and let it go. No need to hold onto it or keep thinking about it. You've set your intention, so let it pass.
- Set a timer for 10 minutes (I recommend using a soft sound as the alarm, not a fire truck siren).
- Close your eyes.
- Focus your attention on your breath. You can do this by either noticing the air filling your belly or concentrating on the bridge of your nose, feeling the air coming in and out of your nasal cavity.

- As you do this, you may experience many thoughts flooding into your mind, like football fans filling a stadium. You don't have to ignore them. Just notice them and let them pass.
- Sometimes, this can be easier said than done. If you're struggling, intensify your focus on your breath by counting. On the inhale, count 1; on the exhale, count 2; inhale, count 3; exhale, count 4, and so on until you reach 10. When you reach 10, start again at 1. If you lose count at any time, return to 1. This will help you divert your attention away from the thoughts and back to your breath.
- With time, your mind will become less distracted by thoughts, and you won't need to count anymore. You'll be able to notice a thought and let it go just as quickly.

You're welcome to meditate for longer, but even just 10 minutes every day may be all you need to cultivate your awareness enough to be more present with women (and people in general). Brandon meditated for just 10 minutes a day for over 5 years and gets numerous comments from women about how at ease they feel with him—and that's because he cultivated that ease in himself first.

Body

Next up is the body. If you're caught up in your head, you're likely losing awareness of how your body is actually interacting with the real world. Your body is like a giant sensor, constantly collecting information. If you don't pay attention to it, you'll miss a lot of valuable signals—like noticing when her cheeks flush or a slight smirk that suggests it might be time for a kiss.

Of course, being aware is not just for her benefit; it's for yours, too! Being aware of the present moment is immensely *pleasurable*, especially during sex. It's the only place where you experience all of the sensations that make sex great. This includes seeing the beautiful curves and movements of the woman in front of you, hearing her moan, beg, and whimper, smelling her pheromones mixed with perfume, tasting her body, sweat, and juices, and feeling the electrifying touch of every single connection when your bodies meet.

No doubt there's been a time when you've experienced sexual performance anxiety—either losing your erection or finishing too quickly because you're so anxious about the situation. That happens when you get stuck in your head, focusing too much on thoughts like hoping you'll stay hard or last longer, and lose awareness of the pleasurable sensations happening in real time.

So, let's start reconnecting with the somatic experience of your body. Essentially, I want you to get out of your head, stop dwelling on the made-up stories about your experience, and connect with what you're actually feeling in your body.

You can do this by improving your **interoception**—your awareness of your bodily and emotional states. Your practice will be to regularly check in with yourself several times a day, identifying body signals and linking them to your emotions. Set alarms, if necessary, to help remind you to check in throughout the day.

You can strengthen your ability to stay connected to your internal state by **practicing body scans:**

- Start by getting into a comfortable position.
- Take a few slow, deep breaths and mindfully bring your attention to your feet. Notice (without judgment or evaluation) any sensations you experience in your feet.
- Move to your lower legs and continue upward through each body part until you reach your head.
- When performing a body scan, it's important to use specific and descriptive words (e.g., squishy, tense, hot, buzzy, relaxed, sharp, heavy) rather than evaluative words (e.g., bad, good, hurt).

The goal here is not to judge a sensation as negative because it's painful or positive because it's pleasurable. Instead, we're simply gaining awareness of what's occurring.

After practicing this for a while, you can start to focus more on pleasurable sensations, which will intensify your sexual experiences.

Seeking Pleasure in the Body:

- Continue the body scan as noted above.
- If you encounter discomfort or tension, think about how you could move or reposition yourself to make it more pleasurable.
- If you experience pleasurable sensations, spend some time fully engaging with those feelings and amplifying them.

Emotions

Next, we move to emotions because there's a chance that you're either too captured by them—blowing up on people for the smallest things—or you're oblivious to them, shutting them out with an iron gate. Mario and Brandon were of the latter.

Too many men believe that being masculine or being a Dom means being a stone-cold killer—no emotions, rigid, and never moved by anything.

But that's not what your woman wants. Turning off your emotions doesn't mean you have control over them. It just flattens you and allows you to avoid them.

What she really wants is for you to feel your emotions fully without losing control when you do. She wants you to let emotions flow through you, be fully felt to your core, and not be triggered into grasping onto them or overreacting.

When she sees that you trust yourself enough to feel your emotions, she will trust you and share her own emotions with you to the fullest extent possible. She knows you can handle both her deepest expressions of joy, bliss, and pleasure as well as her anger, sadness, and despair. If you want her positive emotions, you need to be able to handle the negative ones too. You don't get to pick and choose.

First, you need to learn how to be present with your emotions, specifically the sensations they create in your body, detached from the stories you assign to them. This requires cultivating awareness (of what is happening) and presence (being in

102

the moment), which you must practice over and over again. Every emotion must be felt fully, especially the ones you'd rather not feel.

When you practice this, in combination with strong self-esteem, you'll see that these emotions don't change who you are at your core. The pain doesn't destroy you. You're okay, even when everything around you feels chaotic.

Learning to be with intense emotions—usually the ones that are overwhelming and triggered by someone or something—can help you realize that they are just energy and sensations, and you don't need to attach a story to them. This can be difficult because when you're believing a story about an emotion—like blaming someone else—it can prevent you from fully feeling the emotion.

Intense Emotions Practice:

- To the best of your ability, separate the thoughts and stories you're assigning from the emotional energy and feeling.
- Invite the emotional energy close, noticing the sensations it creates in your body.
- Feel the raw energy of the emotion itself—whether it's joy, excitement, anger, fear, desire, or frustration.
- Let the emotion pulse and surge through your body as it wants to express itself, being sure not to grasp onto it or push it away.
- Neither own nor deny ownership of the emotion. Find the sweet spot where it won't get caught, allowing it to move all the way through your body.
- If you begin to own or grasp onto the emotion, or if it feels stuck in some part of your body, there's a story you're seeing or believing about the emotion that needs to be set aside.
- When you feel the emotion has been fully felt, ground yourself back into the moment by doing a body scan, as we learned previously.

With practice, you can do this exercise in just five minutes during any situation where you find yourself triggered and overwhelmed by emotions. Setting aside time to do this also ensures that you're not bottling emotions up and avoiding them.

Cultivating Awareness of Others

We're now going to shift our focus from the internal world to the external—starting with the vibe or energy we project, awareness of the social fabric we're embedded in, and awareness of other people's internal states.

Vibe

This word can be frustrating for anyone who wants a concrete thing to improve (which, let's be honest, is most guys). The truth is, vibe isn't one specific thing you can point to, but it can definitely be felt. You've heard it before: "That guy just gave me bad vibes," "I only want good vibes," "I like the vibe of this place." In the most esoteric sense, a vibe is like the interface between someone's internal world and the external world. Within the context of sexual dynamics, it's how you're presenting your internal world and the reaction or feeling that women get from perceiving it.

If you're not aware of your vibe, you could be projecting something others perceive as negative, off-putting, or just generally unappealing. You know the guy who's always sharing negative thoughts or letting his emotions overwhelm him? Yeah, that guy has a bad vibe.

So what should you be aware of that will affect your vibe?

- **Personality**: Certain traits of your personality may clash with others. For example, being either highly disagreeable or overly agreeable can be abrasive for some. It doesn't mean you need to change who you are, but you do need to know how it's perceived by others so you can adjust it as necessary.

- **Thoughts**: If you're always lost in your own head, people may perceive you as spacey or like you don't care about them. This isn't helpful when building meaningful connections.
- **Emotions**: If you're clinging to negative thoughts that stir up anger or depression, that energy will leak into your interactions. People will feel that from you.
- **Energy**: You're almost an entirely different person depending on whether you're tired, worn out, or hungry vs. when you feel like the Energizer Bunny—fully alive and recharged.
- **Actions**: All of the above influences how you move, talk, and behave in the world. It's the first thing people notice and judge. It signals what's going on in your inner world.
- **Looks**: How you dress, how you take care of yourself, and how you present your body. People will judge these aspects quickly. They signal how you perceive yourself and what you value.

The reason vibe is grouped into cultivating an awareness of others, even though it's tied to your own presentation, is because it's hard to determine your own vibe at first. The quickest way to gain awareness of your vibe is by using other people as mirrors, because vibe is just as much about your perception as it is theirs.

At any given time, you can check your vibe by simply asking someone. It's that simple. The more you do it, the more feedback you'll receive.

Ask people:

- How do I look?
- What do you feel when you're with me?
- If you were just meeting me, what would you think about me?

While you can do this with anyone, it's especially useful if you do it with the type of submissive women you're interested in.

Whenever someone offers feedback about you, don't take it personally. Instead, note what your internal state is and how you're presenting yourself. It's entirely possible that these internal states are influencing your vibe and how the other person perceives you.

Social Awareness

Understanding your vibe is the first step toward gaining awareness of the social fabric you're a part of. Extending that further, being aware of your social context allows you to choose how you want to present yourself within it and understand the implications it will have on how people perceive you—positively or negatively, or more accurately, as "cool" or "lame." Additionally, being aware of how people interact and govern their behavior allows you to actively decide whether to follow the norm or go against it, depending on what's more advantageous.

The social fabric is made up of:

- **Social norms** (e.g., having sex on the first date vs. after multiple dates)
- **Rules** (e.g., laws)
- **Systems that allow people to interact and cooperate with each other** (e.g., government, social media, economies)
- **Culture** (e.g., what people like/dislike)
- **Values** (e.g., sexual freedom vs. no sex until marriage)
- **Hierarchies** (e.g., boss and employees)

Engaging in BDSM involves two levels of social context: the BDSM community (often called the "scene") and the greater society. BDSM has gained greater popularity as many cultures have become more sexually liberal and it has been depicted in mainstream media, such as in books and movies like *Fifty Shades of Grey*. However, it's still not widely accepted, and power dynamics—particularly male-over-female dynamics, as discussed in this book with male Doms and female submissives—can be taboo or touchy subjects.

Although many in the BDSM scene consider themselves alternative to mainstream culture, labeling themselves as misfits, rebels, and so on, they still exhibit the same qualities of social fabric listed above. It's just that these qualities usually exist in opposition to the mainstream. Covering the entire social fabric is beyond the scope of this book.

Our advice is to:

1. **Embed yourself in these social fabrics and observe.** Don't judge. Don't bring your preconceived notions. Just observe. Within BDSM, you can attend munches, events, play parties, and conferences to see how people conduct themselves.
2. **Consume some of the culture of these social fabrics.** You're already doing so by reading this book, but also check out other influencers within the scene on YouTube, blogs, forums, or FetLife.
3. **Be fluid with how you present yourself.** Don't get dogmatic. Be able to adapt to your social environment. You can still stick to your ideals, and we suggest that you do, but be aware of how they will be perceived and be open to shifting if necessary. Or not—and accept the social consequences of doing so, whether positive or negative. The point is, you're making the choice and staying in control.

Have you ever just sat on a bench in a busy place and watched people? It's actually a great way to understand a culture. You can observe people's behavior, how they dress, who talks to whom, how they interact with each other, and so much more. Most of the time, we take this for granted and push it out of our awareness because it would simply be information overload to pay attention to everyone.

Take an hour or two to just watch people. Brandon enjoys walking, taking the bus, and going to very public places just to observe others. Notice as much as you can about each person you observe. Don't judge them—just observe. If you visit a place often and do this repeatedly, you'll begin to understand the culture of that place. You can apply this skill to environments you care about most, such as the BDSM scene, by going to the same events and observing the people there over and over again.

Empathy

We've started with your internal state, expanded outward to the broader social context, and now we want to zoom in on our target audience: a beautiful submissive woman. To do this, we need to build our capacity for empathy.

Empathy is the ability to sense other people's emotions, coupled with the ability to imagine what someone else might be thinking or feeling. In other words, it's being aware of another person's internal state.

Let's return to the scenario where we were spanking our sub at the beginning of this chapter. You're spanking away happily but don't hear anything from your sub. It's starting to get to her threshold and become too much for her, but she doesn't want to say "yellow" or "red" because she wants to be a "good submissive." You swat her again, and her body tenses hard; she flinches more than she has been. Although she hasn't said anything, if you continue, the submissive may regret the interaction later.

In this situation, your awareness of her *potential state* can help you make a more informed decision about whether or not to keep going. You're aware of how much pain she can tolerate, you understand what pain feels like, you know the anxiety she might feel about possibly upsetting or disappointing you if she asks to stop, and you're aware of what regret may feel like later. You also notice a signal that something could be occurring: her body tensing and flinching.

Now, we say "potential state" because we can't be sure with certainty what she is feeling or will feel in the future. We're not mind readers. We can only make educated guesses based on limited information and then ask if our guesses are correct.

So, in this instance, you might pause the interaction and ask her how she's feeling and if the spanking is becoming too much. If you're right, you'll know your awareness is attuned. If you're wrong, great — you've gained an opportunity for greater awareness.

Of course, awareness will not only serve you during play; it's going to be helpful in the entire relationship with her. Having empathy, specifically knowing how your actions will affect her, is going to influence how you treat her.

You've already begun the process of gaining greater empathy when you learned to become aware of your own emotional states and to feel them fully. During this process, you realized that because you are a human being with emotions, just like everyone else. We all share the same emotions, including the painful ones. This is where empathy is born. You begin to attune yourself to others' states, not because you're afraid of them, like an anxious person might be, or because you're trying to avoid upsetting them, but because you understand and accept that it's okay for them to feel those emotions. You don't try to change, manage, or control their emotions.

You become more vulnerable in the sense that you've increased your sensitivity to others' emotions, emotions that may have previously triggered you. Now, having done the work to control your own emotions and not be triggered by them, you can approach a woman with an open heart. One where she can fully express her emotions without you trying to change, manage, or control them. She knows that regardless of whether she's happy, angry, sad, or experiencing any other emotion, you're not going to shut down or blow up. You'll accept her and still lead, taking care of what needs to be done in her best interest. She feels seen, known, and safe— all prerequisites for her to submit and sink fully into her feminine.

Building empathy can actually be quite simple. To gain an understanding of what other people might feel in any given situation, you can either:

- Experience the situation for yourself and observe how you feel, or
- Talk with the other person about their experience, asking questions to understand how they felt in that situation.

Neither approach is foolproof for gaining a full understanding, but doing both can be beneficial.

There used to be a popular practice in the BDSM scene where, in order to become a Dom, you first had to submit to another Dom. This allowed you to experience what it would be like to be a submissive, so that when you were the Dom for someone else, you would not abuse that power. Although this practice is less common now, it's always helpful to test things out on yourself first. Hit yourself with a flogger, tie yourself up, put the gag in your own mouth.

For things that you may not be able to personally experience, you can ask her what it's like to experience something. A great time to do so is right after you've had sex. Ask her anything about what it's like to be her. You can ask what it was like to experience something you did that night, what it's like to be a woman, what it's like to be in her family, job, or society, or what it's like to date you— or anything else you'd want to know. Most women are happy to talk about their internal world and emotional states, but if they are shy, you can open them up by being vulnerable and sharing your own internal experience.

STORY TIME

When Two Kinky Wanderlusts Part

A real story of Brandon's. To protect the privacy of those involved, all names and identifying details have been altered. The individuals described in these stories were all consenting adults who participated of their own free will. If you choose to engage in similar activities, it is imperative that all parties involved are of legal age, fully informed, and consenting.

It was the last night I'd spend with Elise before embarking on my big adventure in the van I had just spent the last six months building out. I was excited to see new places and meet new people. It just so happened that the algorithm would deliver a wanderlust with an equally adventurous soul to enjoy my final days in Austin.

Elise and I first connected on Bumble after she immediately recognized me from my not-so-subtle profile hinting I was part of the scene. She said she'd been meaning to make it to the munch I lead, but hadn't been able to.

She was a beautiful brunette with big hazel eyes that had seen all around the world, having lots of photos of exotic places. In most photos she was dressed quite modest until her bikini photo which revealed the tattoo that wrapped the curves of her short, petite body from her shoulder, down her back, over her tight ass, and to her thigh. Those kinds of tattoos are so hot to me.

I texted her, "I knew that innocent looking girl on Bumble was just a facade. Of course there was a kinky girl in there.

"Me? No really, I'm a very good girl," she replied

I sent her a voice message mockingly saying, "Suuuuure you are..."

Our first night together was electric. The connection both physically and emotionally felt natural, like neither of us were forcing it or trying to play some role. We just naturally sank into our respective sides of the slash. I purposely slowed down every moment to fully savor it and wanted her to be physically begging me to take her.

Our bodies flowed effortlessly together as I picked her small body up, manhandled her, and moved her in whatever way I needed her while she actively followed suit, no resistance, she just completely trusted what I was doing.

Watching her get so turned on and lustful drove me animalistic. I turned my brain off, got lost in the moment, and bit her neck as I roughly fucked her like an animal from behind.

Afterwards, she said "I just want you to know, that I almost never orgasm the first time for a new partner." She had plenty for me. She could barely stand afterwards and we laughed at how much I had smeared her massacre everywhere.

When Elise came over for our second night together I had already laid out a few impact toys on the end of the bed: a flogger, a riding crop, and a paddle.

I loved undressing her and running my calloused hands along her soft skin and toned body. I shoved her forward over the end of the bed and firmly started groping and stroking her firm cheeks and thighs, getting them warmed up for what was to come. I gave a few light taps, followed by some light spanking with my hands and she melted into the bed, moving her hips towards my hand and turning her head to gaze those big hazel eyes back at me.

I kept spanking her, with ever growing intensity, and then commanded her in a firm tone, "spread your legs."

112

She was then graciously given relief as I cupped my fingers between her quivering legs and stroked her wet lips between the spankings. I continued this rhythm with the riding crop which filled the room with noise from the impact of the crop hitting her rosy red cheeks.

Snap. Snap. She'd gasp and moan.

As I started to reach for the paddle and bring it back to lay across her beaming ass, she softly opened her mouth, "...yellow."

I moved beside her to see her eyes starting to well up with tears, becoming overwhelmed by the sensations and emotions arising.

"Can... can we take a moment"

We crawled to the top of the bed where I held her in my arms, "it's ok to cry. Feel whatever has come up. You're so beautiful right now for being vulnerable with me."

She buried herself deeper into me and let out a few more alligator tears as I lightly kissed her shoulder.

She then softly spoke, "Thank you for holding space and being so kind to me..."

Our cuddling became kissing. Our kissing became petting. Our petting became fucking like animals once again with her head pinned into the bed by my hand grabbing a fist full of hair and smothering her face into the comforter as she screamed in pleasure.

These sexcapades continued over the course of a couple months where I relished in Elise's juxtaposition of being modest and then feral and kinky.

I remember the evening she came over in a cute pink sweater with hearts that covered her lovely curves, only to find an enticing set of lingerie underneath that made my blood boil with desire.

I remember standing over her, her kneeling before me, and pulling her slobbery, dripping mouth of my cock, kissing her passionately, and then picking her up off the floor and throwing her on the bed.

Quickly, I crawled on top of her and pinned her arms firmly above her head as she squirmed trying to get away. I teased her, dry rubbing my cock over her panties while gripping tighter on her wrists. She moaned and continued resisting. I let her "win" for a second, letting off pressure, before pinning her completely down, ripping her panties off, sliding a condom on, and proceeding to fuck her without abandon.

Of course the next day she sends me such a modest text thanking me for the night, like we didn't just have kinky wild sex. Cute girl.

However, our time was now coming to an end and we'd have one final embrace before continuing our nomadic ways. Before she came over to my apartment, I attached heavy boat chains to the legs of the bed and placed a chair on the opposite side of the room facing the bed.

When Elise arrived, she nervously joked that she knew red lingerie was my favorite, but she didn't have any, so instead brought a bikini set. She looked decadent in it, but I had to tease her about it some.

This did not stop me though from pulling her into me, passionately kissing her, and then quickly turning her around and pushing her into the wall like I was about to arrest her. I devoured her body with my hands and kissed and nibbled along the way in my exploration.

"Hands on the wall. Spread your legs. Stay." I demanded.

I grabbed the set of leather cuff restraints. I cuffed each of her outstretched hands that were patiently placed on the wall. As I moved to attach the thigh cuffs, I let my hand wander and inch closely to her groin, already feeling the heat between her legs. Instead of giving her the satisfaction of touching her, I took a bite of her plump ass cheek before moving on to the other thigh. I finished, kissed her hard, and moved her over to the edge of the bed.

Enter the Dom

"On your knees. Now." I commanded her.

Of course she thought she'd get the satisfaction of having my cock in her mouth again. I had other plans.

I attached the chains to her wrist restraints and told her to wait. I took a step back and undressed in front of her as she silently gazed up at me, eagerly waiting. I took a few more steps back, sat down in the chair, and began nursing the erection that had been begging to be released from my pants earlier when I had her against the wall.

I could tell she was getting antsy. I grinned and commanded her, "Crawl over here and come suck my cock."

As if she couldn't wait one second longer, she eagerly began crawling over with the heavy chains clanking as they dragged across the hardwood floor. Now she knew what was finally going on as she ran out of slack in the chains, extending her arms behind her, and only being able to reach my cock with her mouth, not an inch of give more.

Still, she eagerly consumed my cock and started sucking quickly. She'd get frustrated and try to pull herself and wiggle her body more towards me, slobber running out of her lips, and chains swinging behind her.

I chuckled and grinned. "You're being such a good little cocksucker for me."

I pulled her head back by her hair. "Open your mouth." I let my spit drizzle out of my mouth into hers before shoving her face back onto my shaft.

After having thoroughly entertained myself with her predicament, I stood up and released her. I pulled her up and moved her over to the closet door, quickly slamming her into it.

BANG. The door closed shut causing her to gasp.

I firmly planted my lips on her, pulled her hands above her head, and moved my hips to rub my cock on her pelvis as I restrained her wrists to the hooks in the doorframe above. I took off her bikini and took my time running my mouth over her perky breasts and rubbing my fingers between her soaked pussy lips. I roughly flipped her, grabbed a condom, and pushed her against the door before slamming my cock into her aching pussy from behind.

I covered her mouth with my hand and whispered in her ear, "This fucking pussy belongs to me now," as she moaned and whimpered.

As I fucked her, the door rattled with every thrust. I could feel her juices running down my legs.

I unclipped the restraints and moved her to the bed to aggressively continue fucking in the way she had come to love, screaming in pleasure with her head smashed to the bed. Every time we changed positions, I never pulled out my cock. Our bodies just danced and flowed.

After the first round, we just laid there with me still inside her and stared into each other's eyes and smiled, each of us getting a slightly bigger grin. No words. *Just bliss.* We cuddled in about a dozen different positions, laughed a lot, and talked about philosophy and the meaning of life.

"It's really unfortunate that we have both been in the same city this whole time and did not know each other existed..." She said

While we were spooning, I started getting hard again. She was all too eager to press herself into me and we went for another glorious round. When we finished, we were sweaty fucking messes and we just held each other for a while.

I got up to drink some water and as I stood in front of her, sweat dripping down my chest, she leaned forward and ran her tongue over my front, getting every last droplet of sweat.

We cuddled for a little while longer and it was starting to get late. Each of us would start the motion to get up and then end up kissing and embracing more, neither of us really wanting her to actually leave.

She looked at me really sadly and whimpered, "We have to break the spell sometime..."

So we kissed again and we got up. As we got dressed we kept interrupting the process by holding each other and locking lips more. Eventually, I walked her out to the front gate and we took one last embrace.

The quiver in her voice as she said goodbye after our last kiss fucking killed me. I grasped her hand tightly, kissed it like a gentleman, and watched the gate slam closed as she walked away.

CHAPTER EIGHT

Confidence

You know the saying, *"Fake it till you make it"*? Yeah, BDSM is **not** one of the domains where that applies. Let's set aside the nontrivial fact that you could seriously hurt her—or yourself—if you attempt certain BDSM acts without proper knowledge or preparation. Remember Mario's story from Chapter 1, when he dropped poor Cami to her knees by spanking her too hard without warming her up?

The only way a submissive woman will feel safe enough to submit to you is if you **actually** know what you're doing. What's even worse than doing something incorrectly is delivering it in a timid, hesitant, or weak manner. If she can't **feel** your power, the entire purpose of the power exchange is lost.

Now, you might be thinking, *"Guys! I've never done this before. How the hell am I supposed to be confident?!"*

When you first step into a Dominant role, it's probably going to feel unnatural—especially if you're not wired that way. Everyone, including Mario and Brandon, goes through the stage of shaky hands and weak verbal commands on their way to becoming more confident Doms. You're going to be bad at it in the beginning, and that's okay. Own it. Be honest with her about where you are in your learning process. I promise, she'll likely be understanding—and more than that, excited—to explore this with you. The worst thing you can do is lie about being a great Dom and then fail to deliver.

So, what do we do? We take responsibility and build ourselves into men who can actually be Dominant—men who can lead and create the lives we want. Confidence means feeling sure of yourself—not in an arrogant way, but in a secure, grounded, and realistic way. And to build confidence, we need to strengthen each part that constitutes the *Self*.

(No, we're not about to get all Freudian and tell you that your fantasies are just repressed desires for your mother.)

The *Self* is a mental construct—how you perceive yourself in relation to the world. A simple way to break it down is by looking at its three core components, which give us a clear roadmap for improving confidence:

The Three Components of the Self:

- **Self-image** = How you think you look
- **Self-efficacy** = What you think you're capable of
- **Self-esteem** = Who you believe you are

Each of these components requires work if you want to be an effective Dom. We're going to break them down in the order that's easiest to tackle first—starting with self-image.

Building self-image

Self-image is the easiest to address because the work is done largely from the outside in. It's also the best place to start because cultivating a strong self-image creates a positive feedback loop for self-efficacy and self-esteem. Put simply: when you *look* like a Dominant man, you start *acting* like a Dominant man, and soon enough, you start *believing* you **are** a Dominant man.

First rule: **Be attractive. Don't be unattractive.**

You can complain all you want about beauty standards, genetics, and how people are too judgmental. The reality is that people **do** judge based on appearance, and they have preferences. If you want to be attractive, you'll need to align with those preferences—while still staying true to your own vision and values. Otherwise, you risk coming across as inauthentic or fake.

Physique

Submissive women want to feel safe. They feel safer when you *look* like you could take down a mountain lion with your bare hands. Your goal should be 10–15% body fat with noticeable muscular definition—especially in the body parts that women find most attractive:

- Neck
- Shoulders
- Arms
- Forearms
- Traps

Don't believe us? Ask a woman how sexy she finds forearms...

Fashion

"It's not cool for guys to care about how they dress." Bullshit.

Try this test: go outside dressed exactly how you do now and observe how people react. Then, put on some clean, well-fitted clothes—something as simple as fitted jeans and a button-down shirt—and notice the difference. Pay attention to how many people smile, compliment you, or treat you differently.

Find a style that aligns with your personality, vision, and values, then dress like you're the **leader** of people who also dress that way.

Grooming

Hair, facial hair, skin, teeth—all of it matters. Otherwise, it's like dressing a homeless man in a designer suit.

Taking care of yourself signals to both *you* and others that you **respect yourself** enough to invest time in your appearance.

Level Up Your Body Language

How you stand, walk, and sit plays a major role in how others perceive your status. A Dominant man's body language is **calm, cool, and collected**—not nervous or fidgety.

- **Minimize movement.** No fidgeting. Move slowly and deliberately.
- **When sitting,** take up space. Stretch out. Own your presence.
- **When standing,** use the *Statue of David* stance—relaxed and comfortable, but not rigid or hunched over.
- **When walking,** move with purpose. Keep a slow, steady pace. Head up, shoulders back, body swaying naturally, and stride with intentional direction.
- **Make eye contact.** Hold it easily with everyone you interact with.

Refine Your Voice

Your voice is just as important as your appearance and body language. Work on:

- **Deepening your tone** for a more commanding presence.
- **Speaking deliberately,** slowly, and directly.
- **Avoiding extremes**— don't be overly loud or timidly quiet.
- **Breathing in your cadence** to maintain control and rhythm.
- **Using pauses**—long deliberate ones—to create emphasis.
- **Varying your speech, pitch, and speed** to add weight to important points.

We promise—if you **dress, walk, and talk** like a different man, people **will** respond to you differently. And soon enough, you'll start to *believe* you **are** that man.

Building self-efficacy

Now, we **look** like the type of person we want to become—but can we **act** like that person? In other words, do we have the ability to actually bring our vision to life?

When people say they want to be confident, what they usually mean is that they want to feel sure of themselves in their ability to do something. But that assurance isn't just confidence—it's **competence**: the skill and ability to execute something successfully.

The path to competence is simple: first, learn the skill. Then, practice it over and over again until you can execute it without much thought.

Take your vision for your life and break it down into the exact skills you need to make it a reality. Then, learn and practice those skills relentlessly.

When you develop the skills necessary to solve your own problems and do what you want in life, you start seeing yourself as someone who can't be fucked with. Outside circumstances don't shake you, because you know you have the tools to handle whatever life throws at you—including whatever your woman throws at you. You'll figure it out. You won't be fazed. *Goodbye, victim mentality.*

Competence as a Dom

This mindset applies directly to being a Dom. There are specific skills Doms must master, and if you want to be an effective one, you need to practice them. We'll cover many of these in Section 3 of this book.

For now, understand this: To gain competence as a Dom, you need to learn techniques from mentors, workshops, videos, or courses—then practice them repeatedly. Brandon flogged a pillow at least a hundred times before ever flogging a woman.

Some techniques will require a partner to practice with. In that case:

- Turn practice into a fun game and get her engaged in the process.
- Or, incorporate it into your regular sex life so you have ample opportunities to refine your technique.

The more you practice Dominant acts, the more comfortable you become owning your desires and reading her reactions. With time, you'll instinctively know how she will respond because you've seen that same reaction a dozen times before.

When this happens, submissive women will feel assured that you know what you're doing. And that's what allows them to surrender completely.

Skill Breakdown

Every goal in life requires specific skills to achieve it.

If you're reading this book, one of your goals is to become a Dom. Lucky for you, we've already broken down the essential skills you need—just flip back to the Table of Contents to see them laid out.

But this is something you need to practice doing on your own. Get your journal and revisit the goals you set in Chapter 1: Leadership.

For each of your goals:

1. **Identify the skills** you need to achieve that goal.
   - If you don't know, research online or—better yet—ask someone who has already achieved it.
2. **Find resources** to learn those skills:
   - Books
   - Courses
   - Podcasts
   - Mentors
   - Coaches
   - YouTube videos
3. **Put the skill into practice** with small side projects.
4. **Accelerate your progress by:**
   - Joining a community of people dedicated to mastering that skill.
   - Finding a coach or mentor who can provide direct feedback on your progress.

If you do this for any goal or challenge in your life, we promise—you'll start to feel *unstoppable*.

Building self-esteem

We save self-esteem for last because it's the hardest and most internal work. You either have low self-esteem, where you place others' value above your own, or you have an overinflated ego, where you place your value above others. Either way, you're insecure and have an ineffective self-perception.

Insecurity in relationships often stems from maladaptive attachment styles. Research on attachment theory dates back to the 1950s, identifying four primary attachment styles:

- Anxious (Preoccupied)
- Avoidant (Dismissive)
- Disorganized (Fearful-Avoidant)
- Secure

Let's briefly discuss each and how they affect your sex life.

Anxious Attachment

If you've ever been told you're clingy or too needy, you likely have an anxious attachment style.

Your behavior stems from a negative self-view but a positive view of others. You think highly of others but often suffer from low self-esteem. You're highly attuned to others' needs and emotions while disregarding your own (hello, people pleasers).

If you have an anxious attachment style, you need constant reassurance that you are loved, worthy, and good enough because your deepest fear is abandonment. This fear may make you desperate and clingy, obsessing over the security of your relationship.

This is where behaviors like worrying about texts, obsessing over her opinion of you, and constantly chasing her come from. When you do have sex, it's often used as external validation of your manhood and attractiveness.

Avoidant Attachment

If you've ever been told you're cold or emotionally unavailable, or if you've been labeled a "fuckboy," you likely have an avoidant attachment style.

Your behavior stems from a positive self-view but a negative view of others. You avoid relying on others, dislike others depending on you, and don't seek approval in relationships.

If you have an avoidant attachment style, you suppress your emotions, distance yourself from intimacy, and prefer to keep people at arm's length. You fear getting hurt or relied upon too much.

For you, sex isn't about emotional closeness or connection. It's often a meaningless act, leading to short-term encounters like one-night stands or friends-with-benefits situations. If unchecked, sex can become a tool for boosting your ego or gaining status among men.

Disorganized Attachment

If you've been told you're unpredictable or unstable, you likely have a disorganized attachment style.

Your behavior is inconsistent, stemming from a negative view of both yourself and others. You struggle with self-worth and trusting others. Relationships are both desirable and terrifying to you.

You may crave intimacy but also fear it, making emotional regulation difficult. Sex often serves as a pursuit of connection but remains devoid of emotion because expressing vulnerability feels dangerous. This style can combine aspects of both anxious and avoidant attachment, and in extreme cases, sex may become an addiction.

Secure Attachment

The goal is to develop a secure attachment, where you see yourself as inherently worthy and view others as valuable without needing to be better than them or tear them down.

When you're secure, you have a positive self-view and don't need external validation to feel worthy of love. You trust others, openly express emotions, and form stable relationships. It's easy to love and be loved. In sex, you're comfortable giving and receiving touch, experimenting without fear, and expressing emotions without insecurity. You are less likely to use sex to manipulate or seek validation.

Having Needs vs. Being Needy

As you build confidence, you come to recognize an essential truth: you are a limited being with needs. No one escapes this reality unless they are a god. Having needs is normal. In fact, a significant part of becoming secure and self-sufficient is realizing that you can fulfill most of your needs yourself. However, certain needs, such as human connection or physical touch, may not be as easily satisfied alone. Expressing these needs to others is both healthy and natural.

That said, there is a razor sharp distinction between having needs and being needy. The key difference lies in how you express those needs and how you react if they are not met.

The Difference:

- **A secure person with needs:** You express a need. If the other person says no, you either find a way to cope without that need being met or seek an alternative way to fulfill it, usually beginning with fulfilling it yourself.
- **An insecure person being needy:** You express a need. If the other person says no, you persist—repeatedly asking, manipulating, coercing, or creating covert agreements where you meet all their needs in hopes they will reciprocate. Alternatively, you suppress your needs entirely, pretending they don't exist.

The fundamental difference comes down to expectations. Just because you express a need does not mean someone else is **obligated** to fulfill it. Other people are autonomous beings with the right to say no.

You cannot control others into meeting your needs. Any effort to do so is ultimately futile.

"Wait a minute, isn't control the whole point of having a submissive—that they will meet my every need on demand?"

No. Wrong. Wrong. *Wrong.*

BDSM and Dominant/submissive (D/s) relationships are built on consent. At some point, you have discussed your needs with your submissive, and they have agreed—or not agreed—to meet them. Even in a 100% total power exchange (TPE) master/slave relationship, the slave consents beforehand, often through an overt contract, to meet whatever needs you have. The key word here is **consent**— without it, any attempt to have your needs met is manipulation.

When you have a need, your options for fulfilling it are limited to the following:

1. Meet the need on your own.
2. Ask your partner for help fulfilling the need and receive a "yes."
3. Find another person to fulfill the need and receive a "yes" from them.
4. Accept that the need will not be fulfilled and cope with it accordingly.

Handling Emotional Needs

When it comes to emotional needs—especially the need for comfort in response to struggles as a man—We recommend seeking support from other men or a group of men. First, only other men can fully understand the experience of developing as a man and can provide true empathy. Second, when sharing emotional challenges with your woman, it is best to do so only after you have formulated a plan to address them. That way, when you share, you are leading by example, showing her how she can support you rather than seeking comfort from her in a way that undermines your Dominance.

This doesn't mean you should never express emotions to your woman. Rather, it's about **how** you share them. You should share emotions without expecting her to solve your problems—that's your responsibility.

Repairing Your Attachment Style

The first step toward repairing your attachment style is awareness. Learn what your attachment style is and recognize the behaviors it triggers in your relationships. This self-awareness will help you better control your actions and begin the process of developing secure attachment. A great resource for in-depth understanding is **The Attachment Project**, which offers articles, workbooks, and full courses on attachment theory.

Once you have identified your attachment style, you can begin working to repair it. Three of the most effective tools for this process include:

- **Attachment Therapy:** A form of talk therapy where you build a secure relationship with a therapist to explore how your early childhood experiences—especially your relationship with your primary caregivers— have shaped your ability to form healthy emotional and physical relationships as an adult. Once trust is established with the therapist, they can help you communicate more openly and work through these past influences.
- **Ideal Parent Figure Protocol:** This method targets early experiences of insecurity in childhood. Through guided meditation and visualization, you create new "memories" in which Ideal Parents provide the care and security you lacked. Over time, your brain begins to rely on these positive, constructed memories rather than the old, insecure patterns because they are more compelling and emotionally satisfying.
- **Internal Family Systems (IFS):** A therapeutic approach that helps you identify and understand the sub-personalities within your psyche.

Imagine yourself as a collection of different "inner selves," each with its own role and emotional needs. Some of these parts may carry wounds from past experiences, leading to internal conflicts. By acknowledging and working with these parts, you can process repressed emotions, reduce self-sabotaging behaviors, and find healthier ways to manage internal and external conflicts.

As you work toward greater security, you must practice new behaviors until they become second nature. Secure attachment should become your default state. This might mean reevaluating existing relationships or taking the leap to put yourself back out there with a new mindset.

A Note from Brandon: You're Actually Just Like Everyone Else

The single most powerful belief that helped me become secure was the realization that, at our core, all humans share the same essence. We may look different, act differently, or pursue different goals, but we all have the same fundamental needs, desires, fears, and emotions. We all experience suffering. Recognizing this allows you to separate your self-worth from external factors like **what you do** (self-efficacy) or **how you look** (self-image). You have intrinsic value simply because you exist—just like everyone else.

This isn't to say that what you do or how you present yourself doesn't matter. On the contrary, we've already established why those aspects are important. But your core **self** transcends them. Your skills, appearance, and achievements are like clothing—you put them on and take them off, learn them and forget them—but **you** remain constant.

If you sit with that awareness long enough, you realize that everything is okay. That it has always been okay. That, no matter what the future brings, it will continue to be okay.

That sense of security is unshakable. It is the foundation upon which Dominance is built. It is the calm that others will feel in your presence. It is the trust, safety, and comfort that a submissive will rely on.

Treat yourself with respect

The way people treat you is often a reflection of how you treat yourself. Showing others that you have confidence largely comes down to treating yourself with respect. If you're self-assured in your value as a person, why wouldn't you show yourself respect?

Treating yourself with respect is crucial for being a Dom. Recall the truth shared in Chapter 1: *women will only submit to men they respect. Women will only respect you if you respect yourself. You can only respect yourself if you take responsibility for your life.* By this point, you have, or are well on your way to becoming, a man you can respect.

Let's take stock:

- You have addressed your problems.
- You've created a positive vision for your life.
- You've defined your values to guide your actions.
- You've built yourself into the person who can actually achieve and embody that vision.
- You're not triggered by your own emotions or those of others.
- You do only what aligns with what you say you want.

Would you respect that man? **Then actually do.**

How do you show others respect? It's time to start showing those same things to yourself.

This includes:

- Honoring your time
- Enforcing your boundaries

- Taking care of yourself
- Valuing your opinions, feelings, perspectives, and insights
- Giving yourself permission
- Physically taking up space
- Speaking of yourself in high regard
- Giving validation to yourself
- Treating yourself equally to others
- Giving yourself the support and resources you need to succeed
- Living up to your own expectations

After all this, you will have reached a point where a submissive woman could actually respect you and offer you her submission.

CHAPTER NINE

Love

Well, you didn't expect this one in a book about Dominance and skyrocketing your Dominance skills, did you?

So why are we talking about love here? Because love is the origin of all things that endure. It is the ultimate force behind every meaningful act, every significant creation, and every lasting connection. Love is the ultimate power.

Without love, any endeavor—no matter how carefully constructed and planned—will eventually falter and fail. Even the book you are reading now is the result of love. It took years for this book to see the light of day, and even more for Mario and Brandon to develop and refine the knowledge and skills that, ultimately, with love, you will master too.

Love is the fuel that sustains the process, and when you fall in love with the process, you align yourself with abundance, resilience, and purpose.

Why does everything start with love? Because without it, motivation withers under the weight of frustration and hardship. Love infuses meaning into even the smallest tasks, transforming drudgery into devotion. Whether you're building a relationship, mastering a skill, or striving for Dominance, love is the force that sustains you through adversity. If you don't fall in love with the process, you are already doomed to fail—not because of a lack of talent or opportunity, but because you've denied yourself the only force strong enough to carry you through the inevitable storms.

Enter the Dom

We've all had infatuations—with hobbies, fleeting passions, or summer flings—that made us think, *Is this the one?* But just as quickly as they arrived, they faded. Why? Because there was no love in them, only the momentum of the situation carrying the weight.

I know this might sound a little too *ethereal*—and for the skeptics among you, maybe even too *woo-woo*—but we promise, from personal experience, that if you start welcoming love into your life and the things you do, you won't believe what you'll see in the mirror soon.

The type of love we are talking about is unconditional love. Loving without asking for anything in return unlocks abundance. It frees you from the constraints of transactional thinking, allowing your efforts to flow freely. When love is given unconditionally, it transforms both the giver and the receiver.

When you are truly in love, you act for the sake of doing what you love, without expecting anything in return. If you love basketball, you play for the love of the game—not because you expect to become a five-time league champion. Loving without *demanding* a return frees you from the burdens of performance and pressure.

This is not to say that love makes you weak, naïve, or some Tibetan monk thriving on love and oxygen alone. On the contrary, it builds a foundation of trust, resilience, and power—one that others sense and gravitate toward, bringing abundance back into your life.

Mario's quest to become a better Dom led him to seek out as many partners as possible, eager to explore different dynamics in the BDSM world. To achieve that, he spoke to as many women as possible in every socially acceptable situation. As you can imagine, he faced a lot of rejection along the way. But Mario never faltered—because he loved the process. He loved the excitement of going out, never knowing what the day would bring. He saw rejection not as failure, but as a signal guiding him forward.

When you love the process without demanding results, *that's* when the magic happens.

How to Feel More Love in Your Life

Feeling more love begins with a simple but profound shift: **focusing on the good rather than the negative.** This doesn't mean ignoring problems or living in denial—we all have bills to pay, personal struggles, and moments when life throws the proverbial chaos our way.

It means choosing to see what is beautiful and meaningful amidst the chaos. Gratitude is one of the most direct pathways to love. Each day, take a moment to reflect on what you're thankful for, no matter how small.

Start with daily gratitude practices—notice the good things others do for you or the kindness that exists in the world. Mario once attended a mindfulness workshop that transformed his outlook. He learned that simply forcing the muscles that trigger a smile, even when he felt sad or frustrated, created an immediate shift in his emotional state.

Another powerful tool is changing your perspective from negative to positive:

- **Situation:** *I'm sad and exhausted because I'm financially broke.*
- **Negative perspective:** *I'm broke and can't afford the things I want.*
- **Positive perspective:** *I'm broke, but because I'm aware of it, I can make a plan. Things will change for the better, and overcoming this challenge will make me stronger and more confident.*

Sometimes, we become so caught up in our own problems that life feels like an overwhelming whirlwind of chaos. We feel as if everything is going wrong, leaving us lost, and disconnected. It can be difficult to feel as if we have any love to give to life.

The fastest way Brandon has learned to feel more love for life is to *give* value to others. Value, in this sense, means doing something that positively impacts another person's life—whether in a small or significant way. Every piece of content he creates comes from a place of love, with the belief that by sharing valuable knowledge, he can create a ripple effect in someone else's life. Not only does it feel good in the moment, but time and time again, he has heard words of deep gratitude from those whose lives have been changed by his efforts.

It's a *feedback loop*: you give value, they express gratitude, and that fuels you to give even more.

How to Feel More Love Towards Others

Unless you choose to live in complete solitude without internet access, you'll inevitably have to interact with other members of the "humans" gang. And let's be honest—dealing with ourselves is hard enough, so navigating relationships with others adds an extra layer of complexity.

It's also likely that other people will be the biggest source of stress, anxiety, anger, and frustration in your life—*if* you don't have the right mindset and approach. Rather than trying to impose your will or expecting others to behave in a way that pleases you, accept the simple truth: you're dealing with *humans*, and humans aren't perfect.

We tend to judge people based on surface-level perceptions, failing to recognize the complexities and struggles that shape their lives. But when you cultivate empathy, acceptance, and love, you begin to see others not as obstacles or adversaries, but as fellow travelers on the same journey.

To love others is like the proverb says—love like the sun. The sun shines and offers its warmth to everyone, simply because it *is* abundant in those things. It doesn't ask for anything in return.

One powerful practice for fostering love toward others is *Metta* meditation, also known as loving-kindness meditation. This practice involves silently repeating phrases of goodwill—first toward yourself, then toward others, and finally toward all beings.

For example:

- *May I be happy.*
- *May I be healthy.*
- *May I be safe.*
- *May I live with ease.*

After focusing on yourself, extend these wishes to someone you care about. Then to someone neutral. Then to someone you find difficult to love. Finally, expand these wishes to everyone, everywhere.

Metta meditation trains your heart to open, helping you replace judgment with compassion and resentment with understanding.

How to Feel More Love Towards Yourself

If you've been doing the work in these chapters, you're likely becoming someone you can be proud of. But pride and love are not the same thing. Loving yourself isn't about what you accomplish or the circumstances you find yourself in—it's about recognizing and embracing the immutable part of yourself that remains worthy of love, no matter what.

Too many people approach personal development from a place of self-hatred. You may have picked up this book because, in some way, you believe you need to *become* a Dominant man before you can love or accept yourself. Brandon and Mario were no different.

But if you don't learn to love yourself as you are, no amount of achievements will ever be enough. You'll reach milestone after milestone, change countless things about yourself, and still find flaws to fix—endlessly trying to fill an ever-expanding void with more "personal development." While we wholeheartedly advocate learning new skills and becoming more effective in life, we *do not* advocate self-loathing as your driving force.

Much of the work in learning to love yourself happens as you separate the three types of Self we discussed in Chapter 8—particularly when you begin identifying yourself on the level of *being* rather than just how you look or what you accomplish.

For Brandon, overcoming his deepest insecurities—believing he wasn't enough and that he didn't matter—led him to a powerful shortcut to self-love: *loving others first*.

Specifically, he trained himself to stop *judging* people—for anything.

There's a crucial difference between **judgment** and **discernment**:

- **Judgment** is based on moral or social norms, labeling people or actions as "good" or "bad."
- **Discernment** is about assessing the effectiveness of someone or something in achieving a specific outcome.

The way you judge others is the same way you'll *inadvertently* judge yourself. If you go around labeling people as bad, evil, or **unlovable** for their actions, at some point, you'll apply those same labels to yourself. But if you start seeing people as simply *less skillful* at navigating life's challenges, you create space to separate *who they are* from *what they do*.

And this is **massively** important.

When you stop judging others, you eventually stop judging yourself. You begin to see yourself *as a human being*, deserving of love just like anyone else—no matter what you do or don't accomplish.

You are *enough*, just as you are, to be loved.

What's funny is that the more you extend love and understanding to others, the more they'll reflect it back to you. This external affirmation will reinforce the most important love of all—the love you have for yourself.

Love and Dominance

Love, among other key elements, is what separates a good Dom from a bad one—just as it distinguishes a wise king from a tyrant. A bad Dom rules from insecurity and malice, wielding power as a shield to hide his own inadequacies. A good Dom, by contrast, leads from a place of love—love for himself, his partners, and the practice of dominance itself.

Similarly, a tyrant seeks control out of fear and greed, while a philosopher-king leads with wisdom, compassion, and a desire for harmony. The difference lies in intent: when love is present, power becomes a tool for creation and connection, rather than destruction and control.

Dominance, when rooted in love, transcends mere authority. It becomes a sacred exchange—an intricate dynamic where trust, care, and strength are woven together. To dominate out of hate or malice is to diminish both yourself and the one you seek to lead. But to dominate out of love is to uplift, to guide, and to create a space where both partners can grow and experience pleasure deeply craved.

A true Dom accepts every part of his submissive and works to elevate the best in her while refining the rest. He loves her not just for who she is, but for who she will become under his guidance. She is safe in his hands because he knows everything about her—every secret, every flaw—and still, he loves her. When she surrenders to him, she knows that this man sees all of her and does not waver. It is this love that allows him to train her. He could not invest so much of himself in someone he did not love completely.

Even in sadism, love is the cornerstone. Ethical sadism is an act of trust and mutual fulfillment—a shared expression of vulnerability and strength. A well-placed strike, a firm restraint, or a whispered command can all be acts of love when given with care and intention. Without love, these dynamics collapse into abuse. With love, they become profound expressions of connection.

Even when your actions are intense, they must come from a place of love—love for your craft, love for the trust your partner places in you, and love for the sacred dance of giving and receiving. Without love, dominance devolves into cruelty; with love, it becomes an art.

Every act of dominance, every decision you make, and every interaction you engage in is an opportunity to give love—to yourself, to others, and to the practice itself. When you lead with love, you inspire trust, command respect, and build a foundation of stability that others can rely upon.

So, begin every action with love. Love the process, even when it's difficult. Love the people around you, even when they challenge you. Love yourself, even when you fall short of your own expectations. And most importantly, love the journey— because it is through love that you find purpose, strength, and fulfillment.

And the road ahead is long, our friend.

STORY TIME

Never Judge a Woman By Her Looks

A real story of Mario's. To protect the privacy of those involved, all names and identifying details have been altered. The individuals described in these stories were all consenting adults who participated of their own free will. If you choose to engage in similar activities, it is imperative that all parties involved are of legal age, fully informed, and consenting.

Sometimes in life, in order to get what you want, you need to act so bold and daring that other people would gasp looking at your actions.

That was definitely the reaction of a workation group of girls when they saw me stopping Elena on the main street straight in front of their table, filled with Macs and iPhones and external mics, where they were having drinks around sunset time in a notorious Andalusian coastal town.

Elena was petite, pale-skinned, blonde but with a twist: she had shoulder-length rastas that were a funny companion to her sweet blue eyes. She had a colorful sleeve tattoo on her right arm and a series of ear and nose piercings (if you are wondering if she had one down there, the answer is yes, I know because I licked it).

So I stopped her and explained that letting her pass without me trying my luck would have been an unforgivable sin, she laughed, and a few minutes later was convinced to give me her number so we could have a drink later on. I was feeling in heaven.

I always had a thing for petite bodies; pair it with Slavic features and some rock and roll attitude, and you have a girl that really tickles my fancy.

Anyway, back on track with this story, she answered immediately to my first text and from the few initial exchanges, I could tell she was putting up some feigned resistance, saying I was a player, I was too smooth, yadda yadda—just agree to everything and have fun with it, that's what we all want eventually. It's just one life, no reason to make it so serious, a philosophy that got me a drink the following evening.

We met in a bar that overlooked the sea with small to large round tables that favored intimacy, rather than the interview-style squared ones. I noticed those are quite apt for a job interview or an MLM attempted sale, not for conversations about whips and blindfolds that shouldn't be heard, but only eavesdropped slightly to turn on the imagination of the other guests.

She was dressed in an all white: white Nike sneakers and a white tight linen dress that left most of her skin exposed to my delight—every time I looked at her I would bite my lower lip in excitement—complete with a white small bag.

We hugged and kissed on the cheeks like we had known each other forever and we jumped into cocktail selection. I felt bold again and ordered a pornstar martini, which prompted the conversation that I was looking to change career and dedicate myself to porn but didn't find the working hours amusing.

She teased me about this topic a few times. The first one was quite easy to see coming when she said, "But to be in porn you need to have..." Yes girl, I know what I need to have, and trust me, I do, but you'll see—was the answer I mentally delivered to her with my eyes and smirk.

Our back and forth was funny and I loved the witty banters this girl was throwing at me. Between a laugh, a drink with a toast to us, and knowing a bit more about her, the conversation moved like every conversation where sex between two or more people is on the table, towards sex.

I spoke about what I liked in a woman, how I adore submissiveness, but I want to enforce my dominance, not just accept it as it is given.

There is no glory in a victory without struggle.

She talked about how she was frustrated with her sex life, where most guys act all macho but in some shape or form, they all have issues with sex, ranging from erectile dysfunction to premature ejaculation or not having any idea that in order to have good sex, before the body, you need to fuck her mind.

A lot of the BDSM principles can sustain themselves only if they are accompanied by a mental component. Otherwise, the pain from flogging is just pain, but the context and the dynamic it is paired with make it pleasurable.

Same as sex, since the body has a tendency to "desensitize" itself from sensations (that's why you forget about pain after a while), the whole act of pumping in and out doesn't alone bring pleasure. It's the mental components associated with it— in substance, what does the other person *feel* in that moment?

So I took my time to explain to Elena that I was doing something called BDSM and she looked puzzled at me, which made me look puzzled at her. She had no idea what I was talking about or how it looked; I couldn't fathom how someone with her looks had no clue what it looked like (yes, I know, I judged and made assumptions, I'm a bad guy, what can I say? Who is without sin.).

I took my sweet time to explain the principles between D/s: the roles available, how they worked, the games that are possible, and how dominating someone boils down to asserting control by changing all the possible variables, from sensorial to movement, from psychological to impact play.

She absorbed my words like a just-out-of-the-wrapper sponge absorbs water in a sink, and I could swear she was taking notes about everything I was saying. When I teased her about secretly knowing all this stuff and just making me talk to make a fool of myself later, she leaned into me, pressed her hand on my thigh, and said it was actually very hot to see me explaining to her with a calm passion, but patience.

"Let's see if you figured out what my style of dominance is then," I smiled while shooting back at the tease which awakened my third leg.

"For sure you must be a daddy. you lighten up when you say Daddy."

Dang, she got me right in the gut.

"So if I want to be with you I have to be a little girl?" she quizzed back. The answer technically is no, you can be anything you want, BUT—

"Of course, you can always be my little girl." It just came out of my mouth. Too good to pass an assist like that, isn't it?

We spoke a bit more about impact play and how safe words, colors, and numbers worked to start/stop/pay attention. Somehow I could find the only girl on earth that didn't hear about *50 Shades of Grey*.

I was starting to develop a mini crush on her before even being in bed with this girl.

After the third round of drinks, I proposed a practical lesson back at my place while casually walking towards it.

I offered a tour of the house, showing the balcony, giving views on the busy street where there was the unmissable Irish bar with the obvious British patrons and a series of tiny clubs that, aside from loud music and cheap alcoholic drinks mixed with rocket fuel, don't offer much other entertainment.

I shooed her back inside to the living room, offering her to freshen up in the bathroom if she needed, and then I opened the door of the bedroom and proclaimed, "And this is Disneyland, where *magic* happens."

I didn't expect Elena to jump straight on my bed and with her legs crossed, she naughtily looked at me and showed more of her leg, saying devilishly, "How does it make you feel having a hot girl in your bed?"

"It makes me feel that she has something on her mind too," I shot back rapidly while looking her in the eyes.

I closed the distance until her face was pretty much facing my cock, which if it could, would have jumped straight away from distance, but I had to set things right.

I reached with my right hand for her sweet angelical face, now flushed with red cheeks.

"I'm going to make you submit to me now," I proclaimed without any tone of permission.

While rubbing my thumb over her forehead, I told her to stop thinking about my cock and how much she would like to suck it; she would have to ask nicely first.

"Daddy, can I suck your cock please?" I was taken aback—she immediately jumped without experience and submitted right away. This felt amazing, and I couldn't contain myself or try to play it out more.

"Yes baby, take my cock out. I cannot wait to try your mouth."

Now, remember when I said Elena had piercings everywhere? This meant also on the tongue. She used it as the centerpiece of her oral pleasure, rubbing the metal sphere against the tip of my cock and then alternating with slightly tapping on it.

"Yes, little baby."

"Please daddy, like this, c'mon harder and faster."

"Yes, yes, yes," I encouraged her to indulge more in pleasing me orally.

Her grip was very firm, holding all the skin of my cock as far back as possible with her hand planted at the base of my dick. She only used her mouth and tongue to pleasure me.

"Your mouth is so good you could make me cum... which is usually impossible with a blowjob," I complimented her.

Enter the Dom

The information must have been well received as she looked up to me and said she would love it if I came in her mouth. Wow, talk about planning the future together.

"No baby, first daddy wants to taste you."

I undressed her body, revealing a pair of small breasts with big nipples standing out, calling my attention right away. However, I was on a mission. I kept pressing the fabric of the linen dress down till I met her panties, a white G-string that was thrown to the floor a second after it had been unveiled, together with her dress and shoes.

I spread her legs wide open while I pushed her back fully flat on the bed, admiring the little brilliant gemstone she had as a piercing for her pussy.

I began on my knees, slowly tapping with my tongue all around her labia, first moving only with my tip, up and down slowly, then moving faster and faster and pressing and flattening more of my tongue against her pussy, making sure that the clit would get most of the attention.

We kept going like this for what I could reckon was a good 10 minutes before I decided to "zigzag" with my tongue quite fast on her clit. This sent her moaning and animating very fast, and she placed her left hand on my head, begging me not to stop.

Her body fluids mixed with my saliva spread all over her labia as I indulged in big long strokes, using more of the muscles of my neck to support the movement to let my other muscles rest, as it's a good idea generally to pace yourself physically for a longer endeavor rather than a short one. Extra energy could always be used later on for something else.

Elena didn't require me to plan too much further in the future about cunnilingus techniques to use though, as I reverted back to the zigzag. She suddenly clenched her thighs around my head and pressed both hands on the top of my skull before releasing a series of loud moans followed by the noise of her mouth sharply sucking in air.

Once the tension in her thighs evaporated and her legs fell to the sides in a butterfly yoga pose, I slowly crawled over her till our eyes made direct contact.

"Suck my tongue so you can taste how good you taste, baby," I murmured before sticking out my tongue, to which she joyfully wrapped her lips around and sucked like it was a baby pacifier.

I proposed to tie a small microfiber towel in a way that would work as a mouth gag and horse bridle at the same time. I explained to Elena that I would fuck her from behind while gagging and riding her, which made her enthusiastic about what I came up with given my limited access to tools and toys (you can't go on holiday always thinking BDSM is around the corner, right?).

After unrolling my condom, I took the improvised bridle in my left hand as I was slapping rhythmically against her ass with my right, everything enhanced with a side of dirty talk saying the nastiest things, none of them good for a Sunday church meeting.

Earlier in our conversations I asked about words that may trigger her in normal contexts but were entirely acceptable in the bedroom. She had told me a few which I made sure to use plenty of times as we fucked. I always found it entertaining while having sex and dirty talking, how someone could get shy but at the same time enjoy being called a whore.

We had fast rough sex in a few positions till I decided to give her a facial shot that covered her pretty sweaty face entirely, and some ended up on her rastas, too. I had no idea how she was going to wash it off, but now maybe I was part of the glue that held her hair together in everyday life.

SECTION THREE

Outer Dominance

Developing the Skills of a Good Dom

CHAPTER TEN

Decide What You Want

If you don't understand your own desires and communicate them to your submissive, how do you think you will ever get what you want? She will repeatedly ask you what she can do to serve you or might even say, "I want you to do whatever you want to me." If you don't know what it is you want, you're both going to have a very unsatisfying experience.

Early in Brandon's journey to becoming a Dom, there were times when this beautiful submissive woman was on her knees or lying helplessly on the bed, big doe eyes peering up at him, seductively asking, "How can I please you, Daddy?" Too many times, more than he'd like to admit, he would draw a blank and have no idea what to say. Not ideal for leading a woman in the bedroom. Eventually, he had to sit down with his journal and start exploring his own erotic mind to discover what truly turned him on.

First, we want you to temporarily forget everything you've learned or seen about what a Dom is supposed to be (well, except for everything in this book!). Just because you've seen *Fifty Shades of Grey* doesn't mean all Doms look and act like Christian Grey. You might also think being dominant is all about pain and being sadistic, but in reality, many Doms don't enjoy delivering pain. If you try to act like the Dom you see in some porn, it will come across as incongruent because it won't stem from your true desires.

She wants you to do what *you* want to do.

Desires

Exploring the erotic mind—that is, the thoughts, memories, fantasies, activities, etc., that turn you on—is a key component in uncovering your core desires and getting the most satisfying sex tailored to your own unique fantasies.

One of Brandon's favorite books on sex is *The Erotic Mind* by Jack Morin. Jack describes the mind as a powerful engine, transforming basic arousal into profound and often transcendent experiences through a blend of imagination, emotion, and memory.

At the heart of Jack Morin's exploration of human eroticism lies the concept of the Core Erotic Theme (CET), a personal and deeply ingrained pattern of arousal unique to each individual. The CET is essential in understanding why certain experiences, fantasies, and interactions trigger intense sexual excitement while others do not. Unlike mere sexual attraction, the CET is influenced by an intricate web of psychological, emotional, and experiential factors.

Understanding one's CET requires looking beyond surface-level desires and probing into the underlying themes that consistently arise in erotic fantasies and experiences. This is exactly what we will explore today.

Erotic Journaling

To begin understanding your own erotic mind, we suggest starting an erotic journal—a place where you can thoughtfully explore personal desires, fantasies, and arousal patterns. The act of journaling itself is a therapeutic process, providing a safe space for you to explore your inner desires without judgment or inhibition. Starting with an erotic journal allows for the purest expression of what turns you on, free from outside influence on how you *should* be turned on.

In this erotic journal, create four columns: *Turn-Ons*, *Feelings*, *Activity Triggers*, and *Partner Triggers*.

EROTIC JOURNAL			
Turn ons (fantasy, experience, thought, porn)	How it makes me feel	Activities that trigger that feeling	Partner qualities that trigger that feeling
			Brandon The Dom

Step 1: Write Down What Turns You On

We'll begin with your *Turn-Ons*. In this column, write down the following items:

- Fantasies
- Favorite sexual experiences
- Thoughts or mental images that really turn you on
- Types of porn or erotica you enjoy

By writing down these thoughts, you can start to identify recurring themes and patterns that resonate deeply with you.

During this process, try to avoid questioning where these desires came from. Just because you have a particular desire doesn't mean you ever have to act on it if you don't want to. This is about understanding your erotic triggers so you can incorporate them into your sex life in a safe and fulfilling way.

After writing some down, we recommend taking a break because you're probably feeling pretty aroused at this point. In the next step, we'll examine some of these items and discern what feelings they evoke in you. That might be a little challenging when you've just gone through your entire mental "spank bank" and feel like fucking *anything* right now. After you've calmed down (or, if you prefer, rubbed one out—no judgment), let's move on to the next column.

Step 2: Write Down How It Makes You Feel

Now, take one fantasy, sexual experience, thought, or favorite porn/erotica, and examine it in closer detail. Practice visualizing this particular erotic image as vividly as possible. Through visualization, you can explore the emotional and sensory details that make your fantasies arousing, thus gaining insights into what fuels their erotic excitement. From here, identify how this erotic image makes you feel or the types of emotions it evokes.

For example, the feelings and emotions that most occur in Brandon's eroticism are:

- Naughty
- Desired
- Appreciated
- Primal
- Respected
- Worshipped

Why do we care about emotions? Because some of our fantasies may be difficult to fulfill—either on our own or with a partner. Some may be considered too dark, and we may never actually want to act on them outside the confines of our minds. However, if we understand the emotion *behind* the fantasy, we may be able to replicate that same emotional experience through different acts, but with less risk. For example, if you have a capture-and-takedown CNC (consensual non-consent) fantasy, starting with some light bondage and heavy dirty talk may help you achieve the same feeling. In some cases, you'll never need to go fully into your fantasy— unless, of course, you want to.

Step 3: Write Down What Triggers That Feeling or Emotion

Next, identify what in that erotic image triggers the emotion you feel. Specifically, look for triggers that make the erotic image arousing to you: the environment, attributes of who you're with, what sexual acts are occurring, etc. Whatever you think makes it *so spicy*.

Now think about what other activities or partner attributes might trigger that feeling—even if they aren't present in the current erotic image. Write those down in their respective columns under *Activities* or *Partner Qualities*. This is where the rubber meets the road: the next time a partner.

Continue with Steps 2 and 3 for the other items you wrote down in Step 1.

Boundaries

Boundaries are the lines between what is acceptable and unacceptable behavior and actions in relationships with others. Often, external factors such as social norms and cultural beliefs influence personal boundaries, as well as individual preferences. Boundaries can—and do—change over time, depending on mood or circumstances.

Some boundaries to consider:

- When and where you feel comfortable engaging in D/s play, such as only in the bedroom or anywhere.
- How much protocol (rules, rituals, service, etc.) you want in your dynamic.
- Whether punishments are used, and how strict they are.
- If and when you would like your sub to wear a collar.
- Whether there is a contract.
- How much the dynamic is a part of your life.
- Where you stand on the spectrum of monogamy to polyamory.
- What forms of address or honorifics, if any, you enjoy being called during sex and play.
- Acting out specific taboo roleplay scenarios.
- Who gets to know about the dynamic.

As a beginner Dom, knowing where you stand on specific actions and behaviors outside of your D/s dynamic will help you better judge whether you want to participate in BDSM activities that may challenge those boundaries.

Take the time to write down some of the boundaries you want to set around your relationships. It will then be your responsibility to communicate these boundaries with your partner; otherwise, they are likely to cross them simply because you haven't spoken up.

Limits

Unlike boundaries, which can be more flexible, limits are hard lines that should never be crossed. Limits act as protective restrictions imposed on actions and behaviors, specifying what is expressly prohibited or hardly tolerable in exploration during play. The difference between boundaries and limits comes down to ideas of safety and harm reduction.

For example, certain sexual acts may trigger past trauma for an individual, in which case engaging in them could cause harm. A generic limit might be your physical flexibility. No matter how flexible you are, if someone were to push you beyond your flexibility limit, it would result in injury.

Some limits to consider are:

- Who you play with
- What activities you perform
- Certain sexual positions (in bondage or otherwise)
- What toys you use
- Chosen contraceptive and barrier methods, etc.
- Words used during sex or play

Crossing someone's limits can cause harm beyond the physical, including emotional or psychological distress. In this sense, you might regard the consequences of crossing someone's limits in BDSM as typically more severe than pushing someone's boundaries. The result could be an irreparably fractured relationship.

As a beginner Dom, you may not know what your limits are yet, and that's okay. If you're unsure about any activity, voice your concerns and apprehensions with your partner.

To help you navigate your uncertainty, you can categorize limits as either 'soft limits' or 'hard limits.' The difference between hard and soft limits is the degree of restriction given to the specific action:

- **Hard Limit**: A firm *NO*. It is understood as 100% prohibited, with no flexibility to perform that action.
- **Soft Limit**: A *maybe*, but most likely not. It is almost entirely prohibited, with any potential exploration of that action only possible after very detailed pre-scene negotiations, under specific circumstances, and with explicit consent from all involved.

As a beginner Dom, it is important to establish your firm "no's" and differentiate those hard limits from possible "maybe" activities (your soft limits). As you explore and learn more about yourself, you can continually update these.

A Note on Polarizing Play

Along your journey as a Dom, you will encounter many play partners who may be very different from you in terms of experience, boundaries, and limits. As you discover more, you might receive requests from your sub about types of activities that Mario calls "polarizing."

Most of the "Consensual Non-Consent" (CNC) activities could be defined as "polarizing" because they leave a deep mark on the psyche of the person experiencing them. Whether your sub has experience with them or not, it's irrelevant to you: firstly, because you are responsible for any consequences (after all, you have to give your consent to make them happen), and secondly, repairing any damage can be extremely difficult. Trust us, someone might say they would enjoy a "mind fuck," where you pretend to break into their home while they're asleep, but the reality is that how we perceive a fantasy and how we handle the aftermath are two very different things.

As a good Dom, your sub's safety is your #1 concern when playing. Giving someone nightmares or negative psychological anchors is not enjoyable for anyone.

Furthermore, engaging in these types of scenarios requires you, as the Dom, to enter into specific headspaces and access parts of yourself that you may not be ready to face. You can cause as much psychological damage to yourself as you can to her. These types of play can be like playing with psychological dynamite if you're not careful. So, if you choose to engage in them, do your due diligence by having plenty of conversations with your sub, and ensure extensive aftercare—likely in the form of days or even weeks, not just some cuddling afterward. Even then, there are no guarantees of no residual effects, so proceed with caution.

Fill Out a Sex Menu

A sex menu is a tool for communicating your desires, turn-ons, and kinks to partners using an extensive list of sexual and BDSM acts, with a corresponding score for how much you would like to participate in each one.

You can find a template on Brandon's website at:
https://www.brandonthedom.com/resources/sex-menu-template.

On the menu, next to each act, you can rate it with categories such as "Hard limit," "Soft limit," "Occasionally," "Love it," "Need it," "Try it," and "Indifferent." This tool will help greatly in communicating with your partner, a topic we'll cover in a later chapter.

Your Style of Dominance

The final topic we want to cover is how your desires might fit within certain D/s archetypes. These archetypes aren't meant to put you into a box or limit your possibilities; rather, they can help you identify the types of submissive women who are more likely to turn you on. They also point you toward skills and areas of education you may want to explore if you wish to engage with those types of submissive women.

Being a Top

A *Top* is someone who has the skills to perform specific acts on another person. A *Dominant* is the why, the intention, *the juice*, behind those acts. Of course, it's necessary to be a skilled *Top* in addition to being a *Dom* if you're going to engage in BDSM.

A good Top has a solid understanding of BDSM principles, techniques, and safety practices. They continually seek to educate themselves about various aspects of BDSM to ensure safe and enjoyable experiences for both partners.

In some circles, a Top is not considered part of the "Dominant" archetypes, as they may deliver kinky actions like a Dom would within a scene, but they're not necessarily fulfilling the broader role of the Dominant, as covered in this book. Being a *Top* is a great place to start when honing your skills and learning how to gain control, harness power, and manage a D/s dynamic.

If this resonates with you, don't worry—there is no shame in being a good Top. In fact, we've seen some incredible Tops who are far more skilled in particular kinks than we are. But know that this is just the starting point for the type of Dom you could become.

Dominant Archetypes

The acronym BDSM, which stands for Bondage & Discipline, Dominance & Submission, and Sadism & Masochism, illuminates several classic archetypes for Dominants.

These include:

- **Rigger**: Enjoys rope bondage or other forms of restraint, either for the visual appeal of seeing the submissive tied up and at their mercy, or for the art form, such as in *shibari*. *Riggers* pair with *rope bunnies* (those who enjoy being tied up).

- **Disciplinarian**: Enjoys rules and punishments (which can be physical, like spanking, or psychological) to control or modify behavior within a BDSM context. *Disciplinarians* often pair with *brats*, *spankees*, or submissives who crave structure and stern handling.
- **Daddy Dom**: Exhibits caregiving tendencies and enjoys the more tender, nurturing qualities of guiding and mentoring their sub. They patiently nurture, punish, and help their sub towards compliant, fruitful behavior in the relationship. *Daddy Doms* pair with *littles*, *middles*, *baby girls*, or any submissive wanting a caring mentor. (It's important to clarify that this is not about pedophilia, which involves attraction to minors.)
- **Master**: Enjoys 24/7 control of their submissive, often treating them as property. Masters might engage in slave training, where the submissive learns their role and duties. *Masters* pair with *slaves*.
- **Owner**: Refers to ownership of a submissive slave or someone who acts like a pet, such as a kitten or puppy.
- **Sadist**: Enjoys inflicting pain on their submissive, who is often referred to as a *masochist* or *pain slut*. This pain can be physical (impact play, needle play) or emotional (humiliation).

Depending on what turns you on, there are specialty archetypes that focus heavily on specific kinks:

- **Fin Dom**: Someone who controls a submissive's finances, requiring them to follow rules or commands to maintain control over their money.
- **Pleasure Dom**: Focuses on taking complete control of the submissive's pleasure, dictating when, where, and how it happens.
- **Primal Predator**: Enjoys the thrill of hunting and "taking down" their submissive like prey, or engaging fully in their animalistic desires during sex, letting their rational mind turn off.

- **Degrader**: Takes pleasure in emotionally belittling their submissive through humiliation, degradation, objectification, and acts that make them feel less than human.
- **Brat Tamer**: Like a *Disciplinarian*, the *Brat Tamer* uses a variety of tools to discipline, educate, and help their brat get back into proper behavior. *Brats* are often craving attention and misbehave on purpose to get it, so it's up to the *Brat Tamer* to uncover and address that deeper need.

These archetypes are just starting points, and the landscape of BDSM and kink is vast. You can mix and match any of these to begin creating your own unique style, which is what we recommend if you want to really stand out to potential submissives.

We also recommend trying them all out. You may not realize you have locked-away kinky desires until you start engaging in activities you never thought you'd enjoy. We promise that the first time you see a woman orgasm from taking a hard spanking, it will change how you think about pain and being a Sadist forever.

CHAPTER ELEVEN

Consent

Why is consent important in BDSM?

There is a fine line between abuse and enjoyable, pleasurable, kinky play—and that line is consent.

In mainstream society, hitting someone, degrading them, or sexually using them are all seen as bad, wrong, and abusive. Holding power over someone is viewed as manipulative and toxic. Rightfully so, as the person on the receiving end of those actions has not given consent for them to occur.

However, for a kinkster, these acts can all be indulged in because all participants have given consent for them to happen.

Consent within BDSM is when a participant agrees to certain acts or types of relationships.

While some may say that consent is simply an "enthusiastic yes," we believe it is far more nuanced, and the ways in which consent can be acquired vary depending on the situation.

The three most recognized types of consent—whether for vanilla or kinky activities—are implied consent, informed consent, and express consent.

None of these models are wrong, and together, they can form a framework for meaningful consent.

Implied Consent

Implied consent occurs when you make an *assumption*—based on body language, physical actions, and inferred words—that the other person is open to what you'd like to do. No one has explicitly or expressly said "yes" to anything.

A large majority of the vanilla dating world operates on implied consent, and it's often the basis of seduction.

Here's an example: You match on a dating app, talk, and decide to grab coffee or drinks to "see if there's chemistry." Since both of you are on a dating app, you *assume* that the other person is open to some type of relationship, possibly a sexual one.

You show up for the date and give each other a hug. Since they were interested enough to agree to a date, you *assume* that a friendly hug is no big deal. You initiate the hug, and they happily embrace you back.

During the date, you flirt with each other, express your attraction, laugh, smile, and make eye contact—maybe even bump legs a few times. You *assume* things are going well, so you reach out to hold their hand or rest your hand on their thigh. They return your touch, placing their hand on yours.

A moment of silence occurs, your eyes lock, and you feel a warm tension between you two, your bodies naturally drawing closer. You *assume* that you both want to kiss, and you lean in. They lean in as well, and you begin kissing.

The date goes great, and you ask them back to your apartment. The agreement to go to your apartment doesn't necessarily imply that they're up for some sexy fun times (though they might be), but at the very least, it suggests they want to get to know you more. They're *assuming* that the principle of "no means no" will be observed.

Once you're back at the apartment, you chat a bit, and then you start heavily making out. You *assume* they're now open to more, so you begin touching them more intimately. They don't pull away, and they return the touch.

You then *assume* it's okay to start removing clothing. They help, eagerly pulling at your clothes.

Now, both of you are naked, touching, and making out. You *assume* that sex is now on the table.

As you can see, **a lot of assumptions** are made along the way. However, that doesn't necessarily mean it's a bad model.

You make assumptions all the time about how to act with other people. For example, when you get in your car, you assume that everyone else on the road will stay in their lane, stop at stop signs, and follow all the rules, standards, and norms that society has agreed upon for driving. It's when these rules or norms are ignored—either out of ignorance, disregard, or ill intention—that accidents happen.

It's the same here. If both parties are implicitly saying "yes" the entire time, enjoying the actions, and willingly going along with each step, then the model works well.

However, the implied consent model breaks down when one of the people involved doesn't follow the rules, standards, and norms underlying the assumptions.

The primary assumptions are:

- If I start doing something, and you enjoy it, don't show signs of disapproval, or say "stop" or "no," I can continue.
- If you start doing something, and I don't want it, I can say "stop," and everything stops, or I can say "no," and you won't pressure, coerce, or force me.

Using implied consent in practice is *difficult and can be problematic*, even in regular dating.

Downsides of using implied consent:

- Building social skills to the point where you're adept at reading people can take considerable time and experience dating many different people.
- The "norms" of society change over time and can differ between cultures. Something as simple as a hug could be seen as a social faux pas.
- The uncertainty of never really being sure if the other person wants what you're doing can cause anxiety.
- "No means no" assumes that you feel safe enough to say "no" and that you are capable of doing so.
- If someone has ill intentions, it can leave room for manipulation, which you need to guard against.
- You're at greater risk of crossing a boundary you didn't even know existed.

Given the activities involved in BDSM, the implied consent model simply falls short. Other models are needed. Let's now move from one extreme, where consent is not discussed at all, to the other end, where everything is explicitly talked about.

Express Consent

Express consent is clear and explicit communication, either verbal or written, in which the other person tells you what they will and will not do. The purest form of express consent is a genuine and enthusiastic "YES!"

The express consent model operates on the principle of "yes means yes," where everything must be requested and consented to.

Here's an example:

- **Person A**: "I'd really love to use wax on you. Would you be interested in something like that?"
- **Person B**: "Maybe, I'm not sure. Where would you like to use it on me?"
- **Person A**: "How about I start with your arms and legs, and if you like the sensation and feel comfortable, we can move to your chest?"
- **Person B**: "That works well for me. I'll let you know when I'm ready for more. Yes, I'd love to!"

Person A asks to do something to Person B, and in the process, Person B expresses a few clarifications before giving an explicit yes to the action. Both parties know what's going to happen, and both know the other person wants it to happen.

Great, right? *Sort of.*

Yes, we've reduced the risk of crossing boundaries significantly, and we don't have to read as much into body language or make as many assumptions.

However, the express consent model also has its drawbacks, mainly that it can lack some of the elements that make seduction so thrilling. *Too much* certainty can kill creativity, suspense, tension, intrigue, and power differentials.

If everything is not discussed entirely beforehand, there may be a barrage of escalating questions: "May I hug you? May I touch you? May I kiss you? May I take your clothes off? May I tie your hands behind your back? May I penetrate you?"

For someone who wants to be ravished, this may come across as unconfident, not very sexy, and maybe even slightly annoying if you're asking for explicit consent the entire time. Furthermore, it hinders your ability to be flexible and creative when the vibe of the moment calls for something you haven't yet gained explicit consent for.

If power dynamics like Dominance and submission are part of your play, it can feel counterintuitive to the dynamic when the Dom must repeatedly ask for permission first from the submissive, pulling both of you out of those headspaces.

Additionally, if someone has never tried something before, it can be hard for them to say yes to it without the experience to know if they'll enjoy it.

So, an enthusiastic "yes" for *everything* isn't foolproof either. That's why BDSM enthusiasts and kinksters often prefer using one of the models of informed consent.

Informed Consent

Informed consent means that you know what is about to happen to you, with a varying degree of understanding about how it's done and the risks associated with it, and can say you'd like to participate in that activity.

Informed consent operates by having a discussion (often called a negotiation) *before* engaging in play. The level and depth of that discussion—which defines all aspects of the play—can vary widely, falling somewhere between implied consent and express consent.

Here are some popular BDSM models of consent:

- **Safe, Sane, Consensual (SSC)**: Everything is based on safe activities, that all participants are of sufficiently sound mind in their conduct, and that all participants give consent.
- **Risk-Aware Consensual Kink (RACK)**: This model emphasizes the personal responsibility of each participant for their own well-being. It places more focus on being your own advocate for your boundaries and understanding what risks you're willing to take—and which ones you're not.
- **Personal Responsibility, Informed, Consensual Kink (PRICK)**: Similar to RACK, this model stresses personal responsibility in kink. If you're engaging in play, it's your responsibility to be aware of the activities and risks associated with them. This doesn't mean you're free from disclosing potential risks to the other person if they're unaware of them, but it does mean that the other participant is equally responsible for asking and learning about the risks before playing.
- **FRIES**: This acronym stands for:
    - **Freely Given** (not coerced)
    - **Rescindable** (consent can be withdrawn)
    - **Informed** (you understand what's about to happen)
    - **Enthusiastic** (no reservations about what's about to happen)

○ **Specific** (consent is given ONLY for this time, this place, this activity, this location, and with these people)

We've seen new models pop up from time to time, so don't expect this to be an exhaustive list.

While all of these models stress consent, you'll notice that in the SSC model, there are still assumptions about what's considered safe or sane activities and each person's tolerance for risk. As we move toward FRIES, the level of informing and specificity increases, requiring express consent for all activities to take place.

The Missing Factor in Consent: Who is Benefitting

So far, we've viewed consent as merely permission: one person granting another permission to perform an action.

However, consent is not just permission; it's an agreement that outlines who is doing what, who it's being done to, what's being done, and **for whose benefit**.

The question of *who* benefits from the action is a critical, yet underrepresented, factor in traditional consent models. It plays a key role in the psychological and emotional well-being of everyone involved, ensuring that the play is fulfilling for both parties.

A model that highlights this aspect is the **Wheel of Consent** by Betty Martin.

The Wheel of Consent differentiates who is doing the action and who the action is being done to—much like how BDSM distinguishes between a *top* (the one doing the action) and a *bottom* (the one having the action done to them). However, it also distinguishes who the action is meant for, as if the action were a freely given gift intended for the other person's benefit.

This model creates four distinct types of actions:

- **Giving**: You perform an action for the benefit of another person (e.g., massaging).
- **Receiving**: You have an action done to you for your benefit (e.g., being massaged).
- **Taking**: You perform an action for your own benefit (e.g., ravishing).
- **Allowing**: You have an action done to you for the other person's benefit (e.g., being ravished).

It's important to note that you can experience pleasure in all four quadrants. Pleasure is not the distinguishing factor. Similarly, the type of touch or activity— whether giving a massage or ravishing someone—may appear similar from the outside. What truly differentiates these actions is *who* the action is intended to benefit.

Why does consent matter here? **Consent is what makes the activity pleasurable.**

Let's look at the four quadrants through the lens of consent:

- **Giving**: You're performing an action for the benefit of another person.
  - *With consent*: You're happily of service, feeling joy from giving to your partner. Seeing them in pleasure lights you up.
  - *Without consent*: You're either forced to give, or you're giving beyond your means, sacrificing your own needs like a martyr, which causes resentment.
- **Receiving**: You're having an action done to you for your benefit.
  - *With consent*: You relish the experience of someone doing something for you and feel gratitude for receiving such a gift.
  - *Without consent*: You're either being given something you don't want, receiving out of obligation, which feels annoying, or expecting your partner to give and serve you regardless of their desires, which can make you feel entitled.
- **Taking**: You're performing an action for your own benefit.

- o   *With consent*: You're indulging your desires, expressing your needs with integrity, and experiencing the thrill of being entirely selfish in your pleasure.
- o   *Without consent*: You take what you want with disregard for the other person, using them. This leads to harmful behaviors like rape and assault.
- **Allowing**: You're having an action done to you for the other person's benefit.
  - o   *With consent*: You willingly surrender to the other person, allowing them to do what they want within your boundaries. You experience the bliss of surrender.
  - o   *Without consent*: You become a doormat or people-pleaser, allowing people to do whatever they want without regard for your needs or boundaries.

Many of the earlier consent models help prevent taking without consent, but they do little to address scenarios where a Dom might become a *kink dispenser* (giving without consent) or a sub might become a *people-pleaser*, allowing things to happen to them they don't truly want, just to please their Dom. It also leaves room for participants to act out of obligation. To be clear, both a Dom and a sub, or any kinky person, can be in any quadrant at different times to have a completely fulfilling erotic life.

So, how can we make the *benefit* of the experience more explicit? By asking your questions differently.

The previous consent models typically asked, *"May I do X to you?"* The implied assumption here is that the person asking the question is the one who will benefit from the action—otherwise, why would they ask? Perhaps because they want to give something to you!

To better communicate intent, you should differentiate your question:

- To ask consent to *take* (for your benefit): *"May I do X **to** you?"*

- To ask consent to *give* (for their benefit): *"May I do X **for** you?"*

Additionally, the person having actions done to them can ensure that the actions are being done out of genuine desire by asking:

- *What would you **like to do** to me?* (for their benefit)
- *What would you be **willing to do** for me?* (for your benefit)

Do you need to explicitly state who the action is for? Not necessarily, but doing so helps ensure that everyone's needs are communicated and met. Too often, couples become confused about who the pleasure is truly for, and both can be left unfulfilled. A classic example is the husband massaging his wife to arouse her for sex. Is he massaging her for her benefit or his? He thinks he's giving, but that's not how she's receiving it. In reality, she's allowing him to touch her body, but because he thinks it's for her, he's not actually taking pleasure from it, since it's not the type of touch he wants. If the couple were more intentional about clarifying who the action was truly for, they might both experience fulfillment.

What Model Should You Use?

That really depends on you and your partners' comfort levels and limits.

When you're first starting out, it's difficult to know everything you may need to be aware of, and you might not know your partner well enough to be making assumptions. In that case, it's safer to start with explicit consent and gradually move toward one of the BDSM models as you gain experience.

We'd also say that the higher the potential for physical, emotional, or psychological harm from a certain action, the more it should be discussed beforehand. But of course, everyone has a different risk tolerance, so it's important to talk with your partner about their comfort level.

CHAPTER TWELVE

Communication

It may be a cliché to say that communication is the foundation of any relationship, but it's absolutely true. Communication is the only way we can understand what another person is feeling, thinking, and believing. It's how we express our visions, needs, and expectations. To successfully lead a Dom/sub relationship, impeccable communication is essential—not only to ensure both partners' needs are met but also to maintain the Dominant frame.

But what is the purpose of communication?

This might seem like a silly question, but think about it for a moment. The purpose of communication is to transfer an idea from our mind to someone else's—because, no matter how much we might wish otherwise, people can't read minds. So why, when it comes to sex and relationships, do we assume our partner instinctively knows what we want?!

This applies to every interaction you'll have with a submissive woman. If you find her attractive and want to take her out, you have to communicate that. If you have a need that must be fulfilled, you'll have to express it. If you want to try a new or crazy sexual act, guess what? You'll have to open your mouth and ask for it.

So why does your mouth stay glued shut when your entire body is screaming at you to speak up?

Simple. You fear they will **judge, reject, or leave you**

Chances are, you've been in relationships where you were anxious about bringing up dominant sexual desires or sharing a taboo fantasy. It's part of your innermost world, and if your partner rejects it, it can feel like they're rejecting *you*.

Do these thoughts sound familiar? *"What will my partner think of me for even contemplating this? They'll probably assume I'm the most depraved sexual deviant in history, pack their things, storm out, and then broadcast to the world what a pervert I am..."*

Of course, this never actually happens. But the anxiety lingers—whether you're asking a partner to try something new sexually, approaching a woman to compliment her, or asserting a boundary.

Although communication can sometimes be as simple as opening your mouth (and honestly, it often is), different situations call for different approaches.

We're going to explore three broad categories of communication:

- Attraction Communication
- Empathetic Communication
- Assertive Communication

If you want your desires fulfilled, mastering all three is essential to effectively express yourself.

Attraction Communication: Seduction

"Flirting is a promise of sexual intercourse without a guarantee." — Milan Kundera

When it comes to dominance, few skills are as captivating or essential as mastering the art of flirting and seduction. These skills aren't just about attracting others or seeking validation—they're about building chemistry, establishing connection, and creating a dynamic that intrigues and excites both parties. And let's be honest—few things are more frustrating than not knowing how to flirt properly in the early stages of meeting potential partners.

Flirting and seduction are tools of influence and playfulness that can elevate your interactions from ordinary to extraordinary. Don't believe us? Have you ever charmed your way to a free hotel upgrade or a better seat on a flight?

Who usually pulls that off? You guessed it—those we call *charismatic* or, in a romantic context, *seductive*. Think about it: Who in your life—or from the media—do you consider charismatic? There's a lot to learn just by observing them.

Before we move on, let's clear up a common misconception: Flirting and seduction aren't about manipulation or deception. At their core, they are authentic expressions of confidence, value, and personality. Learning to flirt better doesn't mean you're tricking anyone. You're still *you*—and that's not something you need to change.

The Truth About Flirting and Seduction

Flirting and seduction are often misunderstood. Some see them as superficial or dishonest, but this couldn't be further from the truth. When practiced with integrity, these skills become powerful ways to:

- **Build connection:** Flirting is a language of attraction. It signals interest and establishes rapport.
- **Demonstrate confidence:** Good flirting **properly** communicates self-assurance. It shows you're comfortable with yourself and willing to take social risks.
- **Show social value:** Seduction introduces an element of mystery and anticipation, making interactions dynamic and engaging—setting you apart from the average man.

You might have noticed *"properly"* emphasized earlier—and for good reason. Like great banter, great flirting is an art. Mistakes are heavily punished.

It's easy to misread a situation and say or do something out of sync with your audience. That's why flirting requires skill, calibration, and emotional intelligence. If you've put in the work from Section 2, you're already in a strong position.

The Time-Tested Principles of Flirting

Mastering flirting requires understanding some fundamental principles. These serve as the foundation for every interaction, ensuring your approach is effective, genuine, and aligned with your intentions.

Flirting Principles:

- **Confidence is magnetic.** Confidence is the cornerstone of effective flirting. It can't be said enough—if you ever doubt yourself, refer back to the chapter on confidence in Section 2.

- **Playfulness is key.** Flirting is a game, not a job interview. It's about having fun, teasing gently, and creating a light-hearted atmosphere. When you're playful, you lower defenses and make others feel at ease. Stop treating dating and seduction like a high-stakes mission. Even if you screw up, screw up *big*—but have fun with it. Nothing's worse than sulking over a bad date.

- **Mystery fuels attraction.** Seduction thrives on curiosity. If someone isn't interested, no amount of flirting will change that. But revealing too much too soon removes intrigue. Keeping an air of mystery makes you more compelling. Imagine if every introduction sounded like: *"Hi, I'm Ronnie from Dallas, I'm 45, I work in investment banking, and my kinks are toys and leather restraints."* Not exactly thrilling, right?

- **Empathy matters.** The best flirts are also great listeners. Pick up on subtle cues, adjust your approach based on the other person's reactions, and make them feel truly seen and understood.

- **Timing and patience.** Seduction isn't about rushing to the finish line. It's about savoring the process and letting tension build naturally. Timing—knowing when to escalate, when to hold back, and when to shift gears—is everything.

Flirting Techniques

As we said before, flirting is an art—a mix of magic and technical skill. Think of it like striking a flint to create sparks. It takes the right tools and a bit of patience.

Atmosphere Matters

Seduction starts with setting the right environment. Lighting, music, scents, and ambiance all play a role in creating the mood. When planning your "logistics," keep this in mind. Nothing kills the mood faster than a 45-minute traffic jam or a loud bar full of drunk people interrupting your conversation.

Pacing and Escalation

Seduction is a slow burn. Start with light, playful interactions, then gradually introduce deeper, more intimate exchanges. Let tension build naturally. If a playful remark about her hands lands well, take it a step further—don't just repeat the same compliment.

The Push-Pull Dynamic

Push-pull is a classic seduction technique that keeps attraction alive by alternating between showing interest and pulling back slightly. When done right, it creates tension and investment.

The mistake many so-called pickup artists make is getting the balance wrong. The emotional build-up and release must be of equal intensity. For example, if you hold intense eye contact, giving her that *"I want you"* look, break the moment with a playful tease: *"Careful, your cheeks are getting red—I didn't know I had that effect on you."* This emotional ebb and flow creates the kind of chemistry that makes flirting exciting.

Vulnerability and Depth

While mystery is crucial, seduction also requires moments of genuine vulnerability. Sharing a personal story or opening up about your dreams can deepen the connection. Balance intrigue with authenticity—reveal something meaningful about yourself to invite trust and encourage her to do the same.

Advanced Flirting Techniques

Now, let's dive into three techniques that combine charm, humor, and imagination to create emotionally charged interactions.

Mini Cold Reads

A favorite trick of tarot readers and street psychics. Offer playful observations about her personality based on small cues. For example:

- *"You seem like the type who knows all the best hidden spots in town—am I wrong?"*
- *"I bet you're adventurous, but you always keep things respectful."*

Cold reads create intrigue and give her a chance to reveal more about herself.

Future Adventure Projections

People are seduced by their own fantasies. Play into that by painting a fun, imaginative picture of a shared experience:

- *"You'd make a great co-pilot for a spontaneous road trip to the French Alps. Think you could handle the playlist?"*

This subtly plants the idea of spending time together in a way that feels exciting and full of potential.

Playful Double Entendres

Use light, cheeky wordplay to add a layer of flirtation without being overtly serious:

- *"Careful, I might take that as a challenge."*
- *"Are you always this charming, or is this a special occasion?"*

Double entendres keep the mood fun and create a sense of mystery.

Nonverbal Seduction

In seduction, what you communicate with your body language is just as important—if not more important—than what you say verbally. Body language in seduction is often referred to as *subcommunication*, pointing to the idea that what you and she are saying aloud may not tell the whole story. A skillful seducer understands that there's an underlying, nonverbal conversation happening simultaneously.

There are four main components you'll want to master in nonverbal communication for seduction: **body movements, tone, eye contact, and touch.** Let's break them down.

Body Movements

Observing a person's body movements can tell you a lot about their mental state in the moment. Let's put it to the test:

Who do you think appears more confident?

- **Person A**: Fidgeting, bouncing their leg, moving their body quickly, or sitting with crossed and closed-off posture.
- **Person B**: Slow, deliberate movements, open and relaxed posture, steady breathing, and an overall *chill* presence.

In this scenario, **Person A** is likely full of anxiety, stuck in self-referential thoughts like *"I hope she likes me..."* rather than being fully present in the interaction. **Person B**, on the other hand, is calm, collected, and unbothered—fully enjoying the moment.

In seduction, you want to embody **Person B**. Your body movements should give off the impression that you're self-assured, in control, and at ease.

Tone

Your tone will instantly convey confidence—or a lack of it.

A nervous or anxious person will:

- Speak quickly and with a high pitch (often because they're speaking from the chest rather than the diaphragm).
- Raise their tone at the end of statements, making everything sound like a question.
- Ramble or rush through words without clear pauses.

A **seductive tone**, on the other hand, is:

- **Deliberate**—you speak slowly and directly.
- **Resonant**—coming from your diaphragm, creating a deeper, more controlled voice.
- **Varied**—you adjust your pitch, speed, and pauses to emphasize key points.

And here's the real secret: **silence is golden**. Occasional, long pauses build tension, allowing unspoken attraction to surface. Most people feel the need to fill silence—but a confident person embraces it.

Eye Contact

Most people struggle with maintaining eye contact. Why? Because prolonged eye contact makes them self-conscious, causing them to wonder, *What is this person thinking about me?*

But here's the thing—eye contact is one of the most intimate and powerful tools of attraction. If you can hold her gaze—especially in a public setting—you demonstrate an unwavering confidence and create a deeper connection.

That said, there's a right and wrong way to do it.

- **Wrong**: Staring wide-eyed like a serial killer.

- **Right**: Resting your eyelids slightly, giving off *bedroom eyes*. Let your gaze subtly communicate attraction and interest.

If you can master eye contact, you can build a magnetic presence without saying a word.

Touch

This is where most guys fumble—either by hesitating too much or moving too aggressively. And let's be honest, touch has a bad reputation because unwanted touch feels terrible for the receiver. In the kink scene, many munches and play parties even have strict rules about asking for consent before *any* physical contact. You'd be wise to follow those.

But here's the key: there are socially calibrated ways to "ask" for touch nonverbally. This is where *social savviness* comes into play.

Some examples:

- When meeting for a date: Open your arms for a hug—she gets to decide whether to accept it.
- Holding out your hand while saying, "Let me see your rings." She will often place her hand in yours voluntarily.
- Making the "come here" motion before a kiss—this invites her to lean in, signaling interest without forcing it.

Most of the time, if the interaction is going well, she will touch you first—on the hands, arm, or, in stronger cases, the thigh or face. A good rule of thumb is to *reciprocate* by touching the same area she just touched you.

Where guys screw this up is by *escalating too quickly and abruptly*. You can't just jump from touching her hand to touching her thigh. You have to progress naturally. A typical touch progression might look like this:

Hug → Hands → Arms → Back → Hair → Thighs → Face

To be clear, you don't *have* to touch all these areas—most of the time, just hands and arms are enough to build attraction. The important thing is to **pay attention to her response** before attempting to escalate.

- If she hesitates when hugging you? **That's a clear signal to slow down.**
- If she pulls her hand away when you touch it? **Don't force further contact.**
- If she rests her hand in yours or plays with it? **That's a green light to continue.**

The key to nonverbal seduction is *reading the room*—understanding her reactions and moving forward only when there's clear receptivity.

Mastering these nonverbal cues will elevate your seduction game far beyond words alone.

Seduction is a Journey

Flirting and seduction aren't just social skills—they're expressions of creativity, confidence, and connection. When approached with authenticity, respect, and playfulness, they become powerful tools for building chemistry and deepening relationships.

Remember, the art of flirting is a *journey*, not a destination. You don't "achieve" it like a gym PR. Embrace the process, learn from every interaction, and most importantly—have fun along the way.

Attraction Communication: Communicating Desires

Communicating your desires is an essential part of attraction communication. When you openly express a particular desire, turn-on, or fantasy, it's akin to planting a flag—signaling to others who share similar interests and inviting deeper connections.

Building a Safe Space for Openness and Non-Judgment

For both you and your partner to feel comfortable sharing your deepest desires, you must first create an environment rooted in openness and non-judgment.

- **Openness** means you are both willing to hear and consider each other's desires. If a desire is mutual, you can explore it together. If only one partner has the desire, but it's not a hard no for the other, there's room for discussion on how to fulfill it.
- **Non-judgment** means that even if one partner doesn't share a particular desire, they do not judge, shame, or belittle the other for having it. This approach may even allow for discussions on how the desire could be explored outside the relationship. It also means that whatever fantasies are shared, they will be met with respect, not disgust or immediate rejection.

Why are these principles of openness and non-judgment critical when discussing your turn-ons?

Because if you react negatively when she says, *"I want you to do X to me,"* you will instantly shut down any future opportunity to experience the full depth of her sexuality.

Sexually, society often shames her desires. She's expected to be *clean* and *pure,* never too wild, never with multiple partners, and certainly not engaging in anything too kinky.

Culturally, she's pressured to feel guilty for wanting to be submissive. She's supposed to be the independent *boss babe* who doesn't *need* a man, can do everything for herself, and leads her own life.

Never shame her for her sexuality or submissive qualities. If you do, you will never see how truly unhinged and passionate she can be sexually, nor how deeply she will submit to you.

As a Dom, your role is to build trust, showing her that it's safe to express her true desires. Give her permission to reveal the hidden parts of herself. You achieve this by fostering a space of openness and non-judgment, encouraging and rewarding her submissive behavior. Help her become completely at ease with sex, her body, and her fantasies. Show her how much you cherish her submission. Remember, one of the core feelings a submissive seeks through submission is *acceptance.*

This trust is built through a continuous cycle of vulnerability and acceptance. Each time one partner shares and the other responds positively, trust deepens. Over time, past experiences serve as reference points, reinforcing safety and security in sharing desires.

How to Practice This: Start small with low-risk desires and gradually work up to deeper fantasies. Mario and Brandon have reached a point where we can comfortably share desires early on, even with new partners or friends. But that confidence came through repetition and experience—we realized that negative outcomes were rare. In time, you will build that same confidence.

Tools for Communicating Desires

These tools are listed in order of increasing intimacy. If you're with a new partner with whom you lack strong rapport, start with a **Desires Statement**—a low-risk way of expressing yourself. As trust builds, you can progress to more intimate methods.

1. Desires Statement

A Desires Statement is your sexy elevator pitch, conveying key information in a short, structured format. It's ideal for new partners or casual encounters, such as pick-up play at a kink event.

A Desires Statement includes:

- Your sexual identity (Dom, sub, switch, or simply a sexual being)
- What you most want to feel

- Your top sexual activities
- Your hard limits
- Your boundaries and relationship parameters

Example Structure:

As a (Dom/sub/switch or sexual person), I want to be... (list core desires). *The top five activities I want to explore are...* (list top sexual activities). *The things I absolutely don't want are...* (list hard limits). *I want our dynamic to be...* (list relationship boundaries and parameters).

Example Statement:

As a Dom, I want to feel naughty, desired, appreciated, primal, respected, and worshiped. The top activities I want to explore are DD/lg roleplay, bondage, slave training, primal play, and erotic photography. My hard limits include sadism, extreme degradation, and disrespectful brattiness. I want our dynamic to be non-monogamous, casual but emotionally connected, with power exchange in the bedroom and occasionally on dates and at play parties.

Not exactly *seductive* communication, but it's clear and unambiguous.

2. Pillow Talk

Post-coitus is an ideal time for sharing desires, as you're both in a neurochemical high—more open and receptive.

While cuddling, try asking:

"What's something you've always wanted to try? If I tell you one, will you tell me one?"

We always advocate for being vulnerable first as it's easier for the other partner to go second.

Start with something mild, like:

"I've always wanted to try using a blindfold."

Encourage their response without judgment. If their desire doesn't align with yours, you can say:

"That's cool you're into that! I don't think I'd want to try it, but I love that you know what excites you. Maybe there's something else we can explore together?"

That will continue the practice of building a safe container. After going back and forth on a few mild desires, you can start divulging more intimate desires.

3. Sexual Bucket List (a.k.a. the F*ck-It List)

A sexual bucket list is a fun and adventurous way to explore fantasies. Early in a relationship, Brandon often suggests this as *sex homework*.

Each partner writes down all the erotic, taboo, kinky, or exciting things they want to try—ranging from simple acts like using a blindfold to elaborate fantasies. Then, you share your lists. This creates an ongoing menu of experiences to explore, keeping things fresh and thrilling.

Most importantly, reinforce the container of trust. Let your partner know they can write anything without fear of judgment. Encourage their vulnerability.

4. Sex Menu

A sex menu is a spreadsheet-style list of sexual and BDSM activities, with ratings indicating interest levels. Brandon prefers Google Sheets for easy sharing with partners.

Benefits of a Sex Menu:

- **Detailed Reference Notes:** Add personal nuances to each act.
- **Discover New Interests:** Research and learn about new activities.
- **Consent Clarity:** Establish explicit boundaries.

- **Rating System:** Move beyond simple yes/no answers to nuanced preferences.

Brandon often assigns sex menus as *homework* for partners he has seen a few times. If you have multiple partners, it helps track individual desires and limits. Typically, he has them complete their menu first—ensuring their responses aren't influenced by his. Once finished, he shares his as a reward. Most partners thank him, having learned a great deal about themselves in the process.

Empathetic communication

Empathetic communication is about building a bridge between you and your submissive woman to ensure both sides communicate their needs clearly, that those needs are taken into account, and that you, as the Dom, can make informed decisions about what action to take. To create this bridge, you first need to listen to her, then speak and give direction.

Listen First

Let's step outside the realm of relationships for a moment. If you're leading a company or a team, don't you want as much data as possible before deciding on a course of action?

In D/s relationships where you've taken on the responsibility of leading, it's equally beneficial to receive all the data you can from your submissive. However, you may find it frustrating that her primary form of communication is emotion. All she may know is that she feels a certain way, and what she believes is causing that emotion may or may not actually be the trigger. Furthermore, she might not even need you to solve a problem—she may just need to express those emotions and have a safe space to do so. You'll need to learn to really listen to discern what actions are necessary for you to take, if any.

First, *encourage* her to be emotional. If you truly want her to embrace her femininity, you must be able to handle her full range of emotions. If she sees that you can't handle emotions like anger, she won't show you her positive emotions either. You want her to express her emotions because they provide valuable feedback about how you're leading the dynamic. Let her express whatever emotion is true for her in the moment, without trying to change, extinguish, or "solve" it. If you attempt to change her emotion, you inadvertently put her in control, because it shows that your emotional state isn't okay unless hers is. In reality, you should feel okay regardless of how she's feeling. Her emotions don't dictate your internal state.

Second, learn to listen fully and facilitate dialogue so she feels seen, heard, and understood. **The Imago Dialogue** process is an excellent tool for understanding how you can react and actively listen to what she's saying. The process, used in therapeutic contexts, can seem robotic if followed to the letter, but as you integrate these skills into your everyday language, it will sound more natural. What's most helpful is learning the skills and phrases associated with mirroring, being curious, checking for accuracy, summarizing, validating, and empathizing.

Some key phrases to learn:

- *"I would like to talk about... Is now a good time?"* This shows respect for her time and energy. If she says no, schedule another time to talk.
- *"If I understand correctly, you said... Is that right?"* After she expresses herself, mirror what she said in your own words. This shows you've listened and understood. Many people, both women and men, simply want to be heard.
- *"Is there more about that?"* Sometimes women hesitate to share everything, especially if they've seen you lose control in the past. This invites her to express herself fully.
- *"You make sense, and what makes sense is..."* Women dislike having their emotions invalidated or dismissed as "crazy." They have every right to feel what they feel, just as you do. By acknowledging why she might feel the way she does, you validate her perspective, making her feel seen and known while also opening her up to hearing your perspective.

- *"I imagine you might be feeling..."* Now, you're empathizing with her, showing that you truly understand her feelings. If you can connect with what her emotions feel like, even in a different context, it will impact the decisions you make because you can empathize with her experience. You won't treat her poorly because you know how it feels to be treated poorly.

This process benefits you because it helps you dig deeper than her surface-level words, giving you more insight. What she says initially is often not the full picture, and you shouldn't take her words at face value.

Third, when you're listening, never start to **DEER** (Defend, Explain, Excuse, Rationalize) with a submissive woman.

- **Defend**: If she's accusing you of something that isn't true, there's no need to defend yourself. You can laugh it off. If it's true, getting defensive shows insecurity in your inner Dominance and the need to take responsibility.
- **Explain**: If you have to explain yourself, it means your vision, values, and actions weren't clear. Use this as a sign to improve communication moving forward.
- **Excuse**: Making excuses positions you as a victim of your circumstances, which erodes your power. Take responsibility for your life.
- **Rationalize**: Rationalizing happens after the fact. A decision or choice is made, and only then do you try to justify it. This shows that you weren't in full control, and she'll notice.

Lastly, for issues that actually need solutions, discernment, and direction, create "containers" where she can express herself fully and provide ample feedback on your decisions. Set aside specific times for these discussions because there's a time and place for deep conversations and feedback. During an event or activity isn't the right time; you should be leading with confidence. Checking in at those moments is often more about seeking validation than receiving constructive feedback. Additionally, if you're in the presence of others, it's disrespectful for either of you to "gut check" the other in front of people. Present yourselves as a strong unit, uplifting and encouraging each other.

Brandon recommends two types of containers:

- **Debriefs**: After you take significant leadership in the relationship, have time afterward to get feedback about how it went for her. Life naturally provides these opportunities. After sex or a scene, get feedback during pillow talk. After a trip, discuss it on the drive home. After dinner, chat while washing the dishes.
- **Relationship Check-ins**: Usually once a week, these are opportunities to gauge the direction of your relationship and life. During these check-ins, set aside the power dynamic so she can fully express herself. You should be gaining both emotional and logistical feedback from her, making logistical decisions on how to lead the relationship, and providing direction for her regarding the upcoming week.

Speak Second

Once you've understood her perspective and needs, it's time to express yours. When you do, we recommend using nonviolent communication. The benefits are:

- It separates objective observations from feelings and unmet needs.
- It keeps you from attacking or blaming her, which would put you in a victim frame, and helps you take responsibility for your feelings and needs.
- It allows you to speak logically by stating objective facts and emotionally by expressing your feelings. You don't conflate the two, which helps you make clear decisions.

Basics of Nonviolent Communication:

- **Observation**: State an objective observation, such as "She texts me in the middle of the workday."
- **Feelings**: State your emotion, not a thought, such as "I feel annoyed and frustrated when she texts me during the workday."
- **Needs**: Express the need causing your emotion, such as the need to stay focused and productive to finish your work.

- **Request**: Make a request, such as "Would you be willing to wait until 5 p.m. to text me?"

The true power of nonviolent communication lies in requesting your needs be fulfilled. Remember what we discussed in Chapter 8 about needs vs. neediness. When you make the request for your needs to be met, there must be **no expectation of her to say yes** and you must be **ok no matter the outcome**. Just because you're in control of her life as the Dom doesn't mean you control her free will. She retains agency, and any attempt to manipulate her to meet your needs reflects insecurity. If she says no, take responsibility for your own needs and find another way to meet them. She owes you nothing.

After hearing her out and expressing your needs, you can decide on what's going to happen. Remember to stay aligned with your integrity and speak honestly. This is when emotional control is crucial. If you're not in control, you may end up trying to placate her to avoid the discomfort of confrontation, which can lead to inauthentic decisions. Don't say anything that's not true. Don't do anything that's not what you truly want.

Finally, give direct commands. You're not asking for permission. You can ask how your decision might affect her and how to help her through it, but you're still making the decision. You're taking leadership and have all the necessary information, right? You know what's best—so act on it and tell her what's going to happen. This applies whether you're deciding on something as small as setting a time and place for a date or as significant as making financial decisions in a long-term D/s relationship.

Assertive Communication

The last form of communication we want to cover is assertiveness. People often shy away from being assertive because they don't want to cause conflict. They mistakenly assume that being assertive will break the relationship, or that it means they have to be rude. Assertiveness is not about pushing your will onto others to get your way. Instead, it's about expressing how you want to be treated and ensuring that your needs are acknowledged.

There is only one person in the world who will care for your needs more than anyone else, and that's you. If you don't assert yourself by speaking up for your wants, needs, and values, then someone else is going to walk over those boundaries. Not out of malice, but simply because they are trying to meet their own needs and are unaware of yours.

Boundary Setting

Boundary setting is about defining what is acceptable and unacceptable behavior toward you. We spoke about boundaries in Chapter 3 in relation to curbing your nice guy tendencies, and in Chapter 10 concerning what you want from sexual dynamics with women. However, boundaries extend far beyond the bedroom and far beyond this one relationship.

The struggle many men face with setting boundaries often stems from one of two issues:

1. They feel insecure and don't believe they deserve to have boundaries. The work from Chapter 8 will help address this.
2. They are afraid of causing friction in the relationship, fearing that the other person will leave if they set a boundary.

Let's address the second issue more closely. Consider this: if you don't establish a boundary, and the other person starts treating you in a way *you don't want to be treated*, do you really want to stay in that relationship? You'll never have your needs fulfilled because that person won't even know they exist. Additionally, you're likely to be used because all the signals you're sending say it's okay to treat you that way.

Furthermore, women—especially submissive women—*love* knowing your boundaries. It's like giving them a manual that says, "Treat him in this way." Sometimes women will "test" your boundaries, particularly if you haven't spoken up about them yet, just to understand where they are. It's similar to a child playing in the yard and going outside the fence. If the parents don't say anything, the child assumes it's okay to do so. However, if the parents set a boundary and explain why it exists, the child is likely to stay within the fence. Submissive women love clear guidelines like this.

Once you overcome these mental hurdles, setting a boundary becomes relatively simple. You'll do it in one of two ways: **preemptively** or **reactively**.

The first way is to set the boundary **preemptively** before it's even tested. For example, Brandon knows that some women like to text a lot. So, early in the communication, he tells them that during the workday, he's quite busy and prefers to stay focused. He lets them know he's not ignoring them (acknowledging their feelings) and that he will respond when he's free (establishing the boundary). This sets expectations for how he wants to be communicated with. When this happens, she doesn't get upset because she knows he's busy, and he doesn't get upset because he's allowed to focus on his work. If a woman ignores this and continues texting excessively, he would likely end the conversation with her because she isn't respecting his boundary.

The second way is to set the boundary **reactively**, after the boundary has been crossed. It's okay to set boundaries reactively, as you won't always know a boundary exists until it's crossed. However, there's a healthy and unhealthy way to do this.

The unhealthy way to set boundaries reactively is by blowing up at her when the boundary is crossed and blaming her for the transgression. If she crosses a boundary that you haven't clearly communicated, it's not her fault—it's yours for not setting it. Blowing up on her is uncalled for. When people feel attacked, they will never care about your needs. Setting boundaries in this way doesn't create a trusting relationship, and trust is everything in a D/s dynamic.

The healthy way to set boundaries is to recognize when you're triggered by an intense emotion, allow that emotion to pass, and then have a conversation later to let her know a boundary was crossed. Explain that it wasn't her fault, but you'd like to be treated differently in the future. The key is to use the intense emotion as a signal for introspection. In doing so, you'll often uncover a boundary or unmet need, one you may not have recognized before. With this newfound understanding, use the tools of empathetic communication discussed previously to address it.

Once you discover a boundary reactively, be sure to set it preemptively in future relationships if you anticipate it might arise.

Negotiations

Negotiating is the process through which you and your partner express your needs, desires, limits, and boundaries, and find a way to navigate them so that both of you win. You're not trying to one-up each other; you're working toward an agreement that is mutually beneficial and fulfilling. Asserting yourself—simply speaking up for your needs—is essential during this process because, if you don't, your needs are likely to be left out of the agreement.

Some people wrongly assume that if you need to negotiate in a relationship, it must not be "meant to be." They think the other person should simply want to meet their needs out of love. But here's the truth: **no one will ever meet your needs 100% of the time**. There will always be limitations, whether from their own boundaries, or simply because they don't share the same desires as you. Relationships require a dance of give and take. The quicker you accept this and learn to negotiate, the more likely you are to get what you want.

One benefit of D/s relationships over traditional ones is that negotiation is expected. You'll need to negotiate things like the kinds of play you'll engage in, how much power exchange will occur, and the boundaries of the relationship. The deeper the dynamic, the more negotiation you'll do, often formalized through a contract, which we'll discuss in Chapter 16.

There are many models for BDSM negotiation, and it would be impractical to try to define the best one. We recommend exploring different models to see which works best for you. Many cities also offer local workshops on negotiation, which can be helpful for practicing with someone. In the meantime, let's go over an example of a "speed negotiation" model with some important talking points.

Speed Negotiation:

- **Desires**: Ask about her favorite or top desires. If this is your first time playing, she may not share her deepest desires but will likely mention things she enjoys and feels comfortable doing with you. As trust builds, you'll learn her true top desires.

- **Safe Words**: Safe words or phrases help you adjust the pace or stop the play altogether. A common system is the "traffic light" system: Red means stop, yellow means slow down, and green means go harder. "Mercy" is also a common safe word, but you can make up your own. Respecting a safe word is critical—ignoring one is a blatant consent violation.

- **Health**: Know your partner's status regarding STDs to ensure safety. Some may request to see your test results, so it's useful to have them saved on your phone. Depending on the type of play, it might be necessary to know other health details, such as mobility issues if you plan on bondage play.

- **Limits**: Ask about her limits for the night. Your goal is to keep her safe, not find loopholes because she forgot to mention something. Respect her limits, and don't cross them.

- **Marks**: If you're prone to leaving marks—whether through biting, impact play, or other methods—ask her where marks are allowed. Many women prefer not to have marks on visible areas like the neck or upper chest, especially if they need to maintain a professional appearance.

- **Emotional State**: Gauge her emotional state to determine if a certain type of play is appropriate. If she's feeling depressed or lonely, or if she has a negative self-image that day, engaging in heavy degradation might not be suitable, even if it's a favorite kink.

The bottom line of negotiation is ensuring that both parties communicate their desires and limits clearly, so that everyone remains safe and fulfilled.

Enter the Dom

The Venezuelan Squirt Queen Gets More Than She Can Handle

A real story of Mario's. To protect the privacy of those involved, all names and identifying details have been altered. The individuals described in these stories were all consenting adults who participated of their own free will. If you choose to engage in similar activities, it is imperative that all parties involved are of legal age, fully informed, and consenting.

It was a sunny day at the beach, the water was crystal blue and the sand beneath my body was warm and soft. I could see a few scattered ball-shaped clouds on the horizon that would transit quickly across my line of sight. My sunglasses tinted everything bluer, making the families enjoying their deserved holiday time look like a group of Smurfs busy building sand villages.

I was completely relaxing, feeling my hands stroking the warm, sticky sand, appreciating the sensation it left on my fingertips. A vibration from my black backpack under my head sent my skull vibrating both physically and mentally, pulling me out of that fully aware-of-my-body moment I was indulging in. Another buzz claimed my attention further and a few seconds later, another one.

Pulled out from that sweet stasis, I cleaned my fingertips from the sand by stroking my right thigh vigorously a few times and reached for my phone, which with the dexterity that comes from performing a mechanical movement hundreds of times, materialized straight in front of my eyes, offering me a very different proposition from the happy vacationers I was just observing.

Luna and I had just matched on a dating app, and I immediately felt the blood flowing to the animalistic side of my brain and body. Luna, thanks to her bikini photos, had a tanned olive skin tone, complemented by a striking figure: toned legs with prominent curves that matched her impressive physique. Pair that with luxurious long hair reaching the middle of her back and full lips, and I couldn't think of anything else.

She sent me two messages straight away, one referring to my bio that had a "read between the lines" meaning and one directly challenging me:

"So you are one of those naughty men" "I'm not sure you are who you say you are," she offered.

"Me? My mom says I'm an angel... you on the other hand..." I replied.

We exchanged a few more texts taking shots at each other until I suggested that this conversation would be much more fun in person, but only if she could keep her hands off me. We met pretty much an hour later for coffee at a bar near the beach, and my impressions from the photo were confirmed on first sight. She showed up wearing a see-through white linen kimono with a green bikini underneath, with her enhanced figure drawing attention.

We sat at a remote table at the end of the L-shaped seating area outside. We joked, laughed, and exchanged information about the place where we were spending time, me as a tourist and her as a resident. Eventually, she confronted me about that line in my bio, to which I replied that I like to do exciting things with interesting people.

"Give me an example of something you like," she questioned me.

"If you and I found ourselves alone, I would start by grabbing this beautiful hair of yours," I said while reaching for a strand of her hair, "and I would pull it in my fist before slamming you against the door." I gently pressed her hair, making her shiver.

"Then I would push you to your knees and use you all night for my own entertainment," I offered in a low, dark tone, looking directly into her eyes for a solid second before releasing her hair and leaning back in my chair, looking amused at her still taken aback, trying to process the emotions I had just generated.

The silence must have lasted at least 10 solid seconds, during which we never broke eye contact, until she interrupted it with, "I like this and I like you."

We continued talking about other things and, to my surprise, this young woman had a passion for elaborate outfits and role-playing scenarios.

"I want you to go to the boutique at the end of the street and find a sexy costume for some role-playing. You could be a nurse, a nanny, a house cleaner," I commanded, to which she gasped in awe.

"Nobody has talked to me like that, so commanding!"

"And second," I interrupted, "bring a bag of ice from the shop near my apartment." Now she looked really puzzled.

"Ice, why?"

"You'll see," I simply offered.

We kept texting a bit and exchanged a few more playful ideas.

We met a few nights after this coffee date, and she showed up at my door in a totally casual outfit with long cotton tracksuit pants, white sneakers, and a tight light sweater, her casual look only betrayed by the elaborate makeup that would have required several hours to apply. She had a bag of ice in her left hand and a small azure backpack in the other.

I kissed both of her cheeks and welcomed her inside, taking both items from her and directing her to sit on the couch while I found a bowl to place the ice in for a later, not yet disclosed purpose.

I prepared two glasses of wine, letting Luna talk about her day and how tense she was before the meeting; she had done some meditation with an app to calm herself.

"Oh, great state of mind to be in," I joked. "Don't worry, as you know, the door is open, and anytime you want to stop and leave, you just need to do so," I smiled and offered her the glass of wine in my left hand.

"Cheers." "Cheers," she offered back, looking at me.

The sexual tension was palpable. Within 2 sips of the wine, she was already naked laying below on the couch, our arms extended above her head with our fingers intertwined, and of course, with my cock pressing hard on her pussy which I could feel was already wet.

I stood up and pinned down both of her hands with my left hand while I grabbed her right cheek, now flushed, with my right hand and caressed it with my thumb.

"Don't you want to change into something else?" I started with a half-smile on my face.

"Oh..." she snapped back to reality. "Let me do that," she complied.

I moved away, and she quickly made her way to the bathroom with the small azure backpack from before... there had to be a reason for that accessory to accompany her.

My erection was fading as she took her time, but when she emerged from the bathroom it immediately came roaring back. She was dressed in a French maid costume with the back of the skirt completely open and bare, and her generous chest almost popping out from the top.

"Helloooooo," she vibrantly said with a big smile all over her face, knowing that it would have a positive impact on me.

"Oh look at you, aren't you late for starting your service?" I replied with a semi-serious tone, implying it was time to role-play.

"Yes, sorry, mister, what do you want me to do?"

"Well, come here first and help me get comfortable."

Enter the Dom

I let her take off my clothes, telling her to go slowly and look me in the eyes while undoing my pants. Once I was only in my boxers, I told her, "I had a stressful day, give me a back massage," to which she complied half-heartedly, saying something like, "I'm supposed to clean."

"Oh, don't worry, you will have plenty to do later."

Once she had massaged me for a few good minutes, I pretended to feel pain because of a nerve she hit. I stood up and looked at her in mock anger, exclaiming, "Now I will have to discipline you for that!" We role-played a little back and forth about how she didn't want to be disciplined, but very shortly, she was positioned with her chest on the arm of the couch, her ass all the way up and me ready to give her a good spanking.

I started massaging the glutes gently and slightly tapping here and there, continuing with more pressing and squeezing. Once I felt she was ready for something stronger, I started a series of controlled movements that would increase in intensity and rhythm. I had a personal favorite pattern of "100 bpm 4/4," like a slow rock song for those not familiar with music theory.

She moaned gently at the beginning, growing more and more vocal. That's when I decided to really change the tempo, but not beat-wise.

I stood up and went to my wardrobe to my flogger and picked up the ice pack she had brought for her own pleasure. I administered a few precise strokes on her right glute and then applied the ice pack, offering her a "It's going to be a long cold night." I repeated on the other side and mixed the sensations. We played with the ice and flogger until her bottom resembled a modern art painting.

Then it was time to begin torturing her big nipples, and I broke a couple of ice cubes from the pack that I started to rub on her breast as she complied with my order to lie on the couch. The ice and the pinching of the nipples made her squirm and gasp hard at every touch. Once I started to pull her nipples hard, she gasped for air with her mouth wide open and released a series of "ahh ahh" in short sequence with her eyes closed.

I threw a cube toward the sink, missing it entirely (proving why my basketball career never took off), and placed my thumb inside her mouth and ordered, "Suck it," to which she obliged eagerly while keeping her eyes closed.

When she opened her eyes, I sat next to her, smiling, and she immediately jumped to kiss me and said in a lower tone of voice, "That was such a good orgasm!" (yes, some women can orgasm from their nipples). "Thank you, thank you, thank you," she said, alternating words and kisses on my right cheek, now smeared with red lipstick.

"Well, how about we go for different type of orgasm?" I offered, looking dead serious into her eyes.

"What do you have in mind, mister?"

"Spread your legs on the edge of the couch."

I stood on her side and spat on my fingers, not really needed because she was dripping wet at this point, but I always thought it added a certain touch of class.

I put my fingers inside her in a come here motion. After a good 15 seconds, she was already squirting out intensely with a sharp "yahhhh."

"Very good, this is one. You are going to count them until I decide to stop."

Numbers two, three, four, and five arrived all in short sequence. At six, she begged for a water break, which was the minimum she could ask, considering the evidence on my floor and the couch cover (I recommend you always have a double layer for situations like this).

"Siiiiiix," she screamed while her pussy was spraying this crystal fluid.

At ten, she was just with her head rolled back, almost in a state of nirvana.

"Very good, very good. I'm pleased with your performance."

We took a long break with some refreshments and water to prepare ourselves for part two of the evening, some good old-school rough fucking to which I stopped

Enter the Dom

3 times before cumming, just to edge as much as possible and then finally pulling out and exploding all over her face.

I took a napkin from the box on the nightstand and offered it to her.

"I told you there was going to be a lot of cleaning."

CHAPTER THIRTEEN

Shame Breaking

What is your deepest fantasy or sexual desire?

You know—the one you don't share with anyone but constantly think about when you're alone...

The one you're so afraid to admit, even to yourself.

How do you feel right now as I ask you this?

For many, there might have been a flicker of excitement at first—followed by a crushing wave of shame, hitting you like a semi-truck. Then come the intrusive thoughts: *I shouldn't be thinking about this. This is wrong. Why does this turn me on?*

Even if you've taken the time to explore your desires, some of them might scare you. They may cause you to question yourself, leading to self-doubt or even self-judgment. As a result, your sexuality becomes repressed, unexplored, or stunted.

To fully enjoy your sex life—and to allow others the same freedom—you must confront the powerful emotion standing in the way: **shame**.

What Is Shame?

Shame is an emotion shaped by external influences—other people's thoughts, beliefs, or actions—that lead you to hide or deny your perceived wrongdoing. It arises when moral weight is placed on your decisions or behavior, and when the fear of judgment by others becomes overwhelming.

When you experience shame, you feel isolated—like an outcast. You associate your very *Self* with deficiency, failure, inferiority, unworthiness, self-loathing, and self-deprecation.

Why Do You Feel Shame About Your Sexual Desires?

Simple: Someone you admire, respect, or listen to told you it was wrong.

That "someone" could have been your mother, your family, your religious community, your government, society at large—any collective of people enforcing a shared belief system.

Every group relies on collectively agreed-upon stories to function. These stories establish values, standards, and acceptable behaviors, all designed to maintain order, cohesion, and reach a collectively agreed upon goal.

When someone transgresses these narratives, they are labeled "bad," and their behavior is deemed "wrong." This social conditioning is meant to bring them back in line with what is deemed acceptable. If individuals do not conform, the shared belief system begins to break down, threatening the stability of the group.

As an individual, you internalize these narratives, believing that *you*—a human being with intrinsic worth—are now "bad" simply because of your desires.

Then, when those desires surface, you *thought* police yourself. *Boom!* Bring on the wave of shaaaaaame!

Shame is one of the most effective social control mechanisms—far more powerful than simply listing rules. It's internalized, self-enforcing, and, for many, inescapable.

"But Isn't My Desire Wrong?"

It *depends*.

What are your values? What kinds of groups do you want to be a part of? What do they value?

This might be a stretch for some, but morality is less about absolute right and wrong and more about what is effective in reality.

Let's step outside the realm of sexuality for a moment.

Would you say Hitler was a "bad" person? Or did he simply have a completely warped view of reality and what was best for humanity? Read *Mein Kampf*, and you'll see he truly believed some wild, disturbing things. It's easy to judge him in hindsight, but if we examine our own deeply held beliefs, we might find that some of them are just as irrational—just in different ways.

Now, what about Gandhi? Would you say he was a "good" person? Or was nonviolence simply the most effective strategy available to him given his circumstances? If you dig deeper into his life, you'll find that he was often fueled by anger. He didn't have access to an army, weapons, or military resources. Given that reality, nonviolence was the best approach. But had he possessed an arsenal of bazookas and a battalion of trained soldiers, would his tactics have remained the same? Maybe. Maybe not.

This isn't about arguing for subjective morality, where everyone just makes up their own rules and anything goes.

It's about asking: *What is your goal?* And are your behaviors helping you achieve that goal?

Reality itself has no inherent goal. It has no concept of good or bad. Reality just *is*.

Society, however, does have a goal. It establishes what is considered "good" or "bad" in order to function cohesively.

And you—you exist within that society. If you want to align with society's goals, you'll do what is deemed "good." If you don't, then those rules become irrelevant to you.

Here's the kicker: *You get to decide which society—or group of people—you want to belong to, if any at all.*

And here's the even bigger kicker: *Society does not define your worth as a human being.* Your value isn't determined by whether your choices fit within the framework of a particular culture or group. You're simply more or less effective at achieving what *that* society values—which, by the way, is just as made-up as the society itself.

So please, stop shaming yourself over rules that were handed to you by other people.

Brandon's Experience with Shame

As I've embraced my Dominant side and explored my sexuality more deeply, I've encountered shame over and over again.

Here are some of the struggles I've had to confront:

- **Desire to be Dominant** – The story I told myself was that dominance was abusive, manipulative, and toxic. I feared that embracing it would make me a monster.
- **Desire to have a lot of sex** – I believed it was hedonistic, unreasonable, and insatiable. I worried that my desires would make me "too much" for others.
- **Desire to have multiple partners** – I grew up believing monogamy was the only acceptable path, that marriage was simply what you *did*. This led me to believe I was a terrible husband and partner for wanting something different.
- **Desire to sexually objectify** – I internalized the idea that this was not how you should treat a woman. This created a deep conflict within me,

reinforcing a Madonna/whore complex in my mind and making me question my own desires.

Every time, I had to sit down and unravel the stories I had been told. Only then could I fully and confidently embrace my desires—and, more importantly, *myself*.

Mario's Experience with Shame

When I first explored BDSM, it was widely seen as degenerate—something only outcasts and social misfits engaged in. Attending my first meetup was a struggle. I had to push myself to go, despite my fear.

But once I was there, I realized something surprising: sexual preferences aside, the people I met were some of the kindest, most genuine, and lovable individuals I had ever encountered.

That experience changed me. It made me realize I had blindly accepted a narrative without ever questioning its validity or examining its source.

And it didn't stop there. That moment of realization didn't just reshape my understanding of sexuality—it made me start questioning other long-held beliefs in every area of my life.

Why You Must Overcome Shame as a Dom

On your journey to becoming a Dom, you're going to come up against deep-seated societal programming—beliefs about how women should be treated and the expectation of equal power dynamics in relationships. If you're anything like us, you'll repeatedly question whether what you're doing is abusive, manipulative, or simply *wrong*. You may even wonder if your desires make you a bad person.

But if you're truly following the principles in this book—if you are a Dom because you want to lead her toward a shared vision, mutual goals, and a dynamic you both desire—then stepping into your role is not just for you; it's for *both* of you. As a

Dom, you've taken responsibility for her, and your decisions are made with her best interests in mind so that you both reach the goals you've agreed upon.

The mindfuck you'll have to walk through is this: what feels "selfish" is actually *selfless*. She derives **pleasure** from being submissive in the relationship, and if you deny her the opportunity to serve you, you are, in fact, denying *her* pleasure.

This is why consent, boundaries, limits, and safewords exist in BDSM—to keep your Dominant power in check so that you don't become a tyrant. Earlier, in the communication chapter, we urged you to seek feedback. Doing so helps you recognize when your Dominance is slipping out of control and no longer serving *either* of you. Trust your submissive. She is a grown woman, fully capable of expressing when she believes you are overstepping.

Think of everything you and your submissive could possibly do together as a sandbox. When you discussed her boundaries and limitations, you built the walls of that sandbox. Within those boundaries, you have complete freedom. You are allowed to do anything inside the sandbox—just don't cross the boundaries (*unless she has explicitly consented to it*).

Now that you know her boundaries, she *wants* you to own your desires fully. She craves for you not to hold back, not to hesitate. She wants you to *take* what's yours, completely. To be blunt—she wants you to lose control, fuck her like an animal, destroy her, and **completely fucking own her with your entire being**. The key, though, is being able to *immediately* regain control if she calls a safeword.

You will never be able to give her that experience if you don't internally own your desires, remove your shame, and recognize that doing so serves both of you. The darker the desires you can alchemize into confidence and control, the more powerful you will become—not just in the bedroom, but in every aspect of life.

Here's the beautiful part about owning your desires: *she can now own hers.*

The more openly, honestly, and directly you communicate your wants and needs, the more she will realize there is nothing to be ashamed of. The more you embody your truth and act in alignment with it, the safer she will feel to do the same. If you give yourself permission to be a kinky degenerate, she is free to be the slutty nympho she may secretly long to be.

You lead by example.

Breaking the Madonna/Whore Complex

Some men at the beginning of their Dom journey will face a unique challenge that is almost exclusive to straight men. In Mario's opinion, the more conservative the environment someone comes from, the stronger this challenge will be. This challenge is known as the Madonna/Whore Complex (MWC).

MWC is a psychological concept first described by Sigmund Freud, referring to a dualistic perception that men traditionally have toward women, dividing them into two opposing categories: saints or whores, but never both coexisting within the same person.

When dealing with sex and sexual dynamics, the stories, beliefs, and mental models we hold in our minds shape how we experience situations. MWC is just another story—much like marriage (and closely linked to it). If you truly want to overcome this complex, you'll have to dismantle the narratives ingrained in you, the ones wired so deeply that it may feel like tearing out the mainframe, burning it, and starting anew.

Frankly, some of you may never be able to do that. You're too caught up in how things "should" be. If you can stop "shoulding" everything, if you recognize that nearly everything in this world (except for the metal, wood, and plastic that make up the chair you're sitting on) is a socially constructed and agreed-upon story, then you gain the ability to decide whether you want to play along with that story or not.

It's all a game. And in games, there are more and less effective ways of "winning" (where the definition of success is also culturally agreed upon). In certain historical contexts, the MWC was a useful tool for structuring society. Today, not so much (a topic for another book, perhaps). The real issue is that you're assigning moral judgment and human value—both your own and that of others, particularly women—based on the rules of a game that was made up!

If someone is bad at playing Clue or Monopoly, do you take them outside, tar and feather them, and burn them at the stake, condemning them to eternal damnation? Of course not. Yet, this is how many operate when it comes to sexual morality and gender roles.

Both Mario and I, to some degree, see no difference between the so-called "whore" and "Madonna." They are just women, just as human as we are. They have as many filthy, depraved, and complex thoughts as we do, and yet they can also be upstanding citizens, loving mothers, and powerful figures in society. Just as we, as men, can indulge in a week-long sex bender and then return to leading, fathering, or excelling in our careers. We are all multifaceted human beings with limitless potential.

Your labels, your stories, and your brain's desire to categorize everything into neat little boxes with clear black-and-white distinctions of good/bad and right/wrong are what hold you back from truly seeing and experiencing life. Your mother, your sister, the OnlyFans model, the grandma next door, the cashier, the stripper, and even your own daughter one day will all be the same: human. When you understand that there are no "good women" or "bad women," just women, your stress and anxiety about the opposite sex will dissolve almost entirely.

Story Time with Mario

Once, I was invited to a prominent sex party hosted by a well-known couple in the local community. As I enjoyed the night of debauchery, I had a chance to befriend the hosts and learn more about their relationship. Frankly, what I discovered took me by surprise.

They had been happily married for over five years. While the husband spent his days working hard in real estate development, his wife was an up-and-coming adult film actress who had already worked with several major people.

I found it difficult to reconcile these two aspects of her identity. Here was a loving wife who cared for her husband, prepared meals, kept their home, and radiated sweetness like an angel—and yet, in front of a camera, she would have sex with five men at once.

This challenged my own deeply ingrained beliefs and forced me to confront the arbitrary nature of the stories I had internalized. It was a pivotal moment in deconstructing the Madonna/Whore Complex within myself.

Tactics for Overcoming Sexual Shame

These concepts apply to all stories, but let's focus specifically on the sexual ones for now. The simple answer to overcoming your sexual shame is to stop believing the story. Simple, but *really hard*.

We must chip away at this shame from multiple angles until we realize that the story just isn't as true as we once thought. Here are some tactics that Brandon used to address his own shame.

Tactic 1: Remove Yourself from Collective Groups Where Sexual Acts Are Shameful

All of us grew up in various groups that each had values, sometimes even competing ones. At some point in your life, you will have to decide what your own values are, independent of those groups. When you do, you may discover that you don't value the same things.

If your sexuality—and the ability to explore and express that sexuality freely—is of high value to you, then you will either need to rebel within the groups you're a part of or remove yourself from them entirely.

These groups could include:

- Religious communities
- Cities with specific laws, policies, and rules

- Cultures
- Families

Personally, Brandon finds it mentally easier to just remove himself. It takes less emotional energy and mental bandwidth. It's like if you're trying to lose weight: it's much easier to just keep the cookies out of the house in the first place than to use mental willpower to resist eating them.

We realize some groups will feel really hard to remove yourself from. For example, if a religious community is a large part of your identity, leaving may feel incredibly difficult. The same is true for family.

In these cases, you can find ways to set boundaries about what you will or will not show or discuss with them. For example, Brandon told his family he's non-monogamous but hasn't shared that he's kinky. It's never really been relevant to his discussions. If a discussion arose where it was relevant, he'd probably share it. But he's done a lot of work unraveling his identity and dropping old stories. You may not have done that work yet, so you might choose to keep it private.

At the end of the day, though, you have the choice of which groups you interact with—and, more importantly, which ones you don't.

Tactic 2: Join Collective Groups Where Sexual Acts Are Accepted

With 8 billion people on the planet, we promise there are others who value the same things you do. In fact, with 8 billion people, we guarantee there's someone into the same kinky, sexual things as you, who unabashedly enjoys them.

Yes, you may have to do some work to find them. You might even have to move, get a new citizenship, or jump through a dozen other socially constructed hoops to be part of that society—*but you can do it.*

Luckily for you, when it comes to sexuality, it's a lot easier than that.

We live in the age of the internet, where you can find plenty of niche groups for whatever your interests are. Reddit and FetLife will be your friends here.

What will really affect your psyche is meeting these people in person (gasp!) and realizing they're just regular, "normal" people, just like you.

Here's what we recommend:

- Visit a meetup, class, event, or munch (a casual, kinky meetup) based on your interests.
- Ask people what their fantasies, desires, or turn-ons are. Trust us—they'll be happy to share.
- Listen to their stories. Some are pretty wild.
- Attend a play party or event where you'll see people engaging in the very things you're interested in. Expose yourself to wonderful, amazing, upstanding people doing the "filthiest" things.

What will happen is you'll start questioning your own stories. Are your desires really that terrible if all these wonderful people share them? You'll see them engaging in these desires and still being treated with respect. You might even see them getting their ass beaten blue on Sunday and back out saving lives in the ER on Monday. (Nurses are notoriously kinky.)

Tactic 3: Journaling

Sometimes it's easier to observe your stories when you get them out of your head and onto paper. It allows you to look at them more objectively, separating yourself from the thoughts in your mind.

What can be helpful is writing out your desires, particularly the ones you feel the most shame about. Then, imagine someone you love told you about those same desires. How would you respond? How would you treat them? Do that for yourself.

Tactic 4: Digest Your Emotions

Even as you engage in some of these other tactics, there will be times when shame still feels overwhelming—so much so that it's debilitating. You need to learn how to digest this emotion.

Digesting emotions means feeling them fully without resistance, not labeling them as positive or negative, and allowing the emotion to fully pass through its cycle.

Here's the process for digesting shame:

- When shame arises, pause.
- Bring awareness to the **sensation** of shame in your body.
- Breathe. Sit with the sensation as fully as possible. Don't resist it or try to force it away. Just sit with it.
- Take as long as necessary to feel the sensation until it dissipates.

You'll notice that during this process, we didn't stop to ask why the shame is occurring. First off, we don't have control over when emotions arise, so even if we knew the reason, it wouldn't stop the emotion from happening. Second, if you start asking why while trying to digest the emotion, your mind often clings to mental stories and loops, intensifying the emotion and preventing it from passing. Instead, use journaling to examine your stories and the "whys" behind the emotion. Then, use the digestion process to work through the shame.

The more you digest shame, the more you'll recognize that feeling this emotion isn't inherently bad. It doesn't kill you. Even if you feel shame again in the future—and you will—it doesn't have to stop you from doing what you want. You'll be okay.

Tactic 5: Exposure

When you reach a point where you're comfortable starting to explore desires that once brought you shame, we recommend starting small and mild and progressively getting more adventurous. Each time you expose yourself to your desire, you'll have the opportunity to work through the shame that arises. You'll also discover that just because you have these desires doesn't mean you're a terrible person. You'll still be yourself on the other side.

Now, some desires you may choose never to act on or fully explore, and that's completely acceptable. For the ones you do wish to explore, take it step by step with a trusted partner. After each time you explore a desire, talk to them and get reassurance that they don't think any differently of you. Spend some time journaling about the shame that arose, then take time to digest that emotion.

Tactic 6: Sexual Disclosure

These conversations can help you articulate your desires and understand the psychological and emotional triggers behind them. By understanding this, you can integrate these themes into your consensual sexual activities in a healthy and empowering way, while addressing any shame that comes up in the process.

Here's how to do a Sexual Disclosure:

- Set up a time (preferably an hour or more) with someone you trust enough that what you share will stay confidential—and who won't judge you.
- Disclose ALL past sexual partners and experiences with them.
- Disclose desires, kinks, and turn-ons.
- Disclose any shame or guilt you feel about past partners, experiences, or desires.

Warning: This process is intense and requires deep emotional work. That's why it's essential to do it in a safe, non-judgmental space with someone who will keep what you share confidential and encourage your vulnerability, such as a coach or therapist.

Tactic 7: Stop Praising Yourself for "Good" Things and Punishing Yourself for "Bad" Things

This is a next-level, advanced tactic, but it will change how you treat yourself—and surprisingly, how you treat others.

Many people look outside themselves for praise and punishment. They wait for others to validate their actions, and when they receive that validation, they apply it to themselves.

Some people move beyond external validation and start seeking internal validation. However, they're often still running stories in their head, stories given to them by society. So, every time they do something socially accepted or revered, they praise themselves. When they do something socially unacceptable, they shame and punish themselves.

Some people manage to stop shaming and punishing themselves, but they still seek praise for doing the "good" thing.

Here's the hard pill to swallow: every time you praise yourself for doing something "good," you're reinforcing the binary structure in your mind. If something is "good," its opposite—"bad"—must exist. Because "bad" exists, you'll never truly escape its shame.

We're not saying you can't ever tell yourself, "Good job." But what we are saying is that you shouldn't let your actions define your value. Doing something "good" doesn't make you a better person than others. You got a raise, worked out, volunteered, or did something for someone else? Those actions don't make you inherently better than anyone else. And if they did, then the opposite would also be true: when you do something "bad," you're suddenly a lesser person.

This is hard to wrap your head around. Personally, Brandon had to start by not judging others. He had to stop thinking he was better than anyone else. He learned that just because he was skilled in some areas or more capable in some domains, it didn't make him a better person. What happened as a result was that he no longer put others above himself or shamed himself for not following their values or being as skilled as they were. He stopped caring about compliments or criticism—they held no weight for him.

As a result, he's become more accepting of others, more loving, and kinder. He's more open-minded. All that energy he once spent outward, he now directs inward too. It's a significant step toward accepting yourself.

CHAPTER FOURTEEN

Sexual Dominance

Finally, the part you probably picked up this book for—how to start becoming a rockstar in the bedroom. By now, we hope you understand that all the previous chapters are crucial to actually making her wet. Dominance starts long before you ever step into the bedroom.

Let us share a little secret... Mario and Brandon, while pretty skilled in the bedroom from a technical standpoint, are probably not the best in the world (though our teenage selves still wish we were).

What sets us apart from most men who step into the bedroom is our understanding of the real key to giving her the most unforgettable experience of her life. The key to making her orgasm again and again, to getting her dripping wet with pleasure, isn't just about fucking her body—*it's about fucking her mind*. You need to become the man of her fantasies, the one who can fulfill her deepest, darkest desires. The ones she touches herself to in the middle of the night when no one else is around.

In a way, this entire book up until now has been preparing you to connect with her mind more than her body. If you can get inside her head, you can make her come without even touching her. And at that point, it doesn't matter what you do physically.

This is why the dance of Dominance and submission is so erotic. It's what transforms otherwise ordinary, run-of-the-mill acts into something electrifying. So while we're going to walk you through some technical skills, keep in mind that the psychological aspects are far more important. Additionally, we're not here to teach you the mechanics of wielding a flogger or hitting her G-spot—there are plenty of videos, courses, and workshops out there for that. Instead, we're going to give you the principles behind the sexual acts you choose to engage in.

She's Begging for You to Be Dominant in the Bedroom

In our experiences as Doms, we've heard literally hundreds of women say they wish their man were more dominant. They wish he'd be more confident, assertive, and take charge in the relationship—especially in the bedroom.

Yes, they love that you're caring, kind, and attentive. That's wonderful. But they also *crave* you to take control and do terrible, ungodly things to them in bed.

For most men in today's society, being dominant actually goes against our social conditioning. From a young age, we're taught to treat women equally, to be kind, to be caring, and to not impose ourselves too much on them. This is further compounded by the fact that many boys are raised in fatherless households, where their mother is the primary influence on their social conditioning. Of course, a mother will teach her son to treat women with respect.

The problem isn't that women are being treated better or that they've made great strides in social progress—that's fantastic! The issue is that societal conditioning lumps **all** masculine or dominant traits into one category, labels them as "toxic," and fails to help young men discern the difference between being a dominant leader and a domineering tyrant. On top of that, collective shame represses our individual desires—both for Dominants and submissives—leading people to swallow societal ideology rather than express their true individual needs.

Since Brandon was raised by a single mom and naturally ranks high in conscientiousness, he knows this struggle all too well. You might recall his story from Chapter One about pinning his ex-wife to the bed and feeling immense shame afterward. It took him forever to realize—and accept—that she actually wanted that.

Beyond that, men have a whole list of fears they must confront before they can truly embody dominance:

- You're afraid she'll think you're a terrible person.
- You're afraid you'll physically hurt or break her.
- You're afraid you won't be able to control yourself if you give in to your desires.
- You're afraid you don't know what you're doing and will mess up.
- You're afraid she'll leave you.

Want to know why consent in BDSM is so sexy? For a woman, it ensures she feels safe—and as we've discussed in previous chapters, safety is a prerequisite for her arousal. But for a man, it provides reassurance that she wants this.

Just hearing her say "yes," or—Brandon's personal favorite—"Oh God, yes, Daddy, please, please, please, PLEASE fuck me!" melts away your fears and insecurities, reminding you: **she wants this.**

So, always make sure you're actually talking with your partner about what she likes, dislikes, and where her boundaries lie. Don't be reckless and start exerting dominance without knowing if she's comfortable exploring those things. You'll both be glad you did.

How to Perform Sexually Dominant Acts

Do you want the secret to being a Dom and creating mind melting orgasms?

How **you perform a kinky action is more important than** *what* **you do.**

Two Doms can perform the exact same actions on the same sub, yet the effects they create will be entirely different. So even if you become technically proficient in every aspect of BDSM, you still need to master the principles of delivery to evoke the emotions and fulfill the desires she craves.

When Brandon first started learning how to be a Dom, he noticed a pattern—some nights were incredibly hot, steamy, and passionate, while others felt as mundane as washing dishes on a Tuesday night. At first, he could have just blamed it on a lack of connection, but his self-improvement mindset told him there was something he could do to change that.

So he studied and refined the principles that made his subs say, "Oh my god, I can't stop touching myself thinking about our session last night." Of course, not every session can be mind-blowing, and sometimes that's not even the goal, but you can at least make it more likely.

Principle 1: Have a General Goal in Mind

This may seem counterintuitive to other sex advice, which tells you *not* to focus on a goal during sex. And it's true—being too fixated on an outcome can create performance anxiety for both you and her.

However, as a Dom, your role is to set the vision and direction for the dynamic— including the scenes you create.

So what's the solution? **Have a goal without the expectation of reaching it.**

Without a goal, you have no direction, no structure, and no way to set up the experience effectively. There are specific actions you can take to make orgasm, subspace, and an unforgettable experience more likely—but without a clear aim, you won't be able to guide her there.

Instead, set a goal, but don't pressure yourself or her to *achieve* it at all costs. Think of it as:

> *"This would be really hot if we reached it, but if we don't, we're still going to have an amazing time along the way."*

Principle 2: Sequencing

Now, you need to sequence your kinky and sexual actions in a way that makes your goal more likely to happen.

It's not just about *what* you do—it's about *when* and *how* you do it. While there's certainly a time and place for a fast, intense quickie, most of the time, you're not going from 0 to 100 right off the bat.

Think of sex like a **symphony**—each action plays its part, slowly building over time, reaching a crescendo, and then easing back down, leaving both of you satisfied and fulfilled.

This mirrors the **orgasm cycle:**

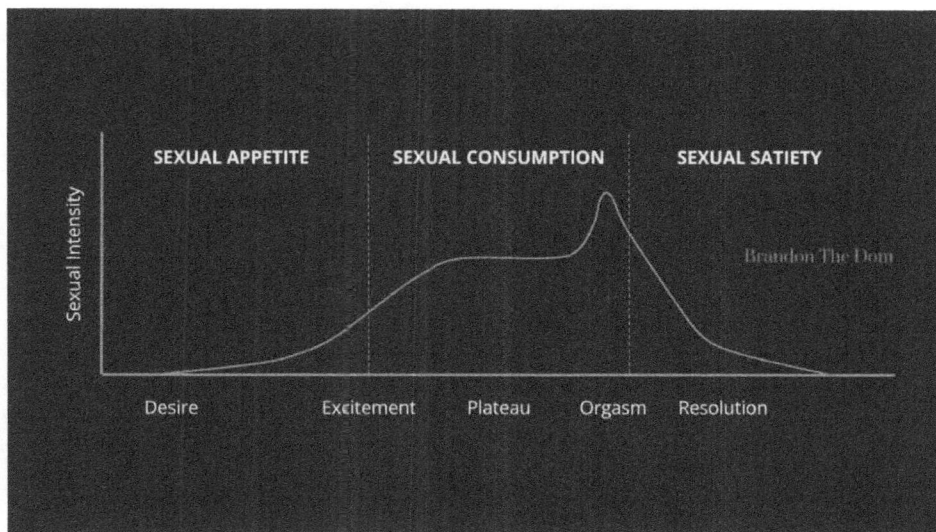

This cycle serves as a good model for how we can start sequencing our scenes in order to create a satisfying experience for the both of us. Chief in his book, *Sensational Scenes,* gives us a model for this, which breaks down into four phases:

1. **Lead-In** – Prepares her mentally for what's to come (*Excitement* phase).
2. **Ramp-Up** – Deepens her mental state and prepares her physically (*Plateau* phase).

3. **Release** – The climax of your scene (*Orgasm* phase).
4. **Relaxation** – Helps her come down and recover (*Resolution* phase).

Your job is to carefully choose actions that:

- **Increase her desire** and get her excited.
- **Maintain her arousal** as she builds toward orgasm.
- **Tip her over the edge** when the moment is right.
- **Bring her back down gently** to help her feel safe and complete.

A great rule of thumb is to **start with low-level dominance and gradually build toward more intense dominance** as the scene progresses.

This benefits both of you:

- **For her** – It helps her ease into submission, relax into the experience, and warm up physically and mentally for deeper dominance.
- **For you** – It gives you time to read her body's responses, build confidence as the scene unfolds, and ensure you have plenty of options to escalate intensity.

Mastering **how** you sequence your scenes is what separates an average Dom from one she *can't stop fantasizing about*.

Principle 3: Perfect Moments

Now, let's fill our scene with the essential building blocks of a powerful sexual encounter. These are the moments both of you will savor and likely replay in your minds later, fueling desire and deepening the connection.

To create a perfect moment, three elements must align seamlessly:

- **Intent:** Why you're performing an action
- **Energy:** How you're performing an action
- **Action:** The specific kinky act you will be executing

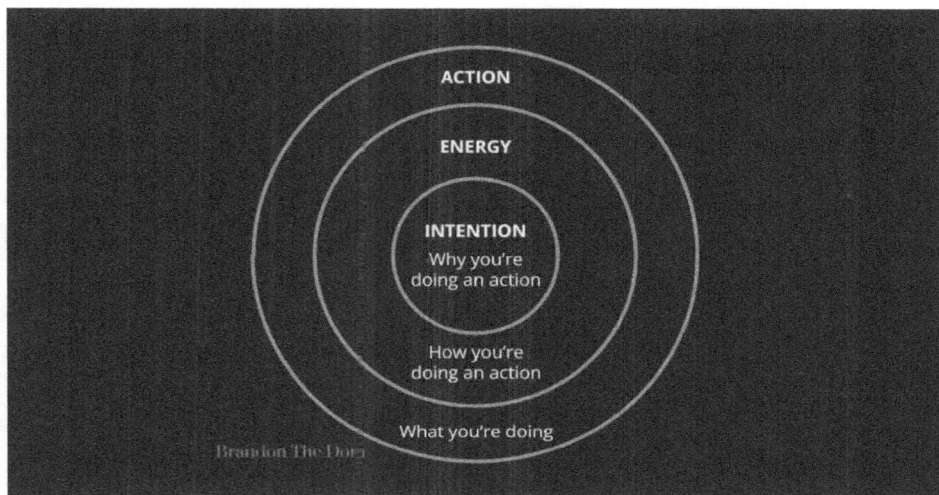

Intention

Like all great things in life, you start with *why* (who knew Simon Sinek was such a kinkster?). Why are you performing this action at this moment? How does this intention move you closer to the goal? What emotions or sensations are you trying to evoke in your submissive?

In *Sensational Scenes*, Chief outlines five core intentions in BDSM:

1. **Pleasure:** Focuses on sensation, arousal, and orgasm.
2. **Pressure:** Increases tension and intensifies the Dom/sub dynamic—this could be physical (e.g., bondage, hair-pulling, choking) or psychological (e.g., degradation, public teasing, enforced begging).
3. **Pain:** Inflicts pain for pleasure or discipline.
4. **Practice:** Helps the Dom or sub develop new skills to enhance future scenes.
5. **Pacify:** Lowers intensity, providing moments of comfort and relaxation, such as aftercare.

A scene might emphasize one intention—like pure pleasure in a sensual worship session—but the most powerful encounters weave multiple intentions together. By alternating between extremes (e.g., pain and pleasure, pressure and pacification), a skilled Dom crafts a dynamic, immersive experience that leads towards the goal.

Energy

If a kinky action is a verb, energy is the adjective that colors it. Energy is the *how*—the passion, intensity, and personality behind each act. Every action can be delivered in different ways, producing distinct responses from your submissive.

Take spanking, for example. Here's how different energies change the experience:

- **Sternly:** A disciplinarian Dom delivers a harsh swat, aiming to correct or punish.
- **Lovingly:** A compassionate Dom delivers rhythmic, pleasurable spanks to ease tension and build anticipation for pleasures to come.
- **Playfully:** A mischievous Dom lands a quick smack to tease and assert control.

The key is alignment—your energy must match your intention. A harsh spanking meant for pleasure on a sub who isn't a pain slut will feel jarring and out of place.

A crucial note: *Competence and confidence* should always be part of your energy. If you're new, you might wonder, *How can I be confident when I've never done this before?*

The answer: **Practice and exposure.**

- **Competence** comes from study—learn techniques from mentors, workshops, and courses. Brandon flogged a pillow a hundred times before ever flogging a woman. Some of the techniques will require her to be there to practice. So, either turn it into a fun game and gain her support in helping you practice, or have it be a regular act you do every time you have sex so you have ample opportunity to practice.
- **Confidence** develops through experience—seeing her responses, learning what works, and gradually making dominance second nature. The more you do it, the easier it becomes.

Every Dom starts somewhere. Shaky hands and uncertain commands are normal. Own it. Be honest with your sub that you're learning—she'll likely be excited to explore with you. The worst thing you can do is pretend to be an expert and fail to deliver.

Action

The final piece of a perfect moment is the action itself. Choose your action and ensure your **energy and intention align** with it.

Every action exists on a spectrum from **mild to wild**. For example:

- **Mild:** Bending her over the bed for a few spanks.
- **Wild:** Taking her into a public changing room, making her hike up her dress, remove her panties, and bend over your knee for a spanking.

As a general rule, start **low and mild** and escalate toward **wild and extremes** as the scene progresses. This allows both of you to ease into the dynamic, making the experience more immersive and satisfying.

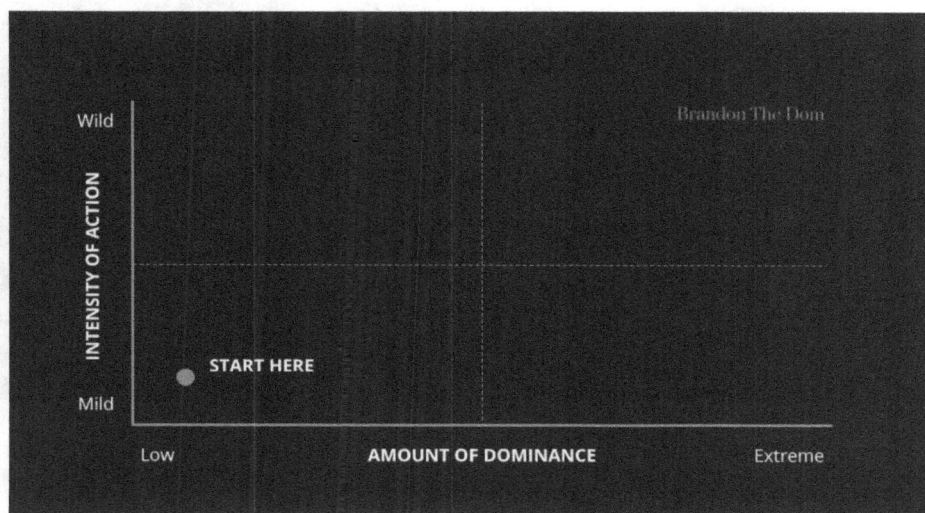

Mastering these three elements—**intent, energy, and action**—is the key to creating electrifying, unforgettable moments. Keep practicing, stay attuned to your partner, and soon you'll be crafting scenes that leave her breathless, longing for more.

Principle 4: Keeping Tension

Dominance and submission are inherently opposite forces that create a natural polarization. The more Dominance you exude, the deeper the submissive reaction you'll receive in return.

Think of D/s like a bungee cord—the more Dominant you are, the more tension you will create. What does tension feel like? It's that warm, electrifying, and slightly nerve-wracking feeling of prolonged eye contact, where anticipation builds and every second stretches with intensity. Your role as a Dom is to maintain that tension throughout the scene.

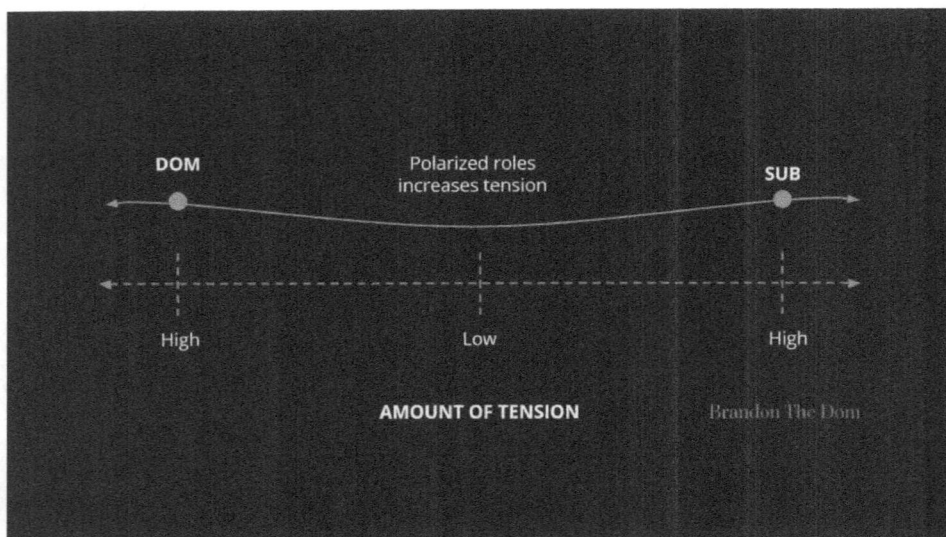

Now, let's extend the bungee cord analogy. If you exert too little Dominance, the cord remains slack, and the experience feels dull. On the other hand, if you push too hard, too fast—maxing out the tension without relief—the cord risks fraying or snapping, leading to discomfort, overwhelm, or even a total break in connection.

The key is to find the sweet spot: a level of tension that keeps the experience exciting without making it either boring or overwhelming.

Your job is to monitor this tension and adjust accordingly—either increasing Dominance to heighten excitement or releasing tension when needed. You can relieve tension through acts that pacify and soothe, like a lingering kiss, a reassuring touch, or even an orgasm. Tools from Tantra—designed to cultivate connection and unity—can also help balance the intensity.

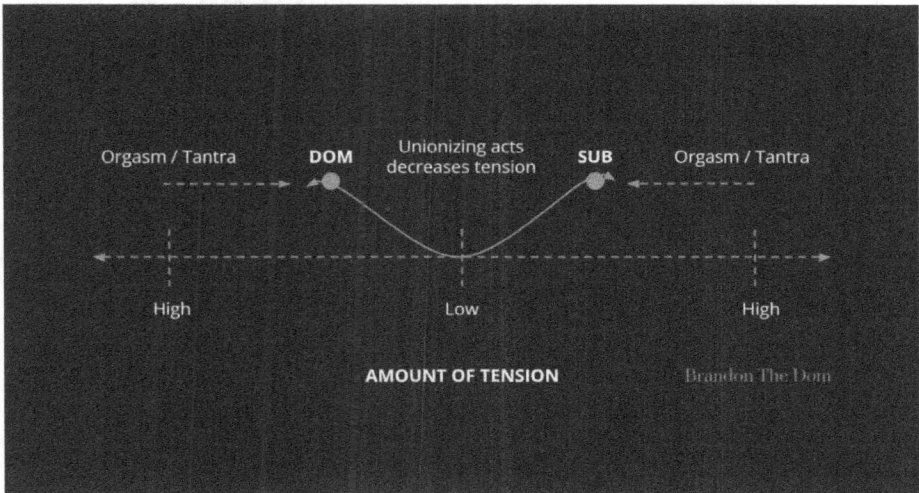

A skilled Dom understands that tension isn't static; it's a rhythm. Just like a bungee jumper, you take her to exhilarating heights, bring her back down, and then launch her into another breathtaking drop. This constant dance between extremes— polarization through Dominance, followed by moments of closeness—creates an emotional and physical rollercoaster. That sounds pretty damn exciting, doesn't it?

Principle 5: Pain & Pleasure

Pain is the body's way of signaling potential harm, much like a car's check engine light. But here's the twist: the brain can interpret the *same sensation* as either pain or pleasure, depending on context and desire. For a willing submissive, pain isn't just tolerable—it can be intensely pleasurable.

Some submissives, often called masochists or "pain sluts," find immense satisfaction in pain. For them, pain isn't just enjoyable—it's essential to their pleasure. Many are chasing the euphoric state known as subspace—a blissed-out, trance-like headspace triggered by BDSM play. Subspace isn't magic; it's biology. It's the result of a potent hormone cocktail: adrenaline, cortisol, endorphins, oxytocin, and dopamine, all working together to create an altered state of pleasure, surrender, and euphoria.

Even a partner who is only lightly kinky—just dipping her toes beyond vanilla—will likely enjoy some level of controlled pain. A sharp spank, a teasing tug of her hair, or the sting of nails on skin can heighten pleasure through contrast. The key lies in the dichotomy between pain and pleasure—a push and pull that builds tension and intensity. This interplay between extremes is what makes the experience electrifying.

Levels of Sexually Dominant Acts

In this section, we'll explore some practical actions you can take in the bedroom that will evoke feelings of submission, as we've discussed throughout the book. This outline is not intended to be an exhaustive list of all the skills you need to master as a Dom, nor does it rank sexual acts definitively. Rather, it offers a rough guide to the types of acts you can perform and the level of dominance you'll be exuding with each one. From there, you can identify your favorites and work on mastering them. It's better to start with a few techniques you excel at and build upon your repertoire over time.

Additionally, don't assume that someone who practices "Extreme Dominance" is inherently better than someone who engages in "Low Dominance." Many submissive women will be content with low to moderate dominance for most of their sexual experiences. In fact, it's quite rare to venture into high or extreme territory. That level of dominance usually requires a deep trust and connection between you two, a developed skill set to perform the acts safely and confidently (so they don't come off as awkward and actually have the desired effect), and a woman who is more kinky than the average person.

Universals

Let's start with the universals. In our experience, these tend to be enjoyed by the majority of women; however, there are always exceptions. Remember to talk with your partner about their desires, limits, and boundaries. We recommend learning these first and getting proficient at them.

Example Universal Acts:

- Sex 101 (kissing, clitoral stimulation, G-spot stimulation, cunnilingus, basic sex positions)
- Spanking
- Hair pulling
- Being manhandled, tossed around between sex positions
- Scratching without drawing blood
- Nibbling (not biting or leaving marks)
- Using hands to hold wrists above her head
- Using body weight to pin her to the bed or restrain her
- Using hands to hold down her hip bones
- Being moved around by the hips
- Teasing or deliberate slow touch
- Doggy style
- Hugging/holding from behind
- Moving her hand on your dick

Low Dominance

These acts are some of the more common Dominance behaviors you can use in the bedroom. They require a little more skill and perhaps a few props from any sex store, but they are relatively easy to add to your repertoire. The focus at this level is to add some spice to acts you're already doing during sex.

Example Low Dominance Acts:

- A-spot, O-spot stimulation
- Blindfolds
- Vibrator
- Hand resting around her throat, no squeezing
- Making her beg for your cock
- Throwing her on the bed
- Biting without leaving marks
- Biting the inside of her thighs, traps, sides of stomach, hip bones
- Grabbing her neck from behind to move her
- Squeezing her breasts
- Making her beg to cum
- Slapping her pussy with your dick
- Making her squirt
- Introducing anal play with a butt plug or finger
- Bondage cuffs
- Collar and leash
- Cumming on her body
- Cumming in her mouth
- Using toys
- Honorifics
- Roleplay

Medium Dominance

At this level, you begin to distinguish yourself from other Doms. You're becoming more intense and taking greater control. The focus is on making her feel the power differential, both physically and psychologically. The acts at this level are becoming slightly more taboo, require more skill, and demand more from her in terms of submission.

Example Moderate Dominance Acts:

- Rough sex
- Making her suck your fingers after fingering
- Spitting on her pussy
- Spitting in her mouth
- Making her clean cum off with her mouth
- Nipple pinching/biting
- Choking
- Anal sex
- Smothering her head into the bed during doggy style
- Mouth gag with panties or ball gag
- Spreader bar
- Impact play without leaving marks
- Orgasm control, denial, and edging
- Rules, punishment/rewards
- Public play

High Dominance

As you reach higher levels of Dominance, you begin to push the envelope on taboos and exert more control, requiring greater skill. These acts will need more trust and connection with her. Unless they are her favorite kink or fetish, they should be done sparingly due to their intensity.

Example High Dominance Acts:

- Face fucking
- Rope bondage
- Slapping her face
- Foot on her head during doggy style
- Leaving marks from impact play, biting, etc.
- Sadism/torture
- Cumming on her face
- Breeding

- Behavior control and modification

Extreme Dominance

At this level, you enter a space where you make her know, without a shadow of a doubt, who is in charge. This can be demonstrated through further control or power exchange or through acts of degradation, humiliation, or objectification. These acts may require more skill and extensive aftercare because of their psychological impact on both of you.

Example Extreme Dominance Acts:

- Master/slave dynamic or Total Power Exchange
- Free use
- CNC (Consensual Non-consent)
- Humiliation
- Degradation
- Edge play

Sexually Dominant Dirty Talk

We want to devote an entire section to dirty talk because it's one of the fastest and most effective ways to get into your submissive's head. As we've discussed throughout the book, that's where the real impact lies. If you can master dirty talk, you'll be leagues ahead of other guys.

For some men—Mario and Brandon included in the beginning—the thought of talking dirty can be nerve-wracking. You have no idea what to say. You worry that you'll come off as embarrassing or crass. Then, you open your mouth, half-heartedly spit out some line, and watch her face contort in response.

Just like any other skill in sex, dirty talk can be learned, practiced, and improved until your submissive is giving you the horniest of bedroom eyes.

Why Dominant Dirty Talk Is Powerful

The brain, specifically the erotic mind, is a treasure trove of sexual arousal. If you can stimulate her mind as much—or even more—than her body, you'll significantly enhance her arousal and, consequently, her pleasure. For example, having you cum inside her may feel good, but evoking the fantasy of breeding her through dirty talk as you do so can send her into uncontrollable ecstasy, if that's one of her turn-ons.

Dirty talk engages her in several powerful ways:

- **Emotions:** She seeks specific emotions and feelings when submitting to you. Dirty talk can trigger and enhance these emotions, making the experience more intense.
- **Imagination:** Using dirty talk, you tap into fantasies that are far more erotic than you are in reality. She's likely carrying years' worth of sexy material in her mind—use it to your advantage.
- **Subconscious:** Societal programming often forces her to repress behaviors she wishes she could act out. Dirty talk can reach into those repressed desires and actively bring them out, including ones she didn't even think she was capable of.

Below, we'll walk you through various levels of dirty talk. The higher levels—those involving commanding, ownership, and degradation—serve to reinforce the power differential between the Dominant and submissive.

Your choice of words can also influence and train your submissive to be exactly how you want. For example, the more often you praise your submissive for how beautiful she looks with your cock in her mouth or her face covered in your cum, the more likely she will want to repeat those acts in the future.

How to Deliver Dominant Dirty Talk

As a Dom, the difference between making her cringe and making her wet when you talk dirty comes down to your delivery. If you have a weak delivery—where you seem uncomfortable or unconfident—your dirty talk may have the opposite effect and repulse her. On the other hand, if you have a strong delivery, with the words coming easily and confidently from your core, she's going to melt in your arms.

Weak Delivery:

- Hesitant
- Shy or avoidant eye contact
- Nervous, erratic body language
- Speaking quickly and mumbling words
- High-pitched vocal tone
- Upward inflection at the end of a sentence, as if it's a question
- Speaking softly

Strong Delivery:

- Directly spoken without hesitation
- Strong, steady eye contact
- Grounded, unflinching body language
- Slowing down and enunciating
- Deep pitch and vocal tone
- Neutral or downward inflection at the end of a sentence
- Speaking loudly (unless close and whispering dirty talk in her ear)

What we recommend is choosing a handful of phrases you'd like to start using and practicing them out loud. You can do this in front of a mirror or while doing something as simple as washing the dishes. It might seem silly, but the goal is to make these phrases feel normal and comfortable for you to say. Then, when you're in the bedroom, it will feel like just another practice rep, and you'll say them with confidence.

How to Dirty Talk as a Dom

Just as we did earlier, we're going to walk you through the lower Dominance dirty talk frameworks first. These will be the easiest for you to say and will help you feel confident in your delivery. As you become more comfortable with dirty talk and begin experiencing its benefits, you can move into the higher levels of Dominant dirty talk.

We recommend having a conversation with your partner about words that may be triggering for them, both positive and negative. Some submissives have specific honorifics they prefer, like being called "little miss" instead of "babygirl." Similarly, words like "slut," "whore," "bitch," or "cunt" can carry different meanings for different women, so be sure to check beforehand. We also suggest discussing how far into degradation they are comfortable going.

Universals

Let's start with the universals. In our experience, these tend to be enjoyed by the majority of women, though there are always exceptions. To each their own. We recommend learning these first and getting proficient at them.

Praise

Praise is the most basic form of dirty talk. It involves telling your submissive that they are a good sub for doing what you want them to do. This not only reinforces their submissive behavior but also lets them know that you're enjoying what they're doing for you. It helps ease any insecurities they may have about doing a good job or how they look in the moment.

Frameworks for Praise Dirty Talk:

- You are x
- You look x when y

Example Praise Dirty Talk:

- "You're such a good girl for me."
- "You look so beautiful with my cock in your mouth."
- "You're doing so good taking Daddy's cock when he's being rough with your little body."

Observations

Observations involve stating the obvious about what's happening in the moment using your senses—sight, hearing, taste, touch, and smell. You can either describe what you observe about yourself or what you observe about her.

Frameworks for Observation Dirty Talk:

- Your x looks/sounds/tastes/feels/smells like y
- How does x look/sound/taste/feel/smell
- You like they way x looks/sounds/tastes/feels/smells, i can tell by how y you are

Example Observation Dirty Talk:

- "Your little pussy is already so wet for me"
- "How does your pussy taste on my fingers?"
- "You love me pinning you down as I fuck you from behind don't you? I can tell by the way your pussy grips my cock as I fuck you into the pillow."

Low Dominance

At this stage, your dirty talk will focus on the basics of being a Dom, which is to command your submissive and evoke her fantasies.

Commands

Straightforward and effective, commands are all about telling her what to do or say. They reinforce your control and make it clear who's in charge.

Frameworks for Commands Dirty Talk:

- Telling her what to do
- Repeat after me "I'm X". then tell her to repeat again louder
- Every time I do "X" I want you to say "Y"

Example Commands Dirty Talk:

- "On your knees, princess. Show me how much you missed me."
- "Repeat after me, 'I'm Daddy's naughty little fuck toy' Louder.'"
- "Every time I spank you I want you to say thank you and ask for another."

Fantasy

Fantasy dirty talk involves using erotic and taboo language to describe future scenarios, roleplays, or fantasies she has. At this stage, you're engaging her erotic imagination to elevate whatever sexual act is taking place in reality. Phrases can be brief or elaborate, depending on the situation.

Frameworks for Fantasy Dirty Talk:

- Imagine what x would feel like
- When x happens you're going to feel y

Example Fantasy Dirty Talk:

- "Imagine my cock pulsating a hot load in your tight little pussy and putting a baby inside you."
- "Imagine walking around in public with my cum dripping out of your holes."
- "Imagine how wet you are gonna be when you lick another girl's juices off my cock."

Medium Dominance

Here, you start to intensify the experience and take more control. The focus at this level is to emphasize the power differential both physically and psychologically.

Ownership

You control her body and what she does with it. Your dirty talk reinforces that you completely own her and that she is there for your pleasure.

Frameworks for Ownership Dirty Talk:

- She has to ask for permission to do x
- She admits that she's yours and you own her

Example Ownership Dirty Talk:

- "Did I say you could suck my cock yet? What are you going to do to earn it?"
- "You're going to be my good little slut, aren't you?"
- While gripping your fingers in her pussy, "Who's pussy does this belong to?" -> "You, Sir!" -> "That's right, I do whatever I want with it, understand?" -> "Yes, Sir!"

High Dominance

As you reach higher levels of Dominance, you begin pushing the envelope on taboos, exerting more control, and requiring deeper trust and connection. Unless these words are specifically her favorites, they should be used sparingly due to their intensity.

Degradation

Degrading dirty talk either highlights her raunchiest and most taboo inner desires or polarizes the power differential by describing her as "less than" you. Degradation can also include objectification and humiliation, pushing boundaries and challenging her sense of self in the most intense ways.

Frameworks for Degradation Dirty Talk:

- You are x
- Say, you are x

Example Degradation Dirty Talk:

- "You like being my little fuck toy, don't you?
- "The only thing you're good for in life is to be my little cum dumpster."
- "Say, 'I am beneath you, Sir'"

Extreme Dominance

At the extreme end of Dominance, you're ensuring she knows, without a shadow of a doubt, who is truly in charge. Here, dirty talk involves more degradation, humiliation, and objectification, and it requires more aftercare due to the psychological impact. We would place public degradation and public humiliation at this level.

Play & Toys

Every Dom worth their name has a toolkit—like a proper craftsman at work. Ultimately, these tools (or toys, depending on how you prefer to call them) become an integral part of the play you perform with your submissive partner(s).

By the way, for those unfamiliar with the term "play," it refers to any activity within BDSM that you engage in, such as impact play, for example. It emphasizes the fact that everyone participating is doing so for *fun*—engaging in these acts purely for enjoyment.

Of course, play always starts with communication. You must negotiate with your partner(s) about their limits and boundaries. It's reckless to include heavy impact play with a flogger if your partner isn't into that at the time.

The Erotic River Flows

Play, when done right, flows like a calm river downstream. It's harmonious and conveys a sense of tranquility. The only difference is that play is intensely erotic, and there's nothing quite like watching a master at work with a submissive partner who is entirely entranced.

To think of your play, imagine it as a river:

- **Boundaries of the river** (negotiation and consent)
- **Where the river starts and ends** (structure and dynamic)
- **What is the water flow** (tempo of the play)
- **What are the river's characteristics, such as rocks, logs, or rapid waters, and how to navigate them** (what tools and toys you'll use)

Once you know these details, structuring your play becomes easier.

Novice Doms often make the mistake of becoming a "Gadget Dom," thinking that the power of play lies in the tools they carry, such as vibrators, ropes, and paddles. These tools are meant to facilitate the flow of the river, not to create it. If you find yourself questioning whether you can perform a good play session without toys or tools, revisit this book while reflecting on why you might feel that way.

How to Build Your Toolkit

Our recommendation is to focus on what excites you as a Dom and build your skills around that. There are shibari masters who aren't interested in spanking, and spankers who aren't drawn to the art of shibari. Trying to master both just to cater to a broader range of subs is a mistake. You risk becoming a "Vending Machine Dom"—a mere service provider, rather than the true Dominant.

Once you understand what excites you and the kind of play you'd like to engage in, you can begin building your toolkit based on that.

For example, let's say you're interested in restraining your sub but don't want to learn the ropes (pun intended) of knot-tying, safety, and maintenance. In that case, leather cuffs or bondage tape could be your go-to.

Or perhaps you want to practice orgasm control and edging. In that case, a magic wand might be better suited to the task than a dildo that requires more physical effort (and we can't stress enough the importance of playing safely).

Figure out what you want from the experience and what you wish to offer your partner(s), then build your toolkit around those desires.

Too Much of a Good Thing Becomes a Bad Thing

Mario once traveled around Europe with 10kg of luggage and was stopped several times by airport security, who gave him puzzled looks. The heartbreak came when he realized a 30cm metal dildo isn't allowed in carry-on luggage. It was a hard lesson that sometimes trying to be everything to everyone just doesn't work.

The best play doesn't require a luggage full of props (a different story for shibari performers, who carry kilograms of rope). In reality, the power exchange lies in the D/s dynamic itself, and your body is fully equipped to experience it viscerally.

Don't have a paddle for impact play or spanking? No problem—your hands are more than capable of handling that. Forgot your handcuffs? Use your hands to pin her down, or even a scarf can do the job.

Don't fall into the trap of thinking you need a toolbox like a mechanic in a muscle car body shop. Most tools rarely get used, and if you partner with someone who has a specific request, that could be your special toy for that person.

Turning a Respectable Woman to Begging Daddy's Girl

A real story of Brandon's. To protect the privacy of those involved, all names and identifying details have been altered. The individuals described in these stories were all consenting adults who participated of their own free will. If you choose to engage in similar activities, it is imperative that all parties involved are of legal age, fully informed, and consenting.

I'm a sucker for a good girl, a willing submissive, a woman who demonstrates respect and wants to be *utterly ruined* in the bedroom. It's by no surprise that I'd find the land of southern hospitality in Texas fertile soil for such wonderful women.

Evelyn was a 25 year old, small town, southern girl who just started her professional career in an extremely male dominated field where it's entirely socially acceptable to play power games. A common trope for women like this that are forced to compete in a hypermasculine world, only wishing to sink fully into the bliss of submission to a man they respect. She had a very cute and endearing face with medium length brunette hair, brown eyes, fair complexion, and always dolled up in a contemporary and fashionable wardrobe covering her petite frame and not showing much to her curvature. Appearances can be deceiving for those that take them at face value, as no one would suspect such an insatiable little girl beneath the proper veneer.

I tend to be quite forthcoming about my sexuality, even if it's a "vanilla" app, so when we matched on Hinge, I was intrigued to discover her interest in Dominance and submission, and with the amount of respect for which she showed.

When we had our date I would only get a glimpse of what she may look like underneath, as she arrived in a flowy blue sundress and joined me in the 100 degree Texas heat in the bar's patio. She was bubbly and full of stories, albeit a little ADHD, but cute nonetheless and took a lot of interest in my passions in education.

Then she asked, "So what are you doing on Hinge?"

I told her I was looking for what I sent her, that I do have other partners, and just keeping things casual, but ok with things developing, however I would be gone in a year.

She said she was also keeping things more casual and in her "lazy phase" meaning she did not want to put so much effort into the dates and have them be garbage. She said she doesn't take the apps too seriously, but will take a relationship seriously if it's worth putting effort into.

She said most people are not as open and direct as I am, which she found refreshing and intriguing. Our conversation moved to sex and I started asking her about her experience in BDSM. She got shy, blushed, and giggly nervous as she was answering.

"Well I'm sure you've already pegged me... uh I mean no pun intended... but I'm probably submissive... Ok, yes I'm very submissive..." as she smiled and looked downward, trying to avoid eye contact.

Her experience was limited to her consumption of smut books and having a Dom online who had set rules and structure for her, but never any real experience in person. She said she's been with other guys and might bring it up on the second or third "hangout", but she was always disappointed to find that none of them were into it and ultimately her burgeoning desires would go unfulfilled.

"I've only done vanilla things. Not by my own desires though..."

I shared some of my experiences with her, being open about what I enjoyed, specifically around enjoying being a Daddy Dom. Her eyes lit up, enamoured by my stories, and began asking a lot of questions.

As we chatted she would sometimes ask a question that others may feel uncomfortable answering, and say "Sorry, you don't have to answer that at all." Of course I did not ever mind and would answer her questions as they were no big deal, because they weren't. I'm assured in who I am and can share that.

Our conversation quieted as I looked at her from across the table, tension rising, and she nervously looked away with a cute grin on her face. I asked if she would like to come back to my place and without hesitation asked if we shall walk or take her car back. Then a pause...

"Would it be acceptable if I finished my drink?"

Acceptable? What a respectable little miss.

"Yes, you may."

We chatted about other random topics as she finished her drink. I continued to tease and verbally play with her, both of us smiling and laughing about things. She finished, we went to her car, and started the short drive back to my place.

When we were back at my place I let her get comfortable as she soaked up the attention from my pitbull lab who is the queen of the home.

"I like your place. Oh! I have a vape. Do you mind if I hit it here?" she said.

"No, I'd prefer that you not." She smiled and left it in her purse.

I sat back and relaxed on the bed as she perused the apartment a bit.

"You have A LOT of books." She had mentioned earlier in the date being introverted and having her nose buried in a book often.

"I also read quite a bit," I calmly remarked.

Then, she sat in the chair across from my bed.

242

Enter the Dom

"Come sit over here." As I tapped on the bed next to me.

She smiled, "Do you want me to take my shoes off?"

I could tell this girl wanted to be led every step of the way.

She came over, sat on the bed next to me, eager for what was to come. She nervously began remarking about something else in the room before I quietly interrupted her, leaning in to kiss her, and her eagerly moving in closer to my lips. Truth be told, she was an ok kisser, darting her tongue into my mouth a little too often. She'd quickly learn to dance her lips with mine in the coming months, though.

As we kissed, I pushed her by the shoulders back onto the comforter of the bed and slid my hands along her arms, pushing them above her head. As I reached her hands, I held them for a moment, kissing her deeply, and bringing them together. I let my hands firmly grasp her wrists, pinning them into the bed, and moving my thigh between her legs. As our tongues now entangled one another, she began pulsing her hips back and forth to grind on my thigh like a belly dancer, softly moaning with each stroke. It was the only movement she was allowed to do.

I pulled her sundress up above her waist to see the soft skin of her lovely legs and flat midriff. Her moans and movements were so enticing. I kissed and nibbled on her body. From the moment my teeth touched her supple skin, she went feral, moaning and moving around like crazy. I firmly pressed one hand into her hip bones as I held the dress in my other, continuing to let my mouth wander.

Her panties were visibly wet and it was not long before I had ripped them down to see how desperately her pussy wanted to be touched. I let my teeth mark the inside of her thighs, moving my mouth back and forth between them, only allowing my mouth to hover and let warm air touch her pussy lips before returning to the other thigh. I teasingly let my lips graze her pussy with soft kisses before I finally gave her the satisfaction of feeling my tongue lick from the bottom of her vulva to her clit, her exhaling in pleasurable relief. As I devoured her, I had to reach around her legs and firmly hold her down as she kept bucking like a wild animal.

She began to pull her dress up more, so I stopped.

"Take that off. Now." I commanded.

Quickly she pulled it over her head, threw it off the bed, followed by her bra. My eyes were delighted as they gazed upon her beautifully round and perky breasts with a delicious set of pierced nipples.

"Oh these are fucking beautiful" as I went into suck and bite her nipples, her gasping everytime I would wrap my tongue round her piercings. As I continued to focus on her breasts, my hand wandered between her legs, rubbing my hand over her mound, and sliding my fingers between her soaked pussy lips.

"OH FUCK! Oh daddy, daddy, daddy... daddyyyyy please don't stop... ooohh fuck I want to cum. PLEASE! Can I cum???"

She begged, squirmed, and moaned as I kept running my fingers inside her, graciously servicing her g-spot.

"Cum for me, babygirl," I demanded.

I felt her grip around my fingers as she moaned in delight, her juices soaking the bed beneath her. I continued my pace, not letting up, pushing her over the edge for a second time.

Now it was my turn. I stood up to take my clothes off as she laid there with a cheeky smile, rocking her hips side to side. I laid back on the bed.

"Come over here and suck Daddy's cock," I ordered.

She eagerly came over and swallowed me in her mouth. She was *very* good, letting her spit shower my throbbing cock and ever so gently running her fingers across my balls.

"You like Daddy's cock in your pretty little mouth, don't you?"

She wouldn't even take it out to answer. She just moaned so loudly and would suck faster. She couldn't take it too deep in before gagging, but she did not care. She kept sacrificing her oxygen for my pleasure. Her bright pink nails shined as the spit dribbled over her fingers that were wrapped around my shaft.

Seeing her with such passion drove me wild and I wanted nothing more than to be deep inside her. I grabbed her hair by the root and pulled her head off my cock. I pushed her over and grabbed a condom from the nightstand.

As she laid back, I held my cock in my hand, and looked into her desperate eyes.

"How badly do you want this inside you?" I teased.

"OH GOD PLEASE! Please please please fuck meeee"

As much as I wanted to keep teasing her with it and hear her beg over and over again, the animal urge to fuck her senseless took over. We vigorously rocked our bodies together, griping each other tight, the only moments of quiet occurring when our lips were locked into one another.

I fucked her hard and fast, one hand tightly gripping her hair, and one arm beneath her reaching across her back to her opposite shoulder, allowing me to grip and push her with force down on my cock as I thrusted. We both came *hard*. We couldn't help ourselves.

As I waited for my refractory period to pass, I kept playing with her, teasing her with the magic wand and letting the vibrations pulsate from her pussy to the rest of her body. She was a girl that enjoyed internal stimulation more than external, so I laid next to her, biting her body as I let my fingers continue to fuck her eager little hole, taking her to a couple more orgasms.

We took a breather for just a brief moment. She spooned with me, tilting her head back so we could make out more. It only took her moving her hips and her ass back into my crotch before I was rock hard and ready to go again.

"Want to feel Daddy deep inside you?" I teasingly asked with a smirk on my face.

"Oh yes Daddy, pleeeease! Please fuck meee."

Told her to grab the condom on the nightstand and she eagerly jumped at it. She watched me with the biggest, cutest smile on her adorable face as I slid it over me.

She laid back down to snuggle back into my body as I cuddled up behind her and pushed my cock into her tight pussy. As I reached around and held her perfect tits in my hand, I slowly moved my body with hers, whispering how good of a little girl she was being for her Daddy.

Our breathing became heavy and movement quicker before I pushed her over and rolled on top of her, pinning her wrists into the bed, and roughly fucking her from behind. I called her the dirtiest things my mind would come up with and shoved my cock as deep as I could. I'd pull her hair back, latch on like an animal with my teeth on her shoulders, and reach around underneath to choke her or use her tits like riding handles.

She'd growl, moan, squirm, and repeatedly keep begging "daddy, daddy, daddy, ohhhh fuck you feel so fucking good... gawddd you're too deep... you're stretching me out..." We fucked like that for what felt like forever and honestly couldn't even count the number of times she orgasmed.

Eventually I needed to recoup, so I rolled over to the edge of the bed and demanded her get on top. She wrapped her arms around me and grinded her petite frame on my cock with enthusiasm as I sat on the edge of the bed. I stood up with my cock still inside her, turned around, and threw her back on the bed. I crawled on top and pinned her legs back to fuck her as deep as I could until she was begging for me to cum.

"Oh daddy, pleeeassse. Please cum inside meee. God please. Oh I want to fill you cum inside my little pussy soo bad. Pleeeeease!"

I pushed her legs back further, thrusted as deeply as I could, and kissed her as every ounce of semen I had left my body. She wrapped her legs around me and did not want me ever to take my cock out, giving a bratty whine any time I motioned to do so.

Afterwards, we cuddled as I softly ran my hands over her glowing skin.

"Someone's so smiley. How come?" I said really cheekily.

She smirked, "Ohhh I don't knc oow. It was just a really good day. The weather was great." followed by a giggle.

Over the course of year I'd show Evelyn a lot of new experiences like bondage, orgasm control, teaching her some Tantra, and taking her to her first play party and fucking her among the sounds of others experiencing pleasure. This nice, respectable, polite girl turned into an incredibly submissive and kinky little miss.

All those vanilla guys *seriously* missed out.

CHAPTER FIFTEEN

Finding a Submissive

This book isn't a pickup guide, and neither Mario nor Brandon intends to be a pickup coach (although Mario admits he spent an excessive amount of time with many of them during his player days).

In this section, we'll provide guidelines and insights to help you maximize your efforts in becoming the Dom you want to be.

Finding a submissive isn't as simple as hanging a "Dom available" sign on your door and waiting. If you thought becoming a good Dom required effort, just wait until you start looking for submissive partners.

The key to successful dating is putting yourself in the right environments where connections can form naturally—without going insane or dreading the process like a job you hate.

In the past, finding play partners (especially submissives) was quite challenging. Any overtly "out of line" club was deemed socially unacceptable, forcing those interested in the lifestyle to "fly under the radar." It wasn't uncommon to travel to another city just to find a discreet venue known only to regulars. These clubs acted as a filtering mechanism, making access to this aspect of sexuality difficult unless you had a personal connection, browsed the adult section of local newspapers, or scoured niche websites.

Over time, technology has revolutionized the dating landscape, streamlining the process to the point of near automation. This shouldn't come as a surprise in an era where most couples meet via dating apps and artificial intelligence is even used to craft profile bios.

The massive success of *Fifty Shades of Grey* demonstrated a widespread desire—particularly among women—for a different kind of erotic connection and dynamic. Twenty years ago, discussing choking and spanking would have been considered scandalous. Today, it's fairly common for two consenting adults to openly share their preferences.

Before diving in, we need to cover a crucial concept that will help you market yourself in the dating scene: archetypes.

The Master Key to Becoming More Attractive to Women: Archetypes

Whether meeting women online or in person, one major pitfall to avoid is being a *JAGG*—"just another generic guy."

Our brains are wired to take cognitive shortcuts, making quick judgments based on available cues. We naturally categorize people into "boxes," attributing certain characteristics to them. This cognitive bias creates a halo effect that enhances attractiveness. That's the power of visual archetypes.

An archetype is the way you present yourself to the world—through appearance and behavior—based on your personality and what women generally find attractive.

For example, if you see a skinny, tanned, long-haired guy walking barefoot from the beach with a surfboard under his arm, what comes to mind? You instinctively project certain beliefs onto him based on his appearance and actions.

Before entering the dating market, crafting a visually compelling persona can make you more attractive from the outset.

What Are the Archetypes Women Find Attractive?

The Bad Boy: Tattoos, chains, leather jackets, and rugged boots. Bad boys have always been attractive because they embody a universal human trait: the need to rebel.

The Gentleman: Tailored suits and impeccable grooming define this archetype. It signals maturity, stability, and social acumen—traits often associated with CEOs, lawyers, and high-status professionals.

The Athlete: Physical fitness has evolutionary and reproductive appeal. Interestingly, there are more millionaires than men with six-pack abs, making fitness a rare and desirable trait.

The Spiritual Yogi: If you prefer white linen and yoga, you channel a sense of calm and introspection that appeals to the spiritually inclined.

The Promoter: Always appearing in Instagram stories and posting about the latest hotspots, the promoter blends elements of the gentleman and the bad boy with a vibrant social life.

The Surfer: Exuding freedom, fitness, and a laid-back attitude, surfers have a natural allure. However, mastering the art of surfing is no easy feat.

The Protector: This category includes muscular men, MMA fighters, military personnel, and archery enthusiasts. Women often seek safety, and nothing feels more secure than a man who can handle himself in tough situations.

The Lover: Romantic Latin love songs were written for this archetype. You'll find him at bachata and salsa nights, effortlessly charming his partners.

Of course, this isn't an exhaustive list. Archetypes evolve with cultural shifts—being a rapper in the '80s wasn't as attractive as it is today. If you doubt the influence of these archetypes, just look at what's trending in romance novels (*Fifty*

Shades of Grey started as a book, after all), pop culture, and social media influencers.

Mix and Match

Like most aspects of personality, archetypes aren't rigid categories. You can—and should—blend elements from different archetypes. This juxtaposition adds depth, mystery, and intrigue to your persona.

Imagine being an entrepreneur by day and a protector by night. Congratulations—you're Batman. You're welcome.

Brandon naturally embodies three distinct archetypes: the bad boy, the spiritual yogi, and the gentleman. When he dresses in all black, with ripped jeans, a chain around his neck, and leather bracelets on his wrists, people don't expect him to be calm and centered. Likewise, when he's in a three-piece suit, they don't anticipate him rolling up his sleeves to reveal a collection of tattoos. This subtle contradiction sparks curiosity, and as we discussed in earlier chapters, curiosity is highly attractive.

The key is authenticity. Brandon isn't faking these archetypes; they're natural extensions of his personality. He is a rebel, a spiritual seeker, and a gentleman—when he chooses to be.

When selecting your archetype, don't just pick one based on perceived attractiveness. Choose something that aligns with who you genuinely are. Women can sense inauthenticity, and nothing is more unattractive than someone pretending to be something they're not.

How to Meet Potential Partners

We'll walk you through various avenues for finding submissive partners. These aren't the only options, but they are the most accessible—especially for beginners.

Meeting Them in Everyday Life

For the sake of everything holy in this world, please don't be the creep who asks random people at a bus stop if they're into BDSM. (If you think this couldn't happen, let me assure you—it did. A friend of Mario's actually tried this in the Bay Area back in the day...)

Meeting potential partners in your everyday life doesn't have to be complicated.

There are hundreds of coaches and YouTube videos on pickup and seduction, but everything they teach boils down to this: walk confidently toward someone you like, maintain strong eye contact with a smirk, and start a conversation by commenting on something you've noticed about them.

You will get rejected—probably a lot—especially if you're not naturally outgoing. But rejection is part of the process. Don't take it personally. Remember, you're being *rejected for what you're offering*, whether that's a date, a relationship, or even just a conversation, along with the value you bring to the interaction. If you struggle with this, revisit the chapter on confidence and continue working on the three parts of the Self.

To put things in perspective, you can expect about one yes for every 100 no's. Sure, some people online will claim they have a better success rate—and we don't doubt it. They've simply put in more time, effort, or have access to better locations, which is beyond the scope of this book.

That said, if you've done the work to become a strong, authentic Dom, you'll find it much easier to attract new partners in everyday interactions than by regurgitating pickup lines from some questionable YouTube coach. When it comes to seduction, eye contact, voice tone, and body language matter far more than the words you say.

But if you're absolutely set on knowing what to say, here's the oldest trick in the book—one that every good salesperson uses: let the prospect talk about themselves. After all, isn't your goal to meet someone new? Give them the space to talk about themselves instead of making the conversation all about you.

Due to the natural polarity between men and women, if things click between you and a potential partner, you can introduce the topic of Dominance and submission during a date—preferably when the mood is right for discussing sexier topics. (We don't recommend bringing up D/s dynamics in a busy coffee shop with someone you just met by complimenting their book selection.) Apply the concepts we've covered throughout this book. It all comes full circle.

Online Dating

Online dating has exploded over the past decade, nearly replacing in-person meetups as the primary way people connect. Add the rise of various social movements and changing cultural dynamics, and it's no surprise that people no longer meet romantic prospects—whether for a relationship or a one-night encounter—the way they used to.

Designed as a simple, elegant solution to a complex problem, online dating has instead created a whole new set of parameters and "rules" that didn't exist before.

Benefits of Online Dating:

- **Less visible rejection:** Dating online feels "easier" because you don't see how many times you get rejected (or swiped left on).
- **Better time management:** If you know what you're doing, you can optimize your time and efforts.
- **Niche BDSM apps:** Some platforms cater specifically to those looking for D/s dynamics, allowing you to connect with pre-screened partners.
- **High volume potential:** With a strong profile and a willingness to "pay to play," the algorithm will put you in front of plenty of potential matches.
- **Marketing principles apply:** If you're skilled at online marketing, the same fundamentals—funnels, copywriting, and visual branding—will work in your favor.

Drawbacks of Online Dating:

- **"Pay to play" reality:** To stand out among the thousands of men vying for her attention, you'll need to invest in premium features.
- **Random bans:** Apps can suspend or ban profiles without warning.
- **High-quality photos are mandatory:** A professional or well-executed photoshoot (even without a pro photographer) is non-negotiable.
- **Fierce competition:** You're up against thousands of other men, many with highly curated profiles.

Picking an App

With dozens of dating apps available, not all of them will work equally well for you. You'll need to assess where to best allocate your time and resources. If Tinder isn't yielding results, try Hinge. If Hinge doesn't work, switch to Bumble. The key is experimentation.

Factors to Consider When Choosing an App:

- **Cost:** If you're serious about success, expect to pay. It's not fair, but life isn't fair.
- **Location:** Some apps perform better than others depending on regional culture.
- **Time investment:** Some apps are quick swipes, while others require more thoughtful engagement.
- **Competition:** Are other men on the app using high-quality, well-composed photos, or is it mostly generic selfies in car mirrors?

Our advice: try all the popular apps in your area. Double down on the ones that get you results and drop the rest.

Crafting a Profile

Online dating is a **visual** game—it's all about **marketing yourself**. You'll need to refine your style, decide what personality you want to project, and invest significant time and effort into making your "packaging" attractive.

A common mistake? Low-effort photos. Too many guys show up with blurry, poorly lit images that look like they were taken with a potato. Consider this: a woman is scrolling through *hundreds* of profiles per minute. If you don't capture her attention in a split second, you'll never even get the chance to start a conversation, let alone take her on a date.

Your first photo is the most important—it needs to hook her and make her want to learn more about you. The rest should reinforce that you're both physically attractive and intriguing enough to be worth her time.

Every photo should have:

- **High-quality resolution** (taken with a professional camera or a well-lit smartphone)
- **Well-fitted, stylish clothing** that reflects a strong archetype
- **Good grooming** (clean shave, trimmed beard, styled hair—whatever suits your look best)
- **A clear view of your face** (one or two with your face blocked is ok, *if* it's interesting in some other way)
- **An interesting background** (think Instagram-worthy framing that directs the eye to you)
- **A subtle hint about your lifestyle or personality**

Your first photo should be a clear, engaging headshot—candid but well-composed.

Best Photo Types (Ranked from Safe to Boldly Dominant)

- **You with a dog** (dog photos outperform cat photos)
- **Low-activity hobbies** (such as reading, art, coffee shop vibes)
- **Travel/interesting locations** (show that you have an adventurous side)
- **Smiling photos** (especially if you have a strong, masculine appearance—Mario and Brandon found that smiling shots softened their image and increased engagement)
- **High-activity hobbies** (such as sports, woodworking, music—especially where your arms, shoulders, or forearms are shown in an attractive way)

- **Physique photos** (but only if you're in top shape with low bodyfat—otherwise, this will backfire)
- **Group photos** (shows social confidence and charisma)
- **Leadership shots** (such as public speaking, leading a group, commanding attention)
- **Photos with attractive women** (signals that women feel comfortable around you and that you're desirable)

Once you've optimized your photos, your bio (or prompts, depending on the app) is your next opportunity to stand out.

- **What not to do:** Don't be the guy who writes, *"Just ask me what you want to know."* That's lazy and makes you look uninspired.
- **What to do:** Frame your personality and attributes in a way that aligns with what she's looking for. This is where copywriting comes into play—think about the value you're offering her, not just listing facts about yourself.

One last tip: imagination is your greatest asset.

When it comes to dating, nothing is more powerful than sparking *curiosity*. No one enjoys reading a book when they already know how it ends—the same applies to attraction.

When crafting your bio and selecting photos, leave room for intrigue. Yes, your archetype should tell people what kind of "movie" you are (are you a thriller, a spy film, or a rom-com?), but never spoil the magic of the plot twist or the grand finale.

FetLife

One challenge with online dating is that you're entering a pool of people who may or may not be interested in all the kinky things you want to explore. This means you'll have to filter potential partners.

Fortunately, there's a website designed specifically for kinky and sexually adventurous individuals: **FetLife**. Often described as the "kinky Facebook," FetLife functions similarly—you create a profile, add friends, and discover events like munches and play parties (which we'll discuss later).

Setting up a FetLife profile follows many of the same principles outlined in the online dating section. However, FetLife has unique aspects that allow you to position yourself better. Let's go over the common mistakes most men make (and what you should avoid) and then discuss the strategies you should use to stand out.

What NOT to Do on FetLife:

- **Do not** use a dick pic as your profile photo (*unless it's exceptionally rare and valuable—think 10"+—but even then, it's still not a great idea*).
- **Do not** spam hundreds of women with messages asking if they want to have sex. Treat FetLife as you would any other dating platform—or better yet, as if you were meeting someone in person. Approach conversations with genuine interest, comment on something unique about them, and find out what they are looking for.
- **Do not** open with your deepest fantasy. Build rapport first.
- **Do not** flood the comments section of dozens of women's pictures with thirsty remarks. Thoughtful comments are okay, but remember that everyone can see your activity feed. Your interactions will be judged.
- **Do not** leave your profile blank. An empty profile signals a lack of credibility and makes it harder for people to trust you.
- **Do not** act entitled. Just because it's a sex-positive platform does not mean anyone owes you sex—even the most sexually open women.

What TO Do on FetLife:

- **Show your face if you're comfortable.** Many users set face photos to "friends only" for privacy reasons, but if you're willing to show yours, it can help establish trust and attraction.

- **Use high-quality photos.** You can repurpose images from your dating profiles, but FetLife also allows you to be more unique and risqué. If you have an impressive physique, showcase it. Display your skills—whether it's shibari (rope bondage), impact play, photography, or another specialty.
- **Craft a compelling bio.** Take the time to write something meaningful. The most common compliment Brandon receives on his profile is about the depth of his bio. At a minimum, include:
  - What you're interested in
  - What Dominance means to you
  - What you're looking for
  - A little about your vanilla life
- **Engage with the community.** The BDSM scene is community-driven, and those who are respected contribute value. You can do this by:
  - Socializing at local munches and events
  - Volunteering at BDSM-related gatherings
  - Posting artistic photos, erotic writings, educational content, or helpful insights online
- **Be charismatic and sociable in direct messages.** Don't be a horndog or a creep. Apply the same principles of seductive communication discussed in earlier chapters. Because FetLife is a sexual site, you can introduce sexual topics a little sooner than on mainstream dating apps—but not in the first couple of messages. Treat these women as people, not as sex dispensers.

If you take the time to build a **valuable** profile—meaning one that is engaging, well-crafted, and provides value to others—you will eventually have submissive women *DMing you*. However, achieving this takes time, effort, and dedication. There are no free lunches.

Munches

A munch is a social gathering for kinky people to meet and make friends with others who are into alternative lifestyles, such as BDSM, polyamory, or swinging. Munches are typically held at social venues like bars, breweries, or restaurants. Have you ever attended a meetup for a hobby club or a business networking event? It's sort of like that—except when you go to a munch, you know all the other people there have a genuine interest in kink. It's not as awkward to discuss being tied up or hit with a paddle in between conversations about the awesome board game you found the other day.

Most munches are pretty low-key, and there's not too much to worry about. However, make sure to read the event description, as some munches may have a few specific rules they would like followed. These rules often revolve around restrictions (such as "submissives only") or specific considerations for the venue.

There are also a few unspoken guidelines to keep in mind:

- **Dress vanilla**: Unless otherwise specified, most munches will be in a public place with regular people around. It's best to dress like anyone else in public, meaning don't show up in your full fetish gear. This is asked because, while you may be comfortable drawing attention to your participation in kink, others at the munch may not be. Additionally, the public may not be comfortable with it either.

- **Confidentiality**: Sometimes, you may run into someone you know from work or a different friend group and have the either awkward or totally amazing realization that you're both kinky. The courteous thing to do is keep that discovery to yourself and not share it with others. Doing so can have real consequences for their personal and professional lives.

- **Don't yuk someone else's yum**: People who come to munches are doing a courageous act by being vulnerable about a side of themselves that many others might judge, criticize, or shame. If someone shares a particular kink or fantasy with you that's not your thing, don't tell them it's disgusting or that they're weird for having it. Imagine sharing one of your most intimate desires—how would you like the other person to respond?

- **Consent**: Before touching someone, ask if it's okay to do so. You'll often hear kinksters asking if they may hug each other. We're all still friendly people, and many will be happy to hug. However, we also respect each other's bodily autonomy. No one will get angry because you asked, but they might get upset if you don't!

Once you click with someone you're interested in, you can ask about their experiences at such events, what they think, and proceed to have a good time together—just like you would on a regular date. Don't be afraid to ask if they want to play with you after the munch has ended. In our experience, munches can be a lot of fun and far more interesting than going to nightclubs.

Play Parties

Play parties are held in clubs with specific dress codes (usually fetish attire) and often have rooms for adults to play or a very "laissez-faire" attitude towards sexual acts. The purpose of these parties is to hang out, be your natural sexual self, and, as the name suggests, to "play" with others.

Let's address one important misconception here: Play parties aren't "get laid easily" events. There's nothing more annoying at those parties than the single, horny guy who pesters couples and single women, trying to get some "action."

Yes, at first, you'll go to these places alone. Yes, the chances of looking like that guy are high, but we'll help you get to the place where you shine like a bright star at these events.

So how do you make these parties work in your favor instead of becoming one of those weirdos who ends up in a corner holding a beer in front of their chest?

Social Hierarchies Are Always in Play

Social hierarchies—how we position ourselves in the rest of society—are always in play. After all, our lizard brain is always at work.

As we discussed the power of visual archetypes and how our brain makes quick decisions, you should be aware that we "judge" people continuously (most of the time subconsciously). The trap of being a "JAGG" (Just Another Guy Guy) is always there.

If we looked at you at the entrance of a party, what would we instinctively think? A lonely, average guy trying to get some action, or an absolute champion? If you're the performer offering free shibari tutorials in the workshop area of the party, how would you be judged? At the top of the hierarchy or at the bottom? What about the bartender? The organizer? Where do they fit in the totem pole of social dominance?

You see, many of the principles we talk about in this book (especially power) have a direct application in today's world—whether in a corporate boardroom or at a swingers club.

"It's Dangerous Out There, Don't Go Alone"

Now, of course, these parties should be safe in terms of personal safety. But at every play party, men showing up alone or with a group of friends are usually frowned upon, and most of the time, they're milked for their money.

The reality is, no matter how new or inexperienced you are at being dominant, showing up with an attractive partner, being in shape, and dressing in a way that grabs attention will give you the "halo effect" of intrigue and attractiveness.

What Are You Famous For?

Mario was once asked at a workshop what the number one skill is to have if you want to shine at these parties. His reply? "A glorious six-pack... or a very specific skill that draws interest in you."

We are wired to be attracted to competent people. There's no other way around that. Simply put, we tend to favor the shibari master who has spent years in Japan studying old-school kinbaku over the guy who's watched a couple of YouTube tutorials.

If you're attending a fetish party where people want to let go and have a great time, why should they choose you? Maybe you're an attractive stud, as discussed above. Maybe you have great social skills and can charm your way into action. Maybe you can offer what submissives are looking for and be the best at it. Are you an expert spanker? A shibari rigger? The list could go on and on. We recommend choosing a specialty and dedicating time to develop it further, so the next time you're at a party, you'll have a line of people waiting to talk to you. Remember, you can be anything—just don't be a JAGG.

CHAPTER SIXTEEN

Structuring Your D/s Dynamic

You, our friend, have come a long way. You've transformed yourself into a powerful Dom, found a woman who wants to be your submissive, and now you're ready for the next step: establishing a Dominant/submissive (D/s) dynamic with her.

D/s relationships differ from traditional ones in two key ways:

1. You are transparent and upfront about what the relationship is going to look like.
2. Sex is an integral part of the relationship at every level.

One of Brandon's favorite pastimes is leaving vanillas (people outside the lifestyle) flabbergasted at what a relationship *could* be. Imagine having complete "free use" of your submissive partner, fulfilling whatever urge strikes you that day. Or being with a woman who gets off on seeing you with other women (they're called *cuckqueans*—you're welcome). Or even having multiple girlfriends, all of whom are fully aware of each other and may even spend time together like sisters. All of this is possible—*if* you fulfill your responsibilities as a Dom, as outlined throughout this book.

But D/s dynamics aren't just about sex. They can also be among the most emotionally fulfilling relationships you'll ever experience. Consider the level of devotion it takes for a woman to call herself your submissive—or even more, your slave. Every effort you make to care for her is explicit and openly rewarded. Vanillas may look down on the lifestyle, but if you really examine their motives for marriage, commitment, and caregiving, you'll find they're often operating under covert contracts to meet the same kinds of needs. The difference? Kinky people are simply more verbal and deliberate about it.

That said, structuring your dynamic—whether casual or long-term—requires purposeful effort. Without it, the relationship will likely crash and burn. As a Dom, it's your responsibility to shape the relationship and lead it in the direction you both desire.

Casual Dynamics

Casual dynamics are relationships where you don't intend for things to be deeply committed—though you might be open to that possibility in the future. These relationships are primarily based on sex, but as Brandon often argues, that doesn't mean they're devoid of emotion. In fact, he always encourages his submissives to express their true emotions, knowing that's the key to experiencing the most authentic version of her.

Most casual dynamics fall into the category of "only in the bedroom" D/s relationships, meaning the power exchange—where you have control over her—occurs exclusively within the confines of your apartment (or wherever you like to get freaky). Outside of that, she retains most of her autonomy.

This might sound simple, almost obvious, but if you want a happy, fulfilling, and ongoing casual relationship, there are a few key practices that can make it more successful.

Practical Tips

- **Be honest.** If you have other partners, tell her. Don't lie. Most are pretty understanding.
- **See each other at least once a week.** Any less, and life will get in the way, making the relationship feel disconnected.

- **Always have variety.** Never do the same thing in the bedroom twice in a row, even if it's her absolute favorite. You don't need to reinvent the wheel each time, but maintaining novelty—whether through different activities or changing locations—keeps things exciting.

- **Be building toward something.** Traditional relationships follow a progression—from dating to marriage to kids, and so on. Even if you've agreed to keep things casual, there should still be a sense of forward movement. Exploring each other's sexualities fully is a great way to do this. Consider creating a sexual bucket list (*or fuck-it list*) and checking off experiences together. You can also focus on improving your respective Dominant and submissive skills.

- **Have open communication about feelings.** The longer you see each other, the more likely it is that one of you will develop deeper feelings. When that happens, have an open conversation and decide how to proceed. Yes, it might mean the relationship ends if one person isn't ready for more. But remember, the goal is a fulfilling, *healthy* casual relationship—not a toxic one where someone is being strung along or growing resentful.

- **Be good at sex.** Let's be real—if your relationship is centered around sex, you need to bring high value in that department. No sugarcoating it—if your skills aren't up to par, she *will* look elsewhere.

- **Extend the D/s dynamic beyond the bedroom.** If both of you are open to it, add rules or fun tasks for your submissive outside the bedroom. For example, one of Brandon's favorite rules is having his submissive masturbate several times in the 48 hours before seeing him—but without being allowed to orgasm. These playful dynamics keep the connection alive between meetups and enhance your time together.

- **Have dates outside the bedroom.** You don't need to make it a habit, but occasional dates can be a great way to strengthen your bond. If your submissive is adventurous, take her to a kink event or play party. Just because the relationship is casual doesn't mean you can't create fun, memorable experiences together.

- **End things as gracefully as you started.** Life happens. People move. Situations change. New relationships begin. That's okay. When the time comes to part ways, communicate openly. Have an honest conversation—whether in person or over a call. Don't just ghost her. That's disrespectful, and no one likes it.

These principles will take you far. But if you want to create *truly memorable* casual dynamics, a little extra effort goes a long way.

Creating a Sanctuary for Her

Think of your bedroom or apartment as a *sanctuary* for her. When she walks through that door, she's no longer in the world of reality—she's in the world of *fantasy*. This is where her deepest desires come to life.

To cultivate this space, you should:

- Have open discussions about her fantasies and desires, then create scenes that bring them to life.
- Set the ambiance with decor, lighting, kink toys, scents, and a clean, stress-free environment.
- Be a non-judgmental presence. The world might judge her, but *you* never do.
- Establish small rituals to help her slip into a submissive mindset—whether it's putting on a play collar or receiving maintenance spankings.
- Tell her what outfits or lingerie to wear when she comes over.
- Tease and text her throughout the day about what's going to happen when she arrives.

Helping Her Grow—Inside and Outside the Bedroom

Helping your submissive become a more confident person—both sexually and emotionally—can deepen your connection, even in a casual dynamic. Not every

Dom enjoys the mentor role, but Brandon and Mario embrace their Daddy personas, making this an integral part of their relationships.

Supporting her sexual exploration can be as simple as introducing her to new kinks, like rope bondage, *proper* anal play, or even a threesome. It can also involve more complex experiences, like helping her understand her deeper desires, dismantling shame around her kinks, or using BDSM as a tool for emotional catharsis.

What you'll often find is that as you lead her through these experiences in the bedroom, she'll begin seeking your guidance in other areas of her life. She sees you as a safe and wise person, and your perspective holds value. The more you bring to the table—even in a casual relationship—the longer it will last and the more fulfilling it will be for both of you.

Multiple Casual Dynamics

Yes, if you'd like to have more than one submissive partner, it is absolutely possible. Welcome to the world of ethical non-monogamy, where it is entirely acceptable to have multiple women—so long as you're honest, transparent, and communicative about it.

The world of non-monogamy, especially when discussing polyamory, can quickly become jargon-heavy and overly complicated with different terms and relationship structures. While those concepts may help you visualize different dynamics, we believe it can be simplified. The bottom line? You and your partners need to openly discuss your boundaries and expectations. What works for you is what matters.

For Brandon, it's simple: He lets his partners know upfront that he has multiple partners, that he will never be exclusive, and that he has no issue with them seeing other people. Others may prefer a primary partner with special boundaries, while some prefer multiple deep, committed relationships within a polyamorous framework. The structure doesn't matter—as long as everyone involved is happy and consenting.

That said, maintaining multiple relationships presents its own challenges. Being a Dom with multiple submissive partners adds an extra layer of complexity. The tips for a single casual relationship still apply, but here are some additional practical considerations:

Practical Tips:

- **Time Management:** If you're following the "at least once per week" guideline for seeing partners, you only have so many free nights in a week. Between your other responsibilities, this realistically limits the number of consistent partners you can maintain. You may also have play partners you connect with less frequently. Regardless, you'll need to be meticulous about managing your time.

- **Emotional Capacity:** Another limitation is your ability to provide emotional connection to each partner. As your number of partners increases, the amount of emotional energy you can devote to each one naturally decreases—unless you're engaging in purely emotionless sex. Be mindful of this to maintain fulfilling relationships.

- **Sexual Satisfaction Setpoint:** Believe it or not, there is such a thing as *too much* sex. You'll know when you've reached that point because it starts feeling... well, meh—like cardboard pizza. To keep your sex life satisfying, stay below that threshold. We recommend incorporating rest days between partners. For example, a practical schedule might be seeing different partners on Monday, Wednesday, and Friday.

- **Introducing Partners:** If your partners are bisexual or open to threesomes, introducing them to one another can be a fun and unique experience. It's also an efficient way to manage time—seeing two partners at once.

- **Using Sex Menus:** As mentioned in an earlier chapter, a sex menu is a great communication tool that outlines each partner's desires and limits. As a Dom, keeping a record of this for each partner ensures you respect their individual preferences and don't mix them up.

Serious, Committed Dynamics

At some point, you may be ready to explore the full depths of a Dominant/submissive relationship. You and your partner might also be prepared to establish a more committed dynamic. This is when you'll most likely create a contract outlining the structure of your relationship.

What Is a Dom/sub Contract?

A Dom/sub contract—sometimes referred to as a Master/slave contract or BDSM contract—is a document that defines the boundaries and agreements between the Dominant and the submissive. This contract can be as simple as a one-page list of rules the submissive agrees to follow, or it can be a detailed, comprehensive breakdown of the entire dynamic.

If you're looking for a template, you can download the one Brandon provides on his website: https://www.brandonthedom.com/resources/dom-sub-contract.

Why Have a Dom/Sub Contract?

"We're just having a little kinky fun—why on earth would we need to bring in a boring document?"

While a contract isn't necessary for every D/s dynamic or for casual kinky play, there are several benefits worth considering.

Benefits of Having a D/s Contract:

- **Psychological Commitment:** Writing down the terms of your relationship requires deeper thought and intentionality, making the dynamic feel more serious and real.
- **Consent:** A clear, written agreement makes it easier for both partners to understand and express their consent.

- **Reference Point:** As a Dominant, leading your submissive becomes easier when expectations are documented. If either of you forgets an agreement, you can refer back to the contract.
- **Clarity and Direction:** Submissives crave clear instructions. A contract eliminates ambiguity, ensuring they know exactly what is expected of them.

One additional benefit—hopefully, one you'll never need—is that in the unlikely event of legal complications, having a written record of consent can be helpful. While these contracts are not legally binding, they can provide context in situations where misunderstandings arise. In fact, some couples even run their contracts by a lawyer as an added precaution.

When Is a Contract Appropriate?

If you're engaging in a **total power exchange, a 24/7 dynamic, or a true Master/slave relationship,** having a contract is highly recommended. In these arrangements, the Dominant assumes near-total control over the submissive's life, making a written framework essential.

Even in everyday life, we don't manage everything in our heads—we use documents and external systems to stay organized. So, taking responsibility for another person's life without at least a basic written plan would be impractical.

But what about the other end of the spectrum—a casual, friends-with-benefits, only-in-the-bedroom dynamic? Does a contract make sense there?

Probably not. However, if you focus on the *purpose* of the contract rather than the formality of it, you can still apply its benefits.

For example, Brandon has had casual dynamics where he and his partner agreed on a few simple rules to enhance the power exchange, including one or two that extended outside the bedroom. Instead of drafting a formal contract, he simply texted her the rules so she could save them on her phone. There was no signing of documents, but he still obtained explicit consent for specific acts and expectations—giving her the structure and guidance that made her a happy little sub.

How to Create a Contract

Giving credit where it's due, Brandon learned this process from Andrew and Dawn at *Infinite Devotion*, who provide some of the best resources on committed D/s dynamics and serve as a stellar example of how these relationships play out. While our contract styles and sections may differ in some areas, the foundational principles remain the same.

Contract Sections

We'll walk you through the process of creating a contract using the sections we believe are most essential. That said, remember that this contract should serve *your* dynamic. In the words of Bruce Lee, *"Absorb what is useful. Reject what is useless. Add what is essentially your own."*

Sections of a D/s Contract:

- **Dynamic**: Defines who is the Dominant and who is the submissive in the relationship.
- **Term**: Specifies when the contract begins, when it expires, and whether there is an opportunity for renewal.
- **Purpose**: States the reason for the dynamic and the vision for the relationship.
- **Parameters**: Outlines the boundaries and contexts in which the dynamic functions.
- **Code of Conduct**: Describes the agreed-upon behaviors for *both* parties.
- **Accountability**: Defines the consequences for violating the Code of Conduct.
- **Communication**: Establishes how discussions about the dynamic will be facilitated.

- **Execution**: Includes the signatures of both the Dominant and the submissive.

A Word of Caution

Before we dive into each section in detail, we want to offer a word of advice. As you go through this process, you'll likely feel incredibly excited about the possibilities for your dynamic. Some of your fantasies may feel within arm's reach, making you eager to implement everything at once.

However, we strongly encourage patience. Start small with your first contract, introducing just one rule at a time. It's much easier to expand and refine the dynamic over time than to overwhelm yourself by trying to do everything at once—only to feel discouraged if it doesn't all come together immediately.

In time, you *will* have everything you desire and more. But remember: *learn to crawl before you walk, walk before you run, and run before you sprint.*

D/s contracts are designed to evolve. That's why we set specific term lengths—so they can be revisited and renegotiated. With each new iteration, you'll incorporate lessons from previous versions, gradually shaping a dynamic beyond what you initially imagined.

Step 1: Determine What You Want as a Dominant

In a Dom/sub relationship, the Dominant must take the lead in all aspects. He is responsible for structuring the dynamic and ensuring its stability.

If you are the Dominant, it is essential to first gain clarity on what you want and why you desire a D/s dynamic. In the next step, we will provide question prompts to guide conversations with your submissive, but we strongly recommend reflecting on them yourself first. Doing so will help you solidify your intentions, allowing you to fully listen to your submissive's responses without simultaneously formulating your own.

For each section of the contract, we suggest following this structured process:

1. Define what you want.
2. Have a conversation with your submissive to gather information about your shared desires and needs.
3. Draft an initial version of that section.
4. Present it to your submissive and discuss her feedback.
5. Evaluate whether revisions are necessary based on her input.
6. Repeat this process until both of you fully consent to the section.
7. Finalize the section and incorporate it into the contract.

This process requires time and multiple discussions—but that is intentional. You are building the foundation of your dynamic. A weak foundation increases the likelihood of failure down the road.

If you are the submissive, your role in creating this contract is to communicate your wants and needs openly and provide honest feedback on the structure your Dominant presents.

Step 2: Have a Conversation with Your Submissive

Once you have a clear idea of what you want, it's time to discuss your submissive's desires. Dominance is not about tyranny—it is about mutual fulfillment. Both partners' needs should be considered when shaping a vision for the relationship.

Below, you'll find a set of guiding questions to help facilitate these discussions. It may be beneficial for both of you to write down your individual answers beforehand. This way, your conversations can focus on gaining deeper insights rather than generating responses on the spot.

While you can go through all these questions at once, breaking them up over several days allows for more thoughtful discussion and reflection.

Purpose Questions

- Why do you want to be in a Dom/sub dynamic?
- What does Dominance mean to you? How do you envision it?
- What does submission mean to you? How do you envision it?
- What do you ultimately want our relationship to be? How do you think a D/s dynamic will help us achieve that?
- What does your ideal, fantasy-version of a D/s dynamic look like? Which aspects are realistic, and which may not be attainable?

Fears Questions

- What fears do you have about being in a Dom/sub dynamic?
- How do you think this will change our relationship?
- How will we support each other when fears arise?

Parameters

- What are your essential needs in this D/s dynamic?
- What are your desires, limits, and boundaries regarding sex and kink play? (Consider completing a sex menu.)
- Where do we fall on the spectrum of monogamy to non-monogamy? What boundaries will we establish regarding others outside the dynamic?
- What aspects of life will be included in the dynamic, and which will be excluded?
- How open or discreet do we want to be about our dynamic? Are there specific people we will or won't share with? How much detail will we divulge?
- Will we incorporate collars into our dynamic? If so, what are the boundaries surrounding them?
- What title or honorific do you prefer as a Dominant? Are there any boundaries around their use?
- What title or honorific do you prefer as a submissive? Are there any boundaries around their use?

- Will we attend play parties? If so, what types of events, and what rules will we set for them?

Code of Conduct

- Who do I want to be as a person in this dynamic?
- Who do we want to be as a couple?
- Where do I need to grow to make this dynamic as fulfilling as possible?
- Where would I like to see my partner grow?
- How will we use challenges in the dynamic as opportunities for personal development?
- How will we integrate this dynamic into our daily lives as they currently exist?
- How can we use the dynamic to enhance our lives and overcome limitations?
- How will we continue to incorporate the dynamic as our lives evolve?
- How do we want to express devotion to each other and the dynamic?

Accountability

- How will the Dominant correct and hold the submissive accountable for following instructions?
- How should a simple mistake be handled versus repeated disobedience?
- What forms of punishment, if any, are acceptable?
- Is bratting allowed? How will we distinguish between punishment and playful "funishment"?
- How will the Dominant be held accountable for his responsibilities and leadership?
- Will the submissive have any veto power? If so, in what situations and to what extent?

Communication

- What is the Dominant's communication style? How will he communicate with the submissive?

- What is the submissive's communication style? How will she be allowed to communicate with the Dominant?
- How will texting and digital communication be handled within the dynamic?
- If a serious conversation as equals is necessary, how and when will the power exchange be temporarily set aside?
- How would the Dominant like to receive ongoing feedback from the submissive regarding the dynamic?
- How will we maintain open, honest communication about what is working and what needs to change for our continued growth?

This structured approach ensures that both partners are heard and that the dynamic is built on a foundation of clarity, consent, and shared understanding.

Step 3: Purpose

The first section we'll discuss in depth is the purpose of the dynamic.

Essentially, we're trying to answer these questions:

- Why does this dynamic exist?
- Why is it worth it for you to take the lead and responsibility for your submissive?
- Why is it worth it for her to submit?
- How will it benefit each of you?
- How good could this dynamic be if you both gave your all?

As the Dominant, you need to create a vision to lead the dynamic and provide direction for both you and your submissive. Of course, you could simply set rules for fun, but you could also leverage them as tools for growth—creating something greater than either of you alone. The purpose section is where you define that vision. Where is this dynamic going, and what will it mean to you? This vision should paint a picture of a D/s relationship that feels inspiring and fulfilling.

Here's an example:

This agreement is intended to guide two individuals on their journey together. While the primary intention is to please the Dominant, it also aims to shape the submissive into a better, happier, and stronger woman, while helping the couple grow together spiritually, emotionally, mentally, and physically. This agreement serves as the foundation or an extension of their relationship, committed in the spirit of love and consent. The dynamic is built on the principles of Dominance and submission, fostering self-awareness, exploration, personal growth, and the mutual enhancement of both partners' lives.

Once you have a draft, share it with your submissive and explain why it excites and inspires you. Tell her what it means to you and allow her to feel the depth of your vision. The emotion behind your words is what will inspire her to embrace and follow this dynamic. Then, seek her feedback and make sure she feels heard. Incorporate her desires as well, and continue refining the purpose until it resonates with both of you.

Step 4: Parameters

Many couples new to a D/s dynamic try to implement everything at once, on top of their already busy lives, in pursuit of the idealized relationship they've imagined. This often leads to overwhelm.

Instead, it's important to integrate the dynamic into your existing relationship structure, using everyday experiences to reinforce it naturally.

The first step is outlining the **parameters** of your relationship—defining where the dynamic starts and ends. If you want it limited to the bedroom with a few specific acts, that's perfectly fine. If you want a total power exchange relationship, that's also an option. However, we strongly encourage starting small and building from there.

Below are some key parameters to consider. This list is not exhaustive, so feel free to modify it based on your specific needs.

Possible Parameters:

- **Play:** Outline your preferences, limits, and boundaries for sexual and kinky activities, or use a sex menu that will be kept with your contract and regularly updated.
- **Monogamy vs. Non-Monogamy:** Define whether either partner will be allowed to see others and what boundaries will be in place.
- **Bedroom vs. Elsewhere:** Decide where the dynamic will be active and where it may be off-limits.
- **Secrecy vs. Openness:** Determine how private you want this aspect of your relationship to be and who, if anyone, will know about it.
- **Collar:** If collars will be incorporated into the dynamic, decide when they will be worn and whether they will take the form of a traditional day collar, a necklace, a bracelet, or another discreet symbol of submission.
- **Honorifics:** Discuss what the Dominant will be called and whether the submissive has any preferences or boundaries regarding names and titles.
- **Play Parties:** If you plan to attend play parties together, define what types you'll go to and establish any specific boundaries for those events.

As with every section, gather information, draft your initial version, discuss it with your submissive, refine as needed, and finalize it once you're both in agreement. Then, add it to your contract.

Step 5: Code of Conduct

Now we've reached the largest portion of the contract: the **Code of Conduct**. This section is designed to outline the ways you both will act and behave within the dynamic to achieve the vision you set forth in the Purpose section. It will include the values you will uphold in the relationship, the Dominant's responsibilities for caring for and leading the submissive, and the submissive's duties for serving the Dominant through commands, assignments, protocols, rituals, and rules.

Values in Action

First, let's discuss your values. Values help create guidelines for the dynamic, enabling you to make decisions and guide actions. Your values should reflect who you both are, what you care about, and where you want the relationship to go.

If you're the Dominant and have taken the steps outlined in this book to become a Dominant man, you should already have a good sense of your personal values. After having had many discussions with your submissive, you should also have an idea of hers. Your task now is to create a list of values—no more than ten, but ideally 5 to 7—that will serve as cornerstones for your dynamic.

To discover your values:

1. First, use the list of values from *Personal Values* or any other list you can find online to brainstorm values that are extremely important to you.
2. Narrow your values down to less than ten.
3. Rank your values from most important to least important. This will provide a framework for making decisions when two values conflict.
4. Finally, be clear about what each value means to you, and write down what this value looks like in action and how each of you will behave.

Present these values to your submissive. Explain why they are important to you and how they will help provide direction for the dynamic. Take her feedback and adjust the values as needed until you both agree and are excited by the list.

Dom's Responsibilities

We don't often see this section in Dom/sub contracts; however, we believe it belongs there just as much as the list of rules for the submissive. If you've ever looked at a real contract for anything else in life, you'll notice that it describes the obligations of **both** parties entering into an agreement. The reason the submissive is submitting is because the Dominant is taking responsibility for her and the dynamic, so why isn't this a standard part of the contract?

In this section, you will list all the ways you agree to take responsibility and how you pledge to act. We place this section before the submissive's duties because, as the Dom, you should be leading by example. She will see your commitment to both of you, which will inspire her submission and her desire to follow the duties that come next. Trust us, if you want to set the right tone of trust and accountability for your submissive, you must include this in your contract.

Submissive's Duties

In the past, Brandon would simply give his submissive a set of rules and call them "rules." However, Brandon came across Diespater's writing on FetLife, which organizes a D/s framework by breaking it down into commands, assignments, protocols, rituals, and rules. What was brilliant about his structure was the clear order of importance or priority between these categories. Let us explain.

A submissive will have the following categories of duties:

- **Commands:** These are direct, immediate statements made by the Dominant, for which the submissive is expected to drop everything and obey.
- **Assignments:** These are ongoing activities or homework tasks given to the submissive to improve the dynamic in some way. Often, these are one-time tasks or have a shorter time frame that doesn't warrant being a protocol, ritual, or rule.
- **Protocols:** These are rules for specific scenarios that may override other rituals or rules normally observed in the dynamic. For example, there may be a ritual in which your submissive kneels on the floor by your side while you're eating at home; however, when in public, she may sit on the same side but not kneel on the floor.
- **Rituals:** These are routines designed to enhance the emotional and psychological aspects of the relationship. They create meaningful moments, reinforce the dynamic, and strengthen the bond between you both.

- **Rules:** These are the foundational, formal, and concrete directions that the submissive is expected to follow. These are the most solid and unchanging duties of the submissive.

The first reason for breaking down the submissive's duties into these categories is to avoid conflicts when the dynamic is put into practice in everyday life. For example, the ritual of kneeling at home may be overridden by the protocol when in public. In this case, the protocol takes precedence. Commands override everything because, as the Dom, you know what's needed at any given time, and you may need to give a command that supersedes one of the submissive's duties to serve the dynamic better in the moment.

The second reason for this breakdown is to allow both flexibility and rigidity. Rules are the most foundational and won't change until the next time the contract is signed. These give your submissive an anchor for her submission. She knows these won't change, and if she follows them, she will make her Dom proud. On the other end of the spectrum are commands, which are fluid, situational, and temporary. This allows the Dominant to move the dynamic in the direction it needs to go in any given situation.

In the contract, you will list the protocols, rituals, and rules you expect your submissive to follow. Commands and assignments are not listed in the contract, as they are short-term and temporary, except for the general expectation that she will follow them when given.

As we've stated before, start small and slow. You may have dozens of duties you want to assign to your submissive but overwhelming her with too many rules right from the start will lead to frustration and resentment. She'll be expected to follow all these rules, and you'll be expected to keep her accountable.

Instead, consider writing down a list of everything you would like her to do at some point, and then pick a select few to start with in your first contract. When you both have a solid handle on those, you can add more in subsequent contracts. We recommend starting with 3-5 rules, 1-2 rituals, and any protocols that may need to override the previously stated rules or rituals.

Unlike other sections of the contract, protocols, rituals, and rules are not up for negotiation. They are either consented to by your submissive or not. You will present them to her to ensure that she understands them clearly and to gain her consent.

The reason for this is that, as the Dominant, you are deciding what behaviors are necessary to guide both of you toward your vision. Sometimes she may struggle to surrender to your leadership because she *thinks* there's a better way to do something, even though what she truly desires is to submit to you. Expect some apprehension toward certain duties. In fact, some of her duties should challenge and stretch her comfort zone if you want to see her grow toward the mutually agreed-upon purpose of the dynamic.

That said, always take her feedback and feelings into consideration. Your job is to support her in following these duties, adjust when necessary, and help her overcome challenges as she begins to follow them.

Step 6: Accountability

Now that you've established your Code of Conduct, it's time to outline the ways in which you both will be held accountable for upholding these standards. The important elements of your accountability plan will include the submissive's accountability, how to handle bratting, the Dominant's accountability, and whether the submissive has any veto powers.

Dominant's Accountability

Once again, this section is often omitted from many contracts, but we believe it has a vital role. The Dominant is also agreeing to the Code of Conduct and has pledged to take responsibility for the dynamic. But how will the Dominant be held accountable? List the ways in which the Dom will be held accountable, which may include external accountability by other Doms, feedback from the submissive, self-improvement, and correcting mistakes.

Submissive's Accountability

To help your submissive understand how she will be held accountable for following her duties, you need to outline how behavior will be corrected, when discipline will be necessary, and what punishments will be applied. In general, it's best to use the least amount of force necessary to correct a behavior, which is why we distinguish between different forms of accountability.

To hold your submissive accountable, use:

- **Corrections:** These are used to address small mistakes. Your submissive is still human. Sometimes she will forget, the rule may be unclear, or she may simply have had a bad day. A simple reminder of the rule from you lets her know you're paying attention, that these rules are important to you, but that you're not being unreasonable.

- **Discipline:** For repeated transgressions, discipline may be necessary. Before disciplining, understand why your submissive is failing to meet her duties. It may be that they are too overwhelming for her life at the moment or they are unclear. It's your responsibility to help resolve this. The goal of discipline is to bring your submissive back in line with the previously agreed-upon rules and behaviors. Be thoughtful in how you apply discipline so that it achieves the goal without damaging her mental state, confidence, or view of the relationship.

- **Punishment:** If you have reached the level of severe punishment, there is a failure occurring somewhere in the dynamic that is equally as much the Dominant's fault as it is the submissive's. The Dominant will need to do restructuring to address this. To hold the submissive accountable on her side, punishments are more severe versions of discipline.

Delivering discipline and punishments can sometimes be difficult, but if you let them slide, the Code of Conduct holds no weight. After delivering these, you should rebuild the connection. Take the time and attention necessary to remind her that she is still your submissive, that she is still good and valuable, and that her mistakes don't define her.

Bratting and "Funishment"

If you and your partner enjoy brat play, you need to delineate when it's acceptable to engage in it and what types of punishments are used for fun in brat play versus those for serious transgressions. This distinction is necessary to maintain the integrity of accountability; otherwise, the line between what constitutes punishment versus "funishment" can blur quickly.

It should be noted that while building a D/s dynamic is serious work, it should also be fun! If your submissive enjoys being a brat, you'll need to make room for her to engage in that. Just be sure to find ways that are enjoyable for you as the Dominant as well.

Submissive's Veto Power

Personally, Brandon doesn't think he could ever engage in a 100% total power exchange. At most, he could do 95%. Within that last 5%, he wants his submissive to still retain some agency. He doesn't feel confident that he would *always* do what's in her best interest. For this reason, he likes to have a veto clause.

A veto clause delineates when and under what circumstances the submissive is allowed to veto anything in the Code of Conduct and suspend the power exchange. This veto power should be used sparingly, if ever. Think of it as the nuclear option. Before using it, the submissive should do everything she can to surrender and follow the Dominant's wishes. The veto clause is considered the last fail-safe against possible tyranny on the Dom's part.

An example of when a veto may be appropriate is:

- Something in the Code of Conduct is no longer helping either person or the dynamic to reach their goals, but the Dominant has repeatedly been oblivious and it's causing damage.

- A duty in the Code of Conduct is causing unwanted harm, either physically or psychologically.

As before, draft the accountability plan, present it to the submissive, gain feedback, make adjustments, and add it to the contract.

Step 7: Communication

It's helpful to set standards and boundaries for how you both will communicate with each other, especially considering the many forms of communication available in the digital age. Doing so will help set clear expectations.

Possible elements to include in the communication section:

- **Dominant's Communication Style:** How will the Dom communicate with the submissive?
- **Submissive's Communication Style:** How will the submissive be allowed to communicate?
- **Texting:** Texting is the most prominent form of digital communication, but you can include any other methods that are relevant to both of you. Discuss how much texting is appropriate, what can be included in texts (logistics, emotional discussions, sexting, etc.), and so on.
- **Communication Safeword:** This is a word that temporarily suspends the power exchange dynamic, making both parties equal during the conversation to resolve any issues.
- **Feedback:** Outline how the submissive can give feedback to the Dominant, ensuring there's a clear mechanism for this exchange.
- **Weekly Check-ins:** Set aside time each week to discuss the dynamic and ensure you're both on the same page.

You're likely familiar with this process by now.

Step 8: Sign + Collar

Once you have the final versions of each section of your contract, it's time to set a term date and sign.

For your first few contracts, we recommend setting short-term dates, such as a one-month term. This allows you enough time to evaluate whether the structure works but doesn't lock you into it if things aren't going as planned. As you gain more experience within your dynamic, you can extend the terms to quarters or half-year intervals. Personally, we think a year is too long to wait before the next review, but if that works for you both, that's all that matters.

Next, you'll both sign the contract. While this contract technically isn't "real," we recommend treating it in your mind *as if it were real*. The more seriously you take the contract and the dynamic, the more you will get out of it. Some couples even treat the contract signing like a marriage, having a celebration or ceremony to mark the occasion. Whatever you choose, make it special and memorable for both of you.

Finally, if you'll be using collars in your dynamic, you can symbolize this moment by collaring your submissive with a collar chosen specifically for her.

Step 9: Sub Training Schedule

Now that you have this document outlining your entire plan for the dynamic, the last step is to implement it. Just like any new habit or routine, it will take consistent effort from both of you to incorporate these new behaviors and ways of being.

We recommend creating a training schedule where the Dominant teaches the submissive the entire Code of Conduct in one intense session over a couple of days, so she understands the purpose of your training. Then, slowly implement each new duty over the course of weeks until the next contract.

For example, let's say you followed our suggestion when creating rules, rituals, and protocols. You decided to start with 3 rules, 1 ritual, and 1 protocol, and your contract term is one month.

Your training schedule might look like this:

- **Day 1 + 2:** Teach her everything, including the rules, ritual, protocol, and accountability if the rules are not followed correctly.
- **Week 1:** Teach her rule 1 and hold her accountable for rule 1 only.
- **Week 2:** Teach her rule 2 and hold her accountable for rules 1 and 2.
- **Week 3:** Teach her rule 3 and hold her accountable for rules 1, 2, and 3.
- **Week 4:** Teach her the ritual and protocol, and hold her accountable for all the rules, the ritual, and the protocol.
- **Day 31:** Revisit the contract and adjust as necessary, including adding or subtracting from the Code of Conduct for the next training period.

This schedule can be easily adapted for any length of time and number of duties. We recommend doing the intensive session at the beginning to set clear expectations, test out the duties, and give both of you a reference point for what you're working towards. Then, break everything down progressively to avoid overwhelming either of you with too much at once.

If you combine this training schedule with weekly check-ins, your submissive will be able to provide feedback about the structure and any challenges she's facing. This feedback can then be used to adjust the contract when the new term date arrives.

The Dynamic of Your Dreams

Building a D/s dynamic is ultimately about creating a space where both partners can thrive—where the Dominant exercises conscious leadership and the submissive finds freedom through consensual surrender. Whether casual or committed, successful dynamics are built on transparency, mutual growth, and intentional design. Remember that your contract isn't just a document; it's a living blueprint for the relationship you're cultivating together. Start small, be patient with yourselves, and allow your dynamic to evolve organically. The journey from fantasy to reality takes time, but with clear communication, consistent accountability, and genuine care for one another's well-being, you'll create something far more fulfilling than what either of you initially imagined. In the end, the true measure of your dynamic's success isn't how closely it resembles someone else's ideal, but how effectively it enhances both of your lives and deepens your connection to one another.

Mastering Dominance

A Journey Without a Destination

CHAPTER SEVENTEEN

The Path of Dominance

Mario always jokes that there is no "Dom's University" or "Dom's certification class" where, once you acquire the skills, you're officially recognized for them. There's no finish line in this. No trophy, no checklist you tick off before someone hands you the title of "Dominant." Dominance isn't something you achieve; it's something you become, something you live day by day.

The reality is that you can read every book, watch every YouTube breakdown, and understand every principle of Dominance inside and out. But it won't make you Dominant. Knowledge is just the foundation; real-world application is the true test.

You don't learn to lead by memorizing strategies; you learn by stepping up and **taking responsibility**.

You don't exude presence by understanding theory. You do it by standing tall, speaking with weight, looking people straight in the eyes, and moving through life like you own your space.

You don't get submissives to submit to you because "You're a Dom," which, by the way, is actually pretty funny when people try to gain power from titles instead of giving power to the titles.

This isn't about just knowing Dominance; it's about *embodying* it.

Every choice, every movement, every interaction is either reinforcing that presence or eroding it. There is no middle ground or gray area.

Pain Was Always Part of the Game

Becoming dominant means evolving, and evolution isn't comfortable. You will be tested. You will have to let go of habits, ideas, and weaknesses that have held you back. That's not easy, if you ask us.

Growth hurts because it forces you to confront where you fall short. It pushes you to refine yourself—physically, mentally, and emotionally—until there's nothing left but strength and certainty.

Some men never make it past this stage. They conform into docile, obedient pawns. They feel the discomfort or social sting and retreat back to safety, to the familiar. But those who push through, who embrace the pain of growth, come out sharper, more solid, more undeniable.

Pain, as part of many BDSM, is also part of personal growth.

It's Not a Hobby; It's a Lifestyle.

From where we stand, we see Dominance not as your Saturday-night hobby. Dominance isn't something you switch on when you want to impress someone. It's not a mask you wear when the situation calls for it. It's how you carry yourself in *everything you do*—the way you walk, the way you speak, the way you handle challenges. It's the discipline in your habits, the weight behind your decisions, and the calm in your presence.

You don't "try" to be Dominant. **You are Dominant**. And that only happens when it's woven into your daily life—when every action reinforces who you are. Then it infuses into your play and interactions with your partners.

This means that you will make new life choices based on your new thinking and behavior. Maybe you'll change jobs, cities, or even leave people behind.

Mario's story below shows you just how far someone sometimes has to go to align with their new version.

Story Time with Mario

I simply had to leave. The city, the people, the routines—they all belonged to an older version of me, one I refused to be anymore. I was feeling trapped in a small place that was only able to show me what I could be, what I could have. I wanted *freedom* above all. I wanted to live life on my own terms.

So, I packed up, changed countries, cut ties with 95% of my 'friends,' emptied a very small bank account, and stepped into the unknown (well, I knew where the airplane was landing, at least) with a backpack and a one-way ticket. New places, new circles, new habits.

It wasn't easy, but I was happy that I was living life as I wanted, where I wanted, and how I wanted it. Every choice I made had to align with who I was becoming.

No half-measures, no looking back.

I didn't just change—I rebuilt myself from the ground up, all while learning a new language. I finally had a chance to hang out more with like-minded people, seeing things I would have never imagined, and yes, a lot more interesting romantic encounters.

All this for the small price of a few mental breakdowns, some sleepless nights, and tears in the shower. But thankfully, from most of those 'breaking' points, I grew stronger and healthier.

I could have just said, 'You know what? *Screw this.* I'm going back to my old life where, if I keep my head down, play nice, and conform, maybe I'll get the comfy life I see my friends craving and the occasional crazy BDSM party extravaganza.'

But this idea scared me more than being a broke, jobless dude who wanted to tie up some girls.

I was asked if I could go back 10–15 years and talk to my younger self. The advice I would give is to push harder and be even more *relentless* in pursuing my life goals and dating goals. We know it may sound obvious: the harder the work upfront, the bigger the reward in the future. But that's exactly why I would say that to my younger self. You think you're tired? Get in the gym. You're sad because your date didn't show up? Get out and try to meet someone. Your play partner stops seeing you and dates a new Master? Get more knowledge and become a better Dom. Everything I wanted was always on the other side of "do more."

Quiet the Noise

Dominance isn't always about force. It's about control, and a part of control is knowing when to act and when to let go. The world is full of noise, distractions, and people who don't even understand their own emotions and motivations, let alone yours. You don't owe anyone an explanation. Sometimes, the situation requires walking away with silent confidence as the ultimate display of power.

You will reach a point where you don't need to explain yourself anymore. There will be people who still see you as who you were, who expect you to conform to their outdated perception of you. That's *their* problem, not *yours*. Trying to convince them otherwise is wasted energy.

Your growth speaks for itself—through your presence, your actions, and your choices. The people who matter will notice, and those who don't? They were never really on your side anyway.

Most people are too caught up in triviality to even recognize what truly matters. They chase validation, argue over meaningless things on social media, and spend their lives in cycles of distraction. If we had a dollar for every meaningless and idiotic comment on social media, we'd probably own some of those platforms.

But once you've stepped outside of that, you'll see it clearly: Society's priorities are not your priorities. Your time is better spent on your purpose, your path, and those few who align with it. It took us a while to understand that you need to invest time in those who choose to be with you.

"Never Argue With a Fool; Onlookers May Not Be Able to Tell the Difference." — Mark Twain

We are living in interesting times, where profound societal changes have occurred over the last 10 years, thanks to the internet, smartphones, and social media.

Mario was once at a play party with a girl he was dating and a friend of his when they were approached by another woman who wanted to introduce herself. They started chatting, and it seemed she and Mario's friend started hitting it off—until she completely lost it when Mario's friend touched her elbow in a completely involuntary manner (note: in Southern cultures, gesticulating and touching others while making a statement is deeply embedded in the culture).

She screamed about consent.

Of course, this dragged his friend into a heated discussion about the episode, which drew the attention of the party's dungeon monitors. The situation escalated into a full meltdown from the woman, with Mario ready to step in and explain things to a fellow dungeon monitor. Thankfully, it resolved into nothing more than someone seeking attention.

But from this experience, we all must learn something: As a Dom, you will have to deal with people—other men, women—that think they know better, more than you, or just want to mess with you. Engaging and wasting energy on them will not only do you no good, but it will lower your overall energy in the aspects of life that matter more.

Mario was once playing with his submissive date at a play party when another Dom/Sub couple nearby started hurling unsolicited advice and borderline passive-aggressive comments.

Obviously, if you're an experienced Dom, you know this is a giant red flag. You don't know the other couple, what dynamic they have, or what they want to do.

So, Mario, initially willing to scold them both and put them in their place, decided instead to double down and flat-out ignore them. They got red in the face and walked away.

Mario also considered writing them a small note on a receipt, suggesting they could get coaching from him because their dynamic was lackluster, but he realized his ego was still in play.

Never, ever, waste your time and energy on causes that don't truly advance you.

Help Others Become Better Doms and Give Back to Your Local Community

When Mario met Brandon, they were just two strangers on an online forum. So, how did they end up a few years later co-writing a book together?

This goes beyond Dominance and submission, but it connects perfectly with the concept of love. There comes a point where your journey isn't just about you anymore, and it can take an interesting turn—you've reached what you consider the top, you've walked the path, fought through the doubts, shed the dead weight, and refined yourself into something sharper. But what's the point of reaching this level if you don't turn around and extend a hand to those behind you? If you climb Mount Everest, is the experience the same if you do it solo versus helping someone reach the top with you?

When Mario met Brandon, he had questions, doubts, ideas—but most of all, he had the brain, energy, and the desire to put in the work. Something that hits hard later in life is the pain of seeing talent go to waste.

Mentoring isn't just about teaching; it's about honoring the process. The younger versions of yourself, the ones hungry for change, truth, and direction, deserve more than just struggle. They deserve guidance. Not everyone will make it, but those who do? They carry your lessons forward, shaping something bigger than just one man's journey.

This isn't charity. This is respect for the craft.

When Brandon stepped into the scene, he wasn't necessarily new to D/s, but he was new to building community and helping others embrace their kinky selves. He started by volunteering in his local community, helping out those who had already been delivering value. When it came time, though, he repeatedly stepped up to make his community in Austin better.

First, he started the Young and Kinky (YAK) munch, a relaxed social environment where 18-39-year-old kinksters could regularly mingle. Whether people were brand new to kink or had been practicing for years, they were welcome. In fact, he gets first-timers in the scene all the time. He tried to create a friendly environment where everyone had an opportunity to speak and express the hidden kinky desires they have to conceal in regular interactions.

As time went on, he was asked to help take over leadership of East Austin Kinksters, a munch that had been taking place for over 15 years, with many regulars and great discussions between veterans and newcomers alike.

However, he continued to see a gap in the knowledge being passed from the old guard to the new generation of kinksters. So, he put together a "leaders' munch" to bring together those who were making the local community happen. They could start discussing ways to strengthen the community as a whole.

Along the way, Brandon has tried to share all the lessons he's learned, whether in discussions with others or in the educational material he creates. Just as Mario helped him understand what it truly means to be a Dom, he wanted to help others. Because the world could use more strong, Dominant men—leaders who transform not only themselves but those around them.

And we hope the book you are holding in your hands has not only helped you, but will inspire you to help others in the future.

One Last Word from Mario "AskTheDom" Tubone

I know how life can hit hard sometimes. I know you'll want to scream, to break, to do nothing, to *cry your soul out*, or just dull yourself and float like a leaf on the water.

There will be nights when you feel crushed under the weight of your own transformation, where the pain feels unbearable and the struggle endless. I know, because I have been there.

I couldn't fall asleep, paralyzed by the crushing weight of feeling defeated (by my own mind). I cried so many tears while kneeling in the corner of the small, moldy studio I was renting while trying to make a living. Believe me, I know life will hit you hard sometimes—losing loved ones, friends, health, and ultimately, hope. I know some folks will have their minds turn against them, hearing the mermaids' dangerous voices. I know, for sure, I've been tempted more than once.

Personally, I found meaning that helped me push through when I discovered Camus. He spoke of Sisyphus, the Greek myth, condemned by the gods to push a boulder up a mountain for eternity. A meaningless, absurd struggle, except for one thing: Sisyphus **does not break**. He does not surrender. He doesn't let the boulder roll over him. He accepts the absurdity of his predicament and the struggle as his own. And in that acceptance, he is *free and finds meaning*.

I really hope, in your struggles and challenges, you will find yours.

Acknowledgments

From Mario

This book would never have seen the light of day without the extraordinary people I've been lucky enough to meet throughout my life. In these pages, you've had the chance to read a few small exchanges with some of them, but my gratitude extends far beyond what's written here. To everyone I've met on this journey—and to those I have yet to meet—I send my deepest thanks and love.

First, I'd like to thank my "inner circle" of friends: Beo, Ivan, Fra, Paw, Ravi, Cam, and Daniel. Thank you for always picking up the phone and helping me navigate life.

I also want to express my gratitude to Matteo, Dylan, and Mirko for introducing me to the lifestyle of a world traveler and seducer. Many of these stories wouldn't have been possible if I hadn't caught the "itch" early on to leave my home country.

A special thanks to a few people from the online world as well:

- Thomas Crown, for being both a friend and a great dating coach—your guidance made a lasting impact.
- Nash, for your blog, which helped me tune out the noise in the dating space.
- Joe, for your clear-headed perspective and ability to see reality for what it is.
- Andy, for building an incredible community and carrying it on your back.

I also want to thank Brandon for taking on this project with me. I've always been more of a talker than a writer, and without him, this book wouldn't exist. Watching his transformation throughout his journey showed me why people love mentoring. He is an amazing guy and a fantastic Dom.

And finally, my deepest thanks to my wonderful girlfriend, K, for supporting me through all my projects, crazy ideas, moods, and decisions.

From Brandon

First and foremost, I want to thank the incredible women who have helped shape me into the man I am today—including my ex-wife. No man walks this path alone, and these beautiful souls have not only made the journey possible but also made every step worth taking. I adore them and will always be grateful.

Next, I want to thank my men's group—Jesse, Haydn, Anthony, Mo, Steven, and the others who have come and gone over the years. You inspire me, challenge me, and continually push me to be a stronger version of myself. Without you, I would have been lost many times over.

I'm also grateful to Joe and Ed for being my peers, mentors, and friends on this journey toward becoming a better seducer. I've cherished the laughter, camaraderie, and the way we've helped each other grow.

A special thanks to Andy for showing me what's possible in dating and for building such a powerful community. Through it, I found many people who offered support during my struggles.

To the leaders of the Austin kink community—I can't thank you enough for welcoming a fledgling Dom into the scene with open arms. Your warmth and generosity helped shape my journey. And to everyone who has attended my munches, play parties, or followed my content online, thank you for trusting me to help guide you toward the kinky lives you seek.

Finally, I want to thank Mario. You saw something in me that I couldn't see in myself, and your encouragement gave me the confidence to let it grow. Writing this book with you has been an honor, and I can only hope it helps others the way you helped me.

Much love to you all.

Extra Resources

BDSM

- Brandon The Dom: https://www.brandonthedom.com/
- Chief: https://kinkyevents.co.uk/
- Andrew & Dawn: https://www.infinitedevotion.com/
- Lola Jean: https://lolajean.com/
- Lina Dune: https://www.askasub.com/

Sex

- Beducated: https://beducated.com/

Dating

- Andy Wells: https://killyourinnerloser.com/
- Jack Napier: https://jacknapier.substack.com
- Thomas Crown: https://thomascrownpua.com/
- Nash: http://Gotalktogirls.com
- Joe: https://www.datingunchained.com/

www.ingramcontent.com/pod-product-compliance
Lightning Source LLC
Chambersburg PA
CBHW070528090426
42735CB00013B/2901